History of Economic Ideas

Panayotis G. Michaelides
Theodoulos Eleftherios Papadakis

History of Economic Ideas

From Adam Smith to Paul Krugman

Panayotis G. Michaelides
National Technical University of Athens
Athens, Greece

Theodoulos Eleftherios Papadakis
National Technical University of Athens
Athens, Greece

ISBN 978-3-031-19696-6   ISBN 978-3-031-19697-3 (eBook)
https://doi.org/10.1007/978-3-031-19697-3

© The Editor(s) (if applicable) and The Author(s), under exclusive licence to Springer Nature Switzerland AG 2023
The translation was done with the help of artificial intelligence (machine translation by the service DeepL.com). A subsequent human revision was done primarily in terms of content.
Translation from the Greek language edition: "ΟΙΚΟΝΟΜΙΚΗ ΘΕΩΡΙΑ: Από τον Adam Smith στον John Nash" by Panayotis G. Michaelides and Theodoulos Eleftherios Papadakis, © Panayotis G. Michaelides and Theodoulos-Eleftherios Papadakis 2021. Published by Tziola. All Rights Reserved.
This work is subject to copyright. All rights are solely and exclusively licensed by the Publisher, whether the whole or part of the material is concerned, specifically the rights of reprinting, reuse of illustrations, recitation, broadcasting, reproduction on microfilms or in any other physical way, and transmission or information storage and retrieval, electronic adaptation, computer software, or by similar or dissimilar methodology now known or hereafter developed.
The use of general descriptive names, registered names, trademarks, service marks, etc. in this publication does not imply, even in the absence of a specific statement, that such names are exempt from the relevant protective laws and regulations and therefore free for general use.
The publisher, the authors, and the editors are safe to assume that the advice and information in this book are believed to be true and accurate at the date of publication. Neither the publisher nor the authors or the editors give a warranty, expressed or implied, with respect to the material contained herein or for any errors or omissions that may have been made. The publisher remains neutral with regard to jurisdictional claims in published maps and institutional affiliations.

This Palgrave Macmillan imprint is published by the registered company Springer Nature Switzerland AG.
The registered company address is: Gewerbestrasse 11, 6330 Cham, Switzerland

Impossible means that you haven't found a solution yet. (Henry Ford)

To our students
teachers
friends
families

Preface

This book is addressed to those who wish to familiarise themselves with basic concepts of *Economic Science* or, simply, *Economics* and in particular with the way these concepts were developed by the great thinkers of the past. In other words, it serves as a *History of Economic Thought* of the last 250 years approximately, beginning with Adam Smith and ending with Paul Krugman.

The different chapters are linked conceptually and in historical order, but can also be read independently. The book presents key points from the work of each economist, together with some brief biographical information, and an attempt has been made to place them in the broader social and historical context of their time.

In addition, the book does not assume prior knowledge and is written in a concise but scholarly way, which should be easily accesible to all, experts as well as non-academic readers. Additionally, it contains some features such as the learning objectives, summaries, key takeaways and some revision questions that cover a very wide range of topics in contemporary *History of Economic Thought*.

Since the book is of an introductory nature, a great deal of effort has been made to keep it as simple and comprehensible as possible, and very little specialised knowledge is required. In order for the text to be readable and not to interrupt the flow of the text, the bibliographical references are listed, in the form of footnotes, at the end of the book.

We believe that a presentation of the main *Schools of Economic Thought* is appropriate for our project and for this reason we have sought to critically analyse the important economists who have dominated *Economics* to date and who are either the main representatives or are important exponents of one of the important *Schools of Economic Thought*. Furthermore, the book gives special emphasis on a critical evaluation of the theoretical controversies between the different *Schools of Economic Thought* as regards the character and role that the state can play in the economic life of societies.

In no way should the economists included in the book be taken either as those to whom we have a preference or as those who fully cover the whole range of *Economics*. Many more economists could have been included.

If we were to present a *History of Economic Ideas* based on Western economic thought, then there are very few women included in the discussion. The fact that there haven't been any in the history of *Economics* is certainly not the case. The great Keynesian economist Joan Robinson, the renowned monetary scholar Anna

Schwartz, the alternative theorist Elinor Ostrom and others have made important contributions to *Economics*. Furthermore, there are also women economists who are involved in the field of 'Feminist Economics'.

Of course, other than the *History of Economic Thought* prior to Adam Smith, future works should also include non-Western economic thought, such as ancient China, India and Islamic Economics, starting probably with ancient Greece.

We hope that readers will be fascinated by the breadth and richness of the theories of the great economists presented in this book, and hopefully, the aforementioned ideas will serve as good examples for future works.

Athens, Greece   Panayotis G. Michaelides
                                                            Theodoulos Eleftherios Papadakis

Acknowledgements

After having considered a number of relevant titles, we opted for *History of Economic Ideas: from Adam Smith to Paul Krugman*, at the urging of many colleagues around the world. Throughout the development of our ideas and arguments in international conferences and meetings, as well as in private conversations, we owe a great deal of gratitude to the people who have debated our viewpoints and encouraged us in our development. We are certain that some crucial omissions will be made if we begin naming them. There is no doubt that any errors or omissions are solely their responsibility! In particular, we are grateful to our families, friends, colleagues and mentors, as well as to those very special students who have inspired us over the years. Furthermore, we would like to thank the three (3) anonymous referees who provided constructive feedback during the prepublication process. Last but not least, we greatly appreciate Palgrave Macmillan's highly efficient processes.

Contents

1. Adam Smith (1723–1790) 1
2. David Ricardo (1772–1823) 17
3. Karl Marx (1818–1883) 29
4. Leon Walras (1834–1910) 45
5. John Maynard Keynes (1883–1946) 55
6. Joseph Schumpeter (1883–1950) 67
7. Friedrich Hayek (1899–1992) 79
8. Milton Friedman (1912–2006) 93
9. Robert Solow (1924–…) 107
10. John Nash (1928–2015) 117
11. Amartya Sen (1933–…) 131
12. Joseph Stiglitz (1943–…) 147
13. Paul Krugman (1953–…) 159

References 175

Index 185

Introduction

Economic Science is the Social Science that studies the activities of people associated with the creation of goods and services, with the real-world economic and financial transactions, both at the individual and collective levels. *Economic Science* is based on one or more theories, which are shaped, co-constructed or replaced with each other with the aid of quantitative analysis (mathematics, statistics, econometrics, experiments, etc.).

Economic Theory, in turn, is an abstract description of the functioning of the extremely complex real world, where new scientific knowledge does not emerge from 'nowhere' but arises out of existing knowledge, in a dialectical relationship with the 'existing' and very often to its negation. Therefore, science develops and evolves as a 'living organism', and often one scientific theory is followed by another in continuity, extension or even opposition to the previous one. Therefore, in order to have a body of knowledge for understanding *Economics*, we must delve into the various individual 'truths' of each theory and, therefore, we must look back to the work of earlier thinkers, within a science that is constantly evolving.

This journey of the formation of *Economic Theory* cannot be seen independently of its social context, since it is within this context that *Economic Science* has developed, in response to the social conditions that prevailed and their evolution. Therefore, an *Economic Theory* without knowledge of the deeper internal as well as external causal relationships that have shaped the existing theories would lead to a sterile view.

After all, as we know, people coexist with society and are shaped by it through this interaction, since humanity is ultimately determined by the totality of its social relations. It is often argued, however, that today's economic society is eternal and ideal, something like a Platonic idea, compatible with the 'speculative nature of man', who appears to have an inherent tendency to maximize his utility. According to this view, there is no inherent solidarity and cooperativeness in 'human nature' but only a tendency to compete and maximise utility.

Also, man, and the individual social and economic unit in general, appears to determine and motivate the total economy and society, and not the other way round, that is to be determined by them. In this context, the economic system appears to be perfectly functioning, since it is seen as not facing generalised economic instabilities and crises emanating from the overall economy, but the individual social and economic unit is seen as imposing its own stable, competitive, maximising behaviour on the economic system.

Finally, money is not considered to play any essential role in the economy, since it is used only as a medium of exchange and to facilitate transactions, since in most analyses in *Economics*, the prices of various commodities are expressed in relation to the prices of other commodities, that is in 'relative prices', and not as exchange for an amount of money. Hence, money is usually absent from analyses at the level of the individual unit, that is the (micro)economic perspective. At the same time, money is usually considered 'neutral' in the overall economy, that is it is believed to have no effect on other economic variables, but only increases the price at the level of the overall economy, that is in the (macro)economic perspective.

But what binds these elements together in the modern economic system? It is the so-called *market*. Markets are those sets of activities where the exchange of goods and services and/or financial assets takes place and determine two very basic elements: the prices and quantities to be sold and purchased, simultaneously. At the same time, *financial markets* also perform the function of pricing products and services and pricing risk. Hence, they provide the incentive to act speculatively on the basis of this information and are often characterised by instability inherent in the economic system, as well as a misunderstanding of the function of money in the theoretical analyses of market transactions.

Therefore, linked, directly or indirectly, to the view or the functioning of the market are: (a) speculation, (b) instability and (c) neglect of money in theoretical analyses. Therefore, we observe that modern *Economic Theory* exhibits a practical difficulty in 'metabolizing', among other things, the aforementioned concepts of *profitability*, *instability* and *money* in a theoretically consistent and coherent conceptual framework. These terms and concepts are absent from almost all textbooks in *Economics* worldwide.

In this way, this book allows us to gain a better understanding of when and how the various ideas, concepts and practices emerged, developed, and were applied in order to come up with the body of modern *Economics*.

Adam Smith (1723–1790)

▶ **Learning Objectives**

After having studied this chapter, the reader should be able to:

- Understand the meaning of the 'invisible hand' in the economy.
- Explain Adam Smith's 'labour theory'.
- Analyse Smith's ideas on the 'division of labour'.
- Give examples on the functioning of a 'free market'.
- Analyse Smith's view on the role of the state.
- Present briefly Adam Smith's contribution to *Economics*.

▶ **Summary**

Smith is widely considered as the 'father' of *Economics*, but also of the Classical School of Political Economy. His theoretical approach to systemic forces in an economic environment led to predictable conclusions, as he was able to construct a 'theory' regarding how systemic forces operate. Consequently, for him, man has a primarily 'economic character', he is homo *oeconomicus*, and his defining qualities are 'economic transaction' and 'trade'. In theory, each individual has a self-interest, which is guided by an 'invisible hand' which directs the personal desires and interests of individuals towards situations that are in the best interests of society. Therefore, Smith believed that society's prosperity is built on the pursuit of individual interests. A key theory of Smith is non-intervention, also known as *laissez faire*, which states that the less the state intervenes in economic activity, the more benefits society receives. The role of the state, according to Smith, should be limited to a few specific activities. A fundamental part of Smith's economic theory was the use of labour as the sole source of value. Further, he considered that specialisation resulting from the division of labour was the main reason for wealth creation in a society, while he was an avid advocate of capital accumulation, but not as an end in itself. According to Smith, the market would eventually stabilise at a point where profits for capitalists would be minimal. Smith's supply should remain unaffected by government intervention since money's function in the market is only to facilitate transactions. Today, Smith is considered by the majority of scholars to be a conservative economist. However, Smith was more hostile to the motives and intentions of the capitalists than most 'progressive' economists are today.

1.1 Introduction

Adam Smith is an iconic figure in *Economics* and a witness to the start of the Industrial Revolution,[1] born in 1723 in the town of Kirkcaldy, a port near Edinburgh, in County Fife, Scotland. His father Adam Smith was a customs officer, and his family had ties with some intellectuals of the time.[2] However, Adam was brought up with by his mother, having lost his father, thanks to whose will, young Adam's education was entrusted to private tutors.[3]

At the age of 14, in 1737, Adam Smith was admitted to the University of Glasgow where he studied *Physics* and *Mathematics*.[4] In 1740, he was awarded a scholarship to Oxford. There he had a book by the philosopher Hume confiscated which argued for the supremacy of reason over theology.[5] In 1751, before he was 28 years old, he took the chair of *Logic* at the University of Glasgow and soon afterwards the chair of *Moral Philosophy*,[6] but was never formally taught *Economics*.[7] Smith then travelled to Europe where he met and became friends with other intellectuals of the time, such as Turgot[8] and Hume,[9] with whom he became close friends.

However, Smith's main stimulus was the great changes that were taking place in the English economy at the time,[10] and the need for a *Political Philosophy* on the basis of which society could justify its existence independent of an authoritarian state.[11]

In 1759, he published his popular[12] *The Theory of Moral Sentiments*, which deals with the way people make moral judgements and which gave Smith a special place as a theoretician of the Enlightenment.[13] In 1776, after 12 years of writing, the *Inquiry into the Nature and Causes of the Wealth of Nations*, or, simply, *The Wealth of Nations,* was published. Although this work is a thorough historical study of how the capitalist system worked, it was Smith's wish that his manuscripts be burned after his[14] death, because of his self-critical disposition.

Smith is considered by most economists as the 'founder' of *Economic Science*, but also of the Classical School of Political Economy. Unlike other great economists, he was able to put some of his ideas on free trade into practice when he was commissioner of customs in Scotland.[15] In his personal life, he never got married and was devoted to his mother; he died in 1790 in Edinburgh, Scotland, six years after her[16] death.

1.2 Individuals and Markets

Smith's economic system revolves around three main axes:[17] the price mechanism, the division of labour and money. With regard to the third axis, the role of money in the market for Smith is simply to facilitate transactions and its supply should be unaffected by government intervention. Let us see how he developed his thoughts regarding the remaining two axes.

Smith asks how society succeeds in performing exactly those functions that are needed in order to survive and expand. He argues that this is not due to a central planning authority nor is it due to the influence of tradition acting as a stabilising influence. Rather, just as capital moves towards the industry that produces the most 'value', each worker seeks the work that will bring him the most money. His goal is his own benefit and so he is guided by 'an invisible hand'.[18] The 'invisible hand' is the one that directs the personal desires and interests of individuals towards a situation in which the interests of society[19] are best served.[20]

▶ The effort to satisfy the individual interest in an environment which consists of individuals with similar aspirations will lead to competition, which in turn will result in the production of exactly the goods that society wants, at exactly the prices that society is willing to pay. This is because self-interest acts as a driving force to direct people to those jobs for which society is willing to pay.[21]

Therefore, society is better served when it is to follow its own instincts and desires, rather than when the state is allowed to interfere.

▶ In this way, we arrive at the idea of a *laissez-faire* system where the combination of the myriad of transactions that take place lead to a better outcome than if the state tried to manage the system.[22]

Of course, Adam Smith's idea that society benefits when competition is developed and encouraged and everyone focuses on their own self-interest sparked off a reaction at the time it was formulated.[23]

Although one would imagine that society would be driven to chaos due to the fact that individuals seek to satisfy their self-interest, this is not the case.[24] In fact, any individual who seeks to achieve the best for himself, without regard to the social consequences, is confronted with a set of individuals who have similar interests and aspirations. If, for example, he sells his products at high prices the result would be, he will be left without buyers; if he is not able to pay his workers as much as others do, the result will be, he will be left without workers. In this way, the self-interested motives of individuals undergo a mutation and because of the interaction, they result in something unexpected: social cohesion and harmony.[25]

For example, suppose there are a thousand glove manufacturers. The self-interest of each one will make him raise the price to a level sufficiently higher than the cost of production in order to make a profit. This is not feasible in the long run, because if he increases his prices excessively, he will lose customers to his competitors, who sell gloves at lower prices. Only in the event that all glove producers join together and agree to sell gloves at very high prices can these prices prevail in the market. However, even in this case, this alliance can be broken by an ambitious manufacturer in another industry, for example, shoes, who decides to allocate his capital to producing gloves, which he will now sell at lower prices and thus has the potential to dominate the market.[26]

The 'laws' of the market make producers keep pace with society's aspirations in terms of the quantities of products it wants. Suppose that buyers want a larger quantity of gloves than those on offer, and at the same time, a smaller quantity of shoes. This will cause the price of gloves to rise, since buyers will make an effort to buy more gloves than are available on the market. Conversely, shoe prices will tend to fall as consumers will seek to buy fewer shoes than are available. As glove prices rise, the glove industry will become increasingly profitable.

Similarly, as shoe prices fall, the shoe industry's profits will fall. This will result in workers employed in the industry being made redundant, as the shoe industry will reduce shoe production to switch to glove production, which is becoming increasingly profitable. Consequently, the socially desirable will happen: glove production will increase and shoe[27] production will decrease. It is the 'laws' of the market, then, that cause products to be sold at the lowest possible prices and producers to produce exactly the quantities that society[28] wants.

When more gloves are produced on the market to meet the increased demand for them, their price will return to normal levels. As soon as smaller quantities of gloves are produced, the surplus will quickly disappear and their prices will return to normal levels. Thanks to the 'market mechanism', society will alter the allocation of its productive forces in order to keep pace with its new demands and desires. Individual interest and competition, each turning against the other, made it possible to achieve equilibrium without the need for any order to be issued and without any production programme to be imposed. Thus, the different interests of individuals, through competition, in a market that functions smoothly, are transformed into an overall social power.[29]

Within this framework, he considered that every good has a 'natural price' which represents its cost of production. This price may differ from the price that is formed in the market under the interaction of the forces of supply and demand. The 'price mechanism' could be distorted either due to unfair practices by firms or due to state intervention. This worried Smith as it would lead to large discrepancies between the 'natural price' and the price at which the product[30] is ultimately sold.

Thus, individuals ultimately serve the collective interest precisely because they pursue their own self-interest, that is, out of self-interest.[31] Therefore, we would say that Smith starts from the view that the development of society is determined by the *interests of* each *individual* who makes up the society and, in turn, these interests derive from the *essence (nature) of man.*[32]

▶ Consequently, Adam Smith formulated a clear version of (rational) 'individualism' where subjects act with a motive of self-interest derived from

1.2 Individuals and Markets

their own inner 'nature'. In this way, 'man' has primarily an economic substance, he is *homo economicus*, and his 'nature' is 'economic transaction' and 'trade'.[33]

At the same time, if an industry is extremely profitable, this will attract other entrepreneurs to that industry until competition reduces profits. If wages are particularly high in a particular type of employment, many people will flock to that job, so that wages will reach the same level as those paid for similar jobs requiring the same level of knowledge and skills. Conversely, if workers' wages or the profitability of entrepreneurs is too low in a sector of the economy, this will result in capital and workers being drawn away from that sector until the quantity supplied is better matched to the quantity[34] demanded. Here, obviously, a 'supply and demand mechanism' is implied but Smith did not put it that[35] way.

The man who, because of his selfish nature, is constantly striving to improve his position, is much more interested in what concerns himself than in what concerns others. In the complex and changing matrix of economic phenomena, we shall find a constant active force: the uniform, constant and unceasing effort of every man to improve his position, the principle from which public and national, as well as private wealth, ultimately arises.[36] In other words, man's 'nature' is understood as an independent commodity producer, while his relations with the other members of society are relations of exchange and competition, and thus society is a society of exchange for the purpose of self-interest.[37]

It is precisely from this 'human nature' that Smith derives his 'labour theory of value' and the 'division of labour'. Thus, Smith's theory takes on the character of an inductive theoretical system, where individuals operate in the context of society, and it is precisely from this natural tendency of the individual that universal 'laws' are derived which regulate the behaviour of the 'whole', despite their individualistic origin. We would say that economic phenomena in Smith's work possess an intrinsic, 'natural', law-like regularity, existing independently of the state and based on the unchanging natural inclinations of the individual.[38] In other words, Smith follows a Newtonian causal method in his work, whereby, relying on a central force, namely individual interest, leads to social evolution.[39] One of the main weaknesses of the theory is that it remained unproven by Smith, who could not prove that equilibrium exists, nor that it is unique (uniqueness), nor that it is stable.[40]

This division of labour—to be studied in what follows—from which so many advantages derive is the consequence of a natural tendency of human nature, which does not aim at a general benefit, that is, the tendency to bargain, to trade and to exchange one thing for another.[41] Thus, every human being in some way becomes a trader.[42]

Finally, Smith was strongly opposed to the abolition of competition and the creation of large, powerful firms and monopolies[43] on the basis of the 'invisible hand' in competitive[44] conditions.

1.3 Labour Theory and Resource Allocation

Smith regarded labour as the only real source of 'value' and followed the Aristotelian division of value between the 'use-value' of goods, which shows how useful a given quantity of a good is, and 'exchange-value', which expresses the quantity of goods with which one good can be exchanged. Note that a good can have a high use value and a low exchange value (e.g. water) or a low use value and a high exchange value (e.g. diamonds).[45]

As Smith wrote, labour is the true measure of the exchange value of all commodities[46] and it is the final and real standard by which the values of all commodities at any time and place can be estimated and compared.[47] Thus, Smith was the first economist to develop and make labour the cornerstone of economic theory.[48]

Therefore, according to Adam Smith, *Political Economy* deals with the independent holders of 'commodities', while commodities include 'labour', which each worker sells to his employer, necessary for the production of certain commodities. Additionally, the economy is based on the *division of labour*, since each commodity holder exchanges the particular commodity he possesses with the commodities of other commodity holders, which he uses to satisfy his needs and is therefore dependent on them. At the same time, *commodities are labour products* and their *value* is proportional to the amount of labour required to produce them.[49]

▶ By exchanging commodities between them, the commodity owners are in fact exchanging their labour, that is, each one 'buys' with a quantity of his own labour an equal quantity of the other's labour, and thus the value of each commodity is proportional to the quantity of labour expended in its production.[50]

Adam Smith was the economist of manufacturing, which was the precursor of the large factory.[51] The manufacture, which was an evolution of the domestic production system, was based on manual technology, whose high level of productivity was due to the segmentation of the production process, the specialisation of workers and the diversification of tools.[52]

With this view, Smith founded the Classical School of Political Economy, as he inaugurated for the first time a new theoretical subject.

▶ In brief, the object of Classical Political Economy is the study of labour-dependent 'value' in a commodity-producing society, where 'labour' itself is a commodity.

▶ Thus, through this theory, he also defined social classes as capitalists, workers and landlords and, for the first time, the corresponding incomes as profit, wages and land rent.[53]

However, Adam Smith displayed theoretical contradictions in his work as well as two versions of the theory of value[54] and thus failed to formulate a fully coherent theory[55] of value. More specifically, according to Smith, value is seen as a quantitative characteristic of commodities, arising from the fact that they are products of

1.3 Labour Theory and Resource Allocation

human labour. The first of Smith's two versions of value theory, in an absolute way, considered value as an expression of the amount of labour 'expended' in the production of commodities,[56] while the second version of his value theory regards value as a quantity derivative of the 'incomes' of the three social classes: capitalists, landlords and workers.[57]

Smith's work, as mentioned above, is undoubtedly influenced by the emergence and dominance of factories in the production process. The division of labour and the specialisation that this entails, Smith sees as the basic cause of the wealth created in a society.[58] Thus, at the beginning of his book *The Wealth of Nations*, he focuses on the division of labour.[59] According to Smith, the division of labour is a process which subdivides a certain productive function into a number of separate functions, usually performed by a different individual or group of individuals, through which the capacity of workers is increased, the time spent in moving workers from one activity to another is reduced, and technological change[60] is promoted.

However, Smith warns of the negative impact of mass production on the human being who spends his entire life performing a few simple functions.[61] At the same time, Smith was a strong advocate of capital accumulation, but not as an end in itself, that is, he was in no way in favour of accumulation for the sake of accumulation. Society would benefit from it, since if one used capital to build machines, one could set in motion the division of labour that becomes the cause of the multiplication of people's productive energies. The pursuit of self-interest would lead to the prosperity of society. However, accumulation would eventually reach a level where further accumulation would seem to be impossible.[62]

This would happen because as accumulation increased, it would create a greater demand for labour and lead capitalists to compete for the workers employed in their industries. But the effect of increasing wages is that profitability decreases and therefore the initial incentive to invest ceases to exist.[63] But with an increase in wages, the number of workers would increase, because, since in Smith's time, there was high infant and child mortality, higher wages would most likely have a significant positive correlation with the number of children reaching working age.

Thus, increased accumulation leads to an increase in workers' wages, which in turn leads to an increase in the number of workers, as the better paid workers can now raise their children, in other words, infant and child mortality is reduced. Consequently, there will be an increase in the supply of workers. But this will put reverse pressure on the level of their wages. Therefore, the barrier of higher wages can be overcome by population growth, which is precisely what the increase in wages has allowed to happen. This would imply that accumulation could continue unhindered and an upward path would start for society provided that there is no state intervention in the market[64] mechanism.

Smith was optimistic that what we mean today when we use the term 'economic development' could be sustained for a long time, but not forever. The reason for this was that population growth would push wages back down to the minimum maintenance level. Nevertheless, Smith believed that over many years, access to goods as well as the welfare of working-class people would improve. This development would come to an end in about 200 years, when society would have fully exhausted its stock of unused resources and achieved the most detailed division of labour possible. Eventually, the market would remain at a point where workers would earn a maintenance wage and capitalists low profits. Landlords would probably be the only ones who would enjoy a more satisfactory income, as the larger population, in order to survive, would need a larger quantity of goods.[65]

1.4 The Role of the State

Contrary to a widely held view, Smith does not support the capitalist class. On the one hand, he clearly supports private property without which there can be no competition, which in turn plays an important role in the accumulation of capital and social welfare.[66] On the other hand, although he stood in admiration of the capitalists' achievements, he was extremely sceptical of their motives and was concerned with the needs of the working class, which he no doubt sympathised with. Those whom he did not like were the landlords, because he considered that they reduced the possibilities of economic development, since they do not contribute in any way to the creation of wealth for the benefit of society, and they have no incentive to accumulate capital.[67]

At the same time, workers also have low wages, and landlords have no real tendency to accumulate. Consequently, the greater the proportion of national income that goes to the profits of the capitalist class, the higher the growth of national wealth due to the increase in economic activity. Thus, the interest of the nation goes hand in hand with that of the capitalist class.[68]

But what Smith is almost exclusively concerned with is to increase the wealth of the whole nation, not to satisfy the interests of any one class. Wealth for Smith is that all members of society should be able to consume goods, even if this is not possible in equal quantities for all,[69] while the individual capitalist interest is transformed into the general interest of society through the individual competition.

The Wealth of Nations was widely recognised early on and its most ardent supporters were the capitalists who were gaining more and more power. It was precisely these people, however, that Smith considered unfit to have a leading and prominent position in humanity, as they were characterised by inhuman and predatory motives.[70] Smith was neither for nor against any class. He fervently supported his ideas and his own system, which could, thanks to the market operating freely and without interference, reach its maximum point of efficiency. Smith was particularly critical and caustic of those systems that supported the interest of producers at the expense of the interest of consumers and believed that production had no reason for existence other than consumption.[71]

Smith, on the basis of his theory, advocates *non-interventionism*, known as *laissez faire*, according to which the less the state intervenes in economic activity, the greater the benefits to society. He believed that governments are irresponsible in the way they allocate their resources and that they usually engage in wasteful spending, reducing the growth potential of the economy. This is because high spending limits the output of the economy that could be invested.[72]

Consistent with the spirit of Enlightenment thinkers, Smith treats the imposition of protectionist measures by the state as an obstacle to the efficient functioning of the market.[73] But it should be emphasised that he was not against certain actions by the state that could promote general welfare. Smith believed that the free market can only ensure positive social outcomes when it interacts smoothly with the state. More specifically, for the free market to function smoothly, it requires the existence of a fair institutional framework and a society whose principles complement those of the market.[74]

Therefore, Smith's role of the state should refer to the following activities: To protect society from the violence that may develop within it, to shield it against the hostile dispositions of other societies, to secure the objective administration of justice for all without exception, and to create and maintain those institutions and projects which may be of special benefit to society and whose form is such that it is economically unprofitable for any private individual or group of private individuals to produce them. Such may be, for example, infrastructure and health care. For Smith, it is the responsibility of the government to provide universal education to offset these effects. He was an advocate of testing in order to maintain high educational standards and stressed the importance of turning to science as a means of liberation from prejudice and superstition.[75]

At the same time, Smith argues that the state should not restrict imports and subsidise exports, nor should it enact laws to protect industry from competition, nor should it make public expenditures for non-productive purposes.[76] However, for Smith, the greatest threat to the system is not the state, but the abolition of free competition and the creation of monopolies.[77] It is necessary, according to Smith, that the market be left free to arrive at its own 'natural' levels of wages, prices, profits and quantities of production, for this will benefit the real wealth of the nation and social harmony and prosperity. It is worth noting, however, that because any legislative action by the government can be interpreted as a restriction on the smooth functioning of the market, arguments drawing their inspiration from the *Wealth of Nations* have often been used to block early attempts to implement laws with a humanitarian content.[78]

The thinker, then, who spoke of the greed of the eighteenth-century industrialists, which led them to exploit the other members of society, came to be considered their supporters. Even today, Smith is still regarded by the vast majority of scholars as a 'conservative' economist. But the reality is that Smith was more hostile to the motives and intentions of capitalists than most economists considered 'progressive' these days.[79]

1.5   Profit, Productive Labour and Taxation

Capitalism in Smith, as in other classical economists, is seen as a system that is ever evolving and expanding. The aim of the entrepreneur in a profit-driven capitalist society is to continually improve and strengthen his position which he hopes will bring him even greater profits. However, whether and on what scale capitalism will continue to grow in a seamless manner is an interesting question.[80]

Smith was the first to study industrial profit as a separate category, which was a major advance for the time.[81] However, Smith believed that in the long run, the market would stabilise at a level where profits for capitalists would be meagre.[82] In fact, profitability for capitalists, over time, would steadily decline to the point where it would even tend to reach zero.

Capitalists still earn some profits but do not live in luxury, as one would expect, based on Smith's work. The capitalist is able to secure for himself a remuneration that exceeds that of the workers he employs within his company as a reward for his business/management skills. According to Smith, even the owner of capital is required to work hard if he wishes to maintain a living standard.[83]

One reason for the long-term downward trend in profitability is that in order to make their products more competitive, capitalists reduce their prices, which in turn reduces profits. Since investment opportunities are not unlimited, the accumulation of capital goods and competition imply a contraction of profits.[84]

At the same time, whenever a sector of production shows potential for high profitability, there will be an attraction of other entrepreneurs to that sector, until profitability is reduced due to competition.[85] Finally, capitalists compete with each other for the workers they wish to attract for employment, resulting in higher wages and lower profitability. Of course, it is true that profits may increase, but profitability, as measured by a variety of metrics, may not.[86]

Meanwhile, Smith divided labour into two categories: productive labour and unproductive labour. Productive labour refers to the production of goods, while non-productive labour refers to the production of services. The first category includes, for example, manual workers, while the second category includes, for example, domestic workers.[87] Similarly, the work of a judge, a military officer or a leader[88] is equally unproductive for Smith. As production is understood as the accumulation of goods, he considers productive labour to be more important for sustaining accumulation than unproductive labour. Therefore, Smith argues that an economy should minimise the proportion of workers engaged in non-productive labor.[89]

Due to the fact that services are consumed immediately after they are produced and cannot be preserved for consumption in the future, according to Smith, they cannot be considered production. Therefore, the workers employed in services are not productive, since their efforts do not contribute to the increase of surplus and subsequent wealth. Contrarily, wage workers engaged in agricultural or industrial activities that generate profits for capitalists can be considered productive since their remuneration is derived from capital. The question of productive and unproductive labour and the relationship between the respective sectors of the economy and economic growth is still debated today.[90]

Finally, Smith recommends that governments should not run deficit budgets, because this increases the public debt, which threatens the independence of the nation and is an obstacle to growth. Budgets should be balanced and public expenditure should be covered entirely by tax revenues and not by borrowing.[91] Moreover, public spending should definitely be directed towards productive purposes and promote the well-being of society.[92]

In Smith's work, reference is made to the elements that should characterise a socially just system of taxation:[93] He develops four basic principles: (a) the principle of *Equality*, according to which citizens should pay taxes in proportion to their incomes; (b) the principle of *Certainty*, according to which what governs the payment of taxes should be strictly defined and clear; (c) the principle of *Convenience*, which requires that the tax should be levied in the most appropriate manner and at the most favourable time for the taxpayer; and (d) the principle of *Economy/Efficiency*, according to which, taxes should be collected at the lowest possible economic cost.

1.6 The Theoretical Legacy of Smith

Initially, Smith's contribution to the emergence of the study of economic phenomena as an independent scientific field was undoubtedly important. Until then, interpretations were given to economic phenomena on a case-by-case basis, without generalisations. Smith was able to 'theorise' the way in which the systematic forces at work in an economic environment operate to arrive at logical conclusions.[94]

In conclusion, Smith's work appears long after the first economic writings which, however, contained only fragmentary theoretical economic thoughts and ideas and prepared the ground for the formulation of the new theoretical field. However, these works did not establish a new theoretical field, partly because their subject matter was not clearly distinguishable from that of *Political Philosophy* and partly because they were approaches that described an ideal economic model that the authors simply envisioned imposing by political means. Smith, by contrast, placed individual economic processes at the heart of the social system as the driving force of all social development and argued, consequently, that the economy is governed by self-sustaining functions that express the intrinsic regularities or 'laws' of economic processes.[95]

Of course, many great economists were influenced by Smith, as we shall see below, directly or indirectly. He is generally famous for his well-known idea that if people are allowed to pursue their own self-interests, society as a whole will eventually benefit.[96] Especially after the collapse of the former Soviet Union and the countries of Eastern Europe, the domination of the state and labour unions was seen as a major obstacle to economic development; therefore, interest in Smith's work was revived. In particular, conservative politicians Ronald Reagan and Margaret Thatcher relied on selected parts of his work to justify policies of limiting the role of the state in the economy and of 'liberalising' markets.[97] However, Smith never advocated 'absolute' laissez-faire as he considered government to have an important role in the economy,[98] while recognising the need for the state to take measures for social welfare, such as in education, health, and so on.

Furthermore, in his analysis of the division of labour, he explained why workers in a large car manufacturer each add their own parts to the vehicle, why busy managers do not answer the phone themselves, but their secretary does, and why we buy pork chops in the shop instead of raising pigs at home.[99] Moreover, his opposition to the big monopolies was in line with the privatisation programmes that turned state monopolies, such as energy production, water supply, public transport, and so on into private enterprises, competing to some extent with each other.

However, we do not know whether an economy that fully adopted *all* of Smith's ideas would be entirely desirable to its citizens. Let us not forget that to date governments seem to have played even a much larger role than Smith might have wished and an indication of this is the fact that in his home country, Britain, about 40 per cent of the economy is in the hands of the state in the form of health, education, and so on.[100] While many may have accepted the existence of a free market, they may also have wanted state intervention to control it. Additionally, many turned against thinkers such as Smith following the financial crisis of the previous decade, believing that a free market without state controls leads to recession.[101] Thus, nowadays, we seem to have drifted away partly from Smith's teachings, even though his work is present, directly or indirectly, in almost all economics textbooks around the world.

Key Takeaways

- Man's defining qualities are 'economic transaction' and 'trade'.
- Labour is the only real source of value in the economy.
- The pursuit of the individual interest leads to the prosperity of society.
- Division of labour and specialisation are the main causes of wealth.
- Economic activity benefits from reduced government intervention.

Revision Questions

- What is the 'invisible hand' in the economy?
- What is the meaning of (rational) 'individualism'?
- What are the main points of Adam Smith's 'labour theory of value'?
- What is the 'division of labour'?
- What is Smith's position on state intervention?
- How does Smith separate work into productive and non-productive?
- What is his view on profitability in the long run?
- Is Adam Smith a conservative economist?
- What is Smith's main contribution to *Economics*?

Notes

1 Yueh (2018).
2 Yueh (2018).
3 Thornton (2014).
4 Yueh (2018).
5 Thornton (2014).
6 Backhouse (2009).

7 Thornton (2014).
 8 Tsoulfidis (2008).
 9 Drakopoulos and Karagiannis (2003).
10 Rubin (1979).
11 Screpanti and Zamagni (2005).
12 Thornton (2014).
13 Yueh (2018).
14 Yueh (2018).
15 Yueh (2018).
16 Thornton (2014).
17 Yueh (2018).
18 Thornton (2014).
19 Heilbroner (2011).
20 Smith (1981).
21 Smith (1981).
22 Thornton (2014).
23 Varoufakis (2007).
24 Tsoulfidis (2010).
25 Tsoulfidis (2010).
26 Heilbroner (2011).
27 Heilbroner (2011).
28 Tsoulfidis (2010).
29 Heilbroner (2011).
30 Yueh (2018).
31 Screpanti and Zamagni (2005).
32 Milios et al. (2018).
33 Milios et al. (2018).
34 Heilbroner (2011).
35 Thornton (2014).
36 Rubin (1979).
37 Rubin (1979).
38 Milios et al. (2018).
39 Karagiannis (2001).
40 Screpanti and Zamagni (2005).
41 Smith (1981).
42 Smith (1981).
43 Thornton (2014).
44 Screpanti and Zamagni (2005).
45 Drakopoulos and Karagiannis (2003).

46 Smith (1981).
47 Smith (1981).
48 Rubin (1979).
49 Milios et al. (2018).
50 Smith (1981).
51 Rubin (1979).
52 Rubin (1979).
53 Rubin (1979).
54 Milios et al. (2018).
55 Screpanti and Zamagni (2005).
56 Rubin (1979).
57 Milios et al. (2018).
58 Yueh (2018).
59 Smith (1981).
60 Screpanti and Zamagni (2005).
61 Smith (1981).
62 Heilbroner (2011).
63 Tsoulfidis (2010).
64 Heilbroner (2011).
65 Heilbroner (2011).
66 Tsoulfidis (2010).
67 Screpanti and Zamagni (2005).
68 Screpanti and Zamagni (2005).
69 Smith (1981).
70 Heilbroner (2011).
71 Heilbroner (2011).
72 Tsoulfidis (2010).
73 Yueh (2018).
74 van Staveren (2021).
75 Yueh (2018).
76 Heilbroner (2011).
77 Smith (1981).
78 Heilbroner (2011).
79 Heilbroner (2011).
80 Tsoulfidis (2010).
81 Rubin (1979).
82 Heilbroner (2011).
83 Tsoulfidis (2010)
84 Tsoulfidis (2010).

85 Heilbroner (2011).
86 Tsoulfidis and Paitaridis (2012).
87 Screpanti and Zamagni (2005).
88 Backhouse (2009).
89 Screpanti and Zamagni (2005).
90 Tsoulfidis (2010).
91 Tsoulfidis (2010).
92 Heilbroner (2011).
93 Tsoulfidis (2010).
94 Tsoulfidis (2010).
95 Milios et al. (2018).
96 Thornton (2014).
97 Thornton (2014).
98 Backhouse (2009).
99 Thornton (2014).
100 Thornton (2014).
101 Thornton (2014).

References

Backhouse, R. E. (2009). *The evolution of economic thought*. Kritiki.
Drakopoulos, S., & Karagiannis, A. (2003). *History of economic thought: An overview*. Kritiki Publications.
Heilbroner, R. L. (2011). *The worldly philosophers: The lives, times and ideas of the great economic thinkers*. Simon and Schuster.
Karagiannis, A. (2001). *Economic methodology*. Kritiki Publications.
Milios, J., Dimoulis, D., & Economakis, G. (2018 [2002]). *Karl Marx and the classics, an essay on value, crises and the capitalist mode of production*. Routledge.
Rubin, I. I. (1979). *A history of economic thought*. Ink links.
Screpanti, E., & Zamagni, S. (2005). *An outline of the history of economic thought*. OUP.
Smith, A. (1981). *An inquiry into the nature and causes of the Wealth of Nations*. Liberty Classics.
Thornton, P. (2014). *The great economists: Ten economists whose thinking changed the way we live*. Pearson UK.
Tsoulfidis, L. (2008). *History of economic theory and policy*. University of Macedonia Publications.
Tsoulfidis, L. (2010). *Competing schools of economic thought*. Springer Science & Business Media.
Tsoulfidis, L., & Paitaridis, D. (2012). Revisiting Adam Smith's theory of the falling rate of profit. *International Journal of Social Economics, 39*(5), 304–313.
van Staveren, I. (2021). *Alternative ideas from 10 (almost) forgotten economists*. Springer Nature Press.
Varoufakis, G. (2007). *Political economy: The economy in the light of criticism*. Gutenberg Publications.
Yueh, L. (2018). *What would the great economists do?* Picador.

David Ricardo (1772–1823)

2

▶ **Learning Objectives**

After studying this chapter, the reader should be able to:

- Understand the meaning of 'comparative advantage'.
- Explain David Ricardo's 'labour theory of value'.
- Distinguish the role of the landlord from that of the capitalist.
- Analyse David Ricardo's views on international trade.
- Present briefly David Ricardo's contribution to Economics.

▶ **Summary**

David Ricardo is often considered the 'father' of systematic and scientific *Economic Analysis*, through his work on the theory of comparative advantage, according to which free trade will reduce prices and economies will become richer if they specialise in what they know how to do best. According to Ricardo, the value of a commodity depends on the amount of labour required to produce it. As a result, capitalists and landlords appropriate part of the value produced by the worker. That is to say, both the profit of the capitalists and the rent of the landlords, which do not contribute to the productive process, are deductions from the value created by the workers. Landlords were seen by Ricardo not only as agents of unproductive consumption but also as obstacles to the development of capitalism. Although Ricardo agreed with Smith's idea on long-term capital accumulation, on the other hand, he believed that competition may not lead to positive results, as those who hold some resources that are in short supply will benefit more and more from the increased demand for products produced using these resources. He considered that the mechanisation of production is beneficial for all social classes, as it increases productivity and reduces production costs and, consequently, prices in competitive conditions. In addition, he believed that government spending was not directed to productive purposes and that, for this reason, their long-term financing through public borrowing would have important social consequences. This is due to the fact that lending to the government prevents one from investing in a business.

2.1 Introduction

David Ricardo, considered by many to be the 'father' of systematic and scientific *Economic Analysis*,[1] was born in London in 1772 and was the third child of a large Jewish family of Dutch descent with seventeen children. As for his education, his parents entrusted the best teachers with the task of providing him with knowledge of immediate practical application necessary for his professional career. At the young age of 14, David worked for the brokerage firm his father owned and never acquired a formal university education.[2] Ricardo's relationship with his parents was disrupted when he entered into a relationship with a woman of another religion.[3] Then, wishing to marry her, he was forced to leave home, as was the Jewish custom of the time. He then joined the ranks of Christianity in order to enter high society.[4]

Ricardo acquired a considerable fortune as an investor during the Napoleonic Wars.[5] Ricardo was such a good investor that he managed to become one of the wealthiest men in Britain. This was helped by the fact that he also made use of his father's connections on the London Stock Exchange, even though his relationship with his family had broken down because of his marriage; but his friends supported him financially.[6] By the age of 43 he already had an enormous fortune for the time and became the owner of land.[7] The very large fortune he acquired[8] enabled him to devote the rest of his life to study, starting with the *Natural Sciences*.[9]

Perhaps he was influenced by the universal and indestructible laws in the *Natural Sciences* when he stated that the fundamental laws of *Political Economy* do not change.[10] The encounter with Adam Smith's Wealth of Nations while attending to his wife in her bed of pain led him entirely to the study of *Economics* in 1799.[11] Ricardo published a series of economic articles in the *Morning Chronicle* that were incorporated into his work entitled *The High Price of Bullion: A Proof of the Depreciation of Banknotes* in 1810. In it, Ricardo argued that the increased printing of money by the Central Bank was the cause of the high inflation that existed at the time. This thesis attracted the interest of some of the leading thinkers of the time, such as Thomas Malthus, Jeremy Bentham and James Mill.[12]

In 1817, Ricardo, at the urging of his friend James Mill and father John Stuart Mill, wrote his most important work, *The Principles of Political Economy and Taxation*. In it, he demonstrated his skill in creating Economic Models aimed at modelling and theorising economic phenomena, criticising the *Wealth of Nations* and expectations of the improvement of society.[13] Unlike Smith, for Ricardo, society was an 'internally divided camp'. This view of his is partly explained by the fact that in his lifetime, in England there was increasing rivalry between the rising classes of capitalists and landlords.[14]

As a personality, Ricardo enjoyed great respect and social recognition and was a close friend of the well-known economist Robert Malthus, with whom he had intense intellectual conflicts.[15] As was often the case at the time, Ricardo bought his parliamentary seat in order to support his views, demonstrating great consistency of words and actions, and did not hesitate to pass bills that were against his personal interests but in line with his philosophy. Ricardo's arguments and proposals were the product of rigorous economic analysis and elaboration such as the proportional tariffs on cereals imported from abroad: with each decrease in price abroad, the tariff increased. As a result, cheaper cereals were kept out of the English market, benefitting domestic landlords.[16] Ricardo held his parliamentary position until his death in 1823 at the age of just 51, brought on by an unexpected infection. In addition to his wife and children, part of his fortune went to his friends Malthus and Mill.[17]

2.2 Labour Theory of Value

The Ricardian system studies all of the basic issues of economic theory, such as those grappled with by—among others—Karl Marx (1818–1883), Leon Walras (1834–1910) and John Maynard Keynes (1883–1946).[18] Ricardo, through his study of *Economics*, sought to discover the mechanisms and internal regularities or 'laws' through which the product is distributed to the social classes. To this end, he first had to clarify the question of 'value'. Ricardo's method of approaching *Economics* has led economists to develop theories that are evaluated more by their ability to be rejected logically than by empirical validation. As a result, it is possible to separate *Economics* from *Ethics*, *Philosophy*, and *History*.[19] In the light of Newtonian *Physics*, he developed a system in which the movement of economic variables is determined by exchange values.[20]

In this context, in the *History of Economic Thought*, Ricardo was particularly popular in terms of the theory of value he developed, as he continued in the line of thought developed by Adam Smith. Ricardo, like Smith, established as the cornerstone of value the amount of labour used in the production of commodities.[21]

According to Ricardo, value is seen as a quantitative characteristic of commodities, arising from the fact that they are products of human labour. However, Ricardo developed one of the two versions of Smith's value theory, which saw value as an expression of the amount of labour 'expended' in the production of commodities[22] and rejected the version of value theory associated with the concept of labour, which took value as a quantity derived from the sum of the incomes of the three social classes: capitalists, landlords and workers.[23]

Ricardo's rejection of Smith's second theory of labour value, also known as the 'cost of production theory of value', is characteristic, since it states that the value of a commodity depends on the amount of labour needed to produce it and not on the greater or lesser remuneration paid for this labour, which would mean that an increase in the level of wages would lead to an increase in the value of the product.[24]

Ricardo's theory of value has the consequence that capitalists and landlords appropriate a part of the value produced by the worker. That is, both the capitalists' profit and the landlords' income are deductions from the labour expended for the benefit of agents who do not themselves contribute to the productive process.[25] In other words, the basis of profit remains the same: the appropriation of part of the products of labour, since neither the capitalist nor the landowner 'really' contribute to the productive process. It is therefore inferred that the core of the organisation of society is the legal institution of private property and, in this sense, profit constitutes the result of the redistribution of labour income in favour of private property.[26]

Moreover, Ricardo explicitly differentiated the capitalist from the landowner, since the former plays a role in the organisation of production and the expansion of the productive capacity of the firm, while the latter simply exploits the 'scarcity' of land for his own benefit. This endogenous character of the capitalist in relation to the production process is due to the fact that there was not a high degree of separation between 'ownership' and 'control', and therefore the role of the capitalist as owner is extended to include, to some extent, the entrepreneur/director/manager. Therefore, technically speaking, the capitalist as entrepreneur/director/manager has a productive contribution, overseeing the production process. Of course, at the same time, he remains an owner who benefits from the appropriation of part of the value produced, from the product of labour. At the same time, landlords, having not contributed to the production process, simply exploit the scarcity of the land they own by getting a land rent[27] (Ricardo's theory of differential rent).

As a result, Ricardo agreed with Smith that long-term capital accumulation is inevitable, but he also argued that competition may not lead to desirable outcomes since those who own scarce resources will benefit from their increased demand.[28]

▶ In this context, based on the fact that prices are shaped by the interaction of the forces of demand and supply, and while the basic condition for the above is the existence of free competition,[29] Ricardo argued that the 'natural price'—that is, the price at which the profit in an industry equals the average rate of profit of the economy as a whole—is determined mainly by the time required to produce a product.[30]

▶ Rate of profit is defined as the ratio of profits earned by a firm to the total capital required to make that production possible over a given period, usually a year.[31]

Thus, according to Ricardo, it is the amount of labour required to produce a commodity—together with its scarcity when we refer to the agrarian sector (i.e. differential rent)—that determines its exchange value,[32] which is not determined by its use value, since the latter is only a condition of exchange.

Finally, Ricardo tried, without success, to identify a commodity whose production always requires the same amount of labour and whose price remains unchanged despite changes in the distribution of income, in order to use it as an 'invariable measure of value'. However, despite his failure in this endeavour, Ricardo hypothesised that gold could, at least in part, play this[33] role.

2.3 Capitalists, Landlords and Profit

In Ricardo's analysis, economic activity shows a continuous tendency to expand and, in principle, his ideas do not seem to be particularly different from those of Smith. However, Ricardo's theoretical analysis differs markedly, as we have seen, with regard to his references to the role of landlords, vis-à-vis, capitalists.[34] Indeed, Ricardo's theory expressed, as we have also seen, the class conflict between capitalists and landlords that characterised English society of the period, between 1816 and 1846, approximately.[35]

Capitalists consider that they save and reinvest their profits for the purpose of accumulating capital, on which their survival depends,[36] by increasing the demand for workers, who until then were paid a living wage that provided them with the bare necessities so that they and their families could survive. With the accumulation that capitalists seek, given that they must constantly be one step ahead of their competitors (since any level of profitability above the 'normal' level, for example, thanks to a new technique or penetration of a new market, is quickly erased by competition)[37], the workers' wage will exceed the living wage. But this is only temporary, as the population increase of workers that will result will bring it back to its previous level, as argued by Smith before Ricardo.

Thus, Ricardo considers the capitalist's profit to be substantially different from the landowner's rent. More specifically, Ricardo's view was that capitalists save and, unlike landlords, do not squander their wealth on consumption. In fact, they retain their profits and reinvest them. And, subsequently, savings become investments, and as such, they play a positive role in capitalist development. In contrast, landlords were identified with 'unproductive' consumption.[38]

According to Ricardo, landlords do not just squander their income, but extract an ever higher rent due to the decreasing fertility and therefore efficiency of the soil as it is cultivated more, the price of agricultural products, especially cereals, will constantly increase and so will the rent of landlords with more fertile soils[39] (differential rent). This will increase the price of the workers' subsistence wage, thus squeezing the capitalists' profit, and hence the rate of capital accumulation. Consequently, the chain of 'cause and effect' that Ricardo had described was as follows: declining soil fertility, rising grain price, rising wages, falling profits, slowing rate of capital accumulation.[40] Thus, Ricardo, through his theory of differential rent, perceived landlords not only as agents of unproductive consumption but also as 'obstacles' to capitalist development.[41]

At the same time, as workers already receive a wage, which is now insufficient to buy the now more expensive food, they will see increases in their wages because otherwise they will not be able to support themselves to work. Increased wages for workers do not mean an improvement in their standard of living, as the price of food is higher, and also the increase in their population and the consequent increase in labour supply will reduce them again.[42]

Therefore, unlike Smith, who believed that the division of labour would benefit all members of society, only landlords benefit from this process, as the increase in wages brought about by the rise in food prices reduces the capitalists' profits and is a disincentive to continue accumulating and to undertake new investments and business activities.[43] Consequently, society reaches a stage of 'stagnation' and the biggest victim is the capitalist, as his actions benefit the other two social classes, but they exert enormous pressure on him, which eventually leads to him seeing his profits approaching zero.[44]

This situation, according to Ricardo, could be reversed by increasing productivity, made possible by improving technology. Another solution he proposed was to reduce the prices of agricultural products and, consequently, wages.[45] Indeed, for some of his ideas, Ricardo acknowledged his intellectual debt to Malthus and the latter, respectively, had no difficulty in accepting many of the conclusions of the former, despite their disagreements on key issues.[46]

2.4 International Trade and Technology

In the context of international trade, Ricardo developed his ideas, starting with Smith's reasoning. This is not surprising, given that Ricardo first became interested in *Economics* thanks to the *Wealth of Nations*.[47]

Smith was in favour of free trade, believing that it promoted the economic prosperity of the trading nations. Therefore, if a country produces a good using fewer resources than the others do, that is, it has an 'absolute advantage' in its production, it should specialise in producing that good and export it to the other countries. In turn, that country will import from the others the good in the production of which they have an absolute advantage, i.e. the ability to produce it at lower cost, and in which they should specialise. Such trade between countries presupposes free trade conditions and will benefit both countries.

Ricardo went further by introducing the concept of comparative advantage as follows: If two countries exchange only two products with each other and one of them has an absolute advantage in the production of both, Ricardo argued that the country that has an advantage in both should export those products to the other. Suppose, for example, that Portugal produces cheaper wine and cloth than England. Consequently, by exporting these products to England, it will extract some of the gold that the latter has, with the result that the money supply in England, and hence the price level, will fall. The opposite will happen in Portugal. As this continues to happen, at some point, England will be able to produce one of the two goods more cheaply, so it will in turn have to specialise in the production of that good, which will benefit both countries. All this will happen on the assumption that the price level in an economy depends on the amount of money in circulation.[48]

Throughout his work, Ricardo attempted to demonstrate that foreign trade is an important factor in the expansion of consumption opportunities.[49] Moreover, Ricardo was one of the first economists to deal specifically with the issue of technology and, indeed, in the course of his work he did not hesitate to revise his views on the impact of the extensive use of machines on the production process. In the first edition of his *Principles of Political Economy,* he considers that the mechanisation of production is beneficial to all social classes, since it increases productivity and reduces production costs and, consequently, prices in competitive conditions. Of course, mechanisation can lead to unemployment, but because of Say's law (codified in that 'supply creates equal demand'), which Ricardo shared, this will be temporary.[50]

Later on, however, he considered that the mechanisation of the production process may be detrimental to the working class, since the unemployment it will bring about will not be temporary. Ricardo, in the end, argued that technological progress in a country should be encouraged and promoted, despite any negative consequences it may cause as, among other things, it makes the country more competitive in international markets due to the reduction of production[51] costs.

2.5 Taxation and Public Debt

▶ Ricardo developed his views on taxation in great detail. The technique he used was what we nowadays call 'comparative statics'. In it, two equilibrium situations are considered. The second situation arises from the first when some of its determinants[52] are changed.

According to Ricardo, taxing workers' wages will result in a reduction in firms' profits since firms will be forced to increase wages in general. This will act as a disincentive for capitalists from further capital accumulation. In terms of profit taxation, Ricardo argued that if it takes place across all sectors of production, it will lead to an increase in the level of prices.[53] With regard to taxes on land rent, although Ricardo could have advocated the view that all taxes should be replaced by a single tax on land rent, he did not do so for the following reasons: (a) because he considered that a tax on land rent would have the same consequences as a tax on profits; (b) because such a tax would not be consistent with the aim of establishing a just tax system; and (c) because it would lead to speculative revaluations in the price of land and to turbulence in economic activity in general.[54]

In addition to direct taxes, i.e. taxes imposed on wages, profits and land, Ricardo also referred in his work to indirect taxes, i.e. those taxes imposed on the prices of products, arguing that they increase the cost of their production and that this is also generalised to other industries or products to the extent that the products on which an indirect tax is imposed are the raw material for others. Also, the increase in the price of products due to indirect taxation leads to increases in wages, as the previous lower wages are no longer sufficient to buy the same 'basket of goods', which reduces the profit of capitalists and their willingness to undertake investments.[55]

Ricardo believed that government spending is not directed to productive purposes and therefore in the long run financing it through public borrowing will have dire social consequences. The reason for this is that by borrowing from the government, one is in effect depriving one's money from being invested in entrepreneurial activity. Instead, he sees his money wasted by the government on unproductive investments.[56] Ricardo, true to his position that *Economics* is scientific in nature—contrary to the prevailing view of his day—proposed taxing capital in order to pay off the national debt. This proposal caused resentment in the Parliament of which he was a respected member, although all the great economists of the eighteenth century were advocates of the idea that drastic measures[57] were needed to deal with the national debt.[58]

2.6 The Theoretical Legacy of Ricardo

Despite his short career as an economist, Ricardo, through his work on the theory of comparative advantage, is often considered the 'father' of international trade[59] theories, since the current system of free trade owes much to Ricardo's thinking, which was influenced by the situation in Britain after the Napoleonic Wars. For example, the idea that when a rich country trades with a poor one, both benefit is at the core of the World Trade Organisation (WTO).[60] It is based on Ricardo's idea that eventually free trade will lower prices, and economies will become richer if they specialise in what they know how to do best.[61] Ricardo assumed a quantitative analogy between production prices and labour values in order to demonstrate that foreign trade under the law of comparative advantage benefits both countries. Therefore, the question of whether the conclusion is ultimately dependent on this condition arises. In addition, he did not address the issue of determining international equilibrium prices.[62]

At the same time, Ricardo's contribution to the theoretical debate on value was remarkable. However, despite its depth and analytical rigour, what led many economists to reject the Ricardian approach was the theory of value it encompassed and, in particular, its 'socialist' expression. Thus, fierce controversy was provoked by the characteristic conclusion of this theory that profits are a 'subtraction' from the goods produced by the worker and therefore an expression of economic exploitation.[63]

Hence, the principles of the Ricardian theory of value that were questioned, prepared the ground for the change of both its theoretical object and the system of concepts on which the whole analytical framework of Political Economy[64] was based.

▶ Furthermore, as a response to Ricardian theory, attempts were made to interpret value in different terms,[65] such as money, supply–demand, utility, and so on which led to other theoretical systems such as Marxist, Keynesian and Neoclassical, respectively.

Key Takeaways
- Prices are influenced by free trade.
- The value of a commodity depends on the amount of labour expanded.
- Landlords are major obstacles to capitalist development.
- Specialisation will lead economies to become richer.
- Mechanicisation of production benefits all social classes.

Revision Questions

- How is the 'exchange value' determined?
- Is the role of the capitalist different from that of the landlord?
- What role does property play in the capitalist system?
- How does the product of labour generate profit?
- What is 'comparative advantage' and what is 'absolute advantage'?
- How does technology affect the economy?
- What is the role of direct and indirect taxes?
- What is Ricardo's main contribution to *Economics*?

Notes

1 Drakopoulos and Karagiannis (2003).
2 Tsoulfidis (2010).
3 Heilbroner (2011).
4 Tsoulfidis (2008).
5 Sotiropoulos et al. (2013).
6 Thornton (2014).
7 Yueh (2018).
8 Heilbroner (2011).
9 Drakopoulos and Karagiannis (2003).
10 Rubin (1979).
11 Thornton (2014).
12 Yueh (2018).
13 Tsoulfidis (2010).
14 Heilbroner (2011).
15 Heilbroner (2011).
16 Heilbroner (2011).
17 Yueh (2018).
18 Mariolis (2010).
19 Karagiannis (2001).
20 Karagiannis (2001).
21 Drakopoulos and Karagiannis (2003).
22 Rubin (1979).
23 Milios et al. (2018).
24 Rubin (1979).
25 Sotiropoulos et al. (2013).
26 Sotiropoulos et al. (2013).

27 Sotiropoulos et al. (2013).
28 Varoufakis (2007).
29 Rubin (1979).
30 Tsoulfidis (2008).
31 Milios et al. (2018).
32 Rubin (1979).
33 Tsoulfidis (2010).
34 Heilbroner (2011).
35 Screpanti and Zamagni (2005).
36 Heilbroner (2011).
37 Tsoulfidis (2010).
38 Sotiropoulos et al. (2013).
39 Heilbroner (2011).
40 Rubin (1979).
41 Sotiropoulos et al. (2013).
42 Tsoulfidis (2010).
43 Heilbroner (2011).
44 Tsoulfidis (2010).
45 Tsoulfidis (2010).
46 Screpanti and Zamagni (2005).
47 Yueh (2018).
48 Tsoulfidis (2010).
49 Mariolis (2010).
50 Tsoulfidis (2010).
51 Tsoulfidis (2010).
52 Tsoulfidis (2010).
53 Tsoulfidis (2010).
54 Tsoulfidis (2010).
55 Tsoulfidis (2010).
56 Tsoulfidis (2010).
57 Yueh (2018).
58 Tsoulfidis (2007).
59 Yueh (2018).
60 Thornton (2014).
61 Thornton (2014).
62 Mariolis (2010).
63 Milios et al. (2018).
64 Milios et al. (2018).
65 Screpanti and Zamagni (2005).

References

Drakopoulos, S., & Karagiannis, A. (2003). *History of economic thought: An overview*. Kritiki Publications.

Heilbroner, R. L. (2011). *The worldly philosophers: The lives, times and ideas of the great economic thinkers*. Simon and Schuster.

Karagiannis, A. (2001). *Economic methodology*. Kritiki Publications.

Mariolis, T. (2010). *Essays in the logical history of political economy*. Matura.

Milios, J., Dimoulis, D., & Economakis, G. (2018 [2002]). *Karl Marx and the classics, an essay on value, crises and the capitalist mode of production*. Routledge.

Rubin, I. I. (1979). *A history of economic thought*. Ink links.

Screpanti, E., & Zamagni, S. (2005). *An outline of the history of economic thought*. OUP.

Sotiropoulos, D. P., Milios, J., & Lapatsioras, S. (2013). *A political economy of contemporary capitalism and its crisis: Demystifying finance*. Routledge.

Thornton, P. (2014). *The great economists: Ten economists whose thinking changed the way we live*. Pearson UK.

Tsoulfidis, L. (2007). Classical economists and public debt. *International Review of Economics, 54*(1), 1–12.

Tsoulfidis, L. (2008). *History of economic theory and policy*. University of Macedonia Publications.

Tsoulfidis, L. (2010). *Competing schools of economic thought*. Springer Science & Business Media.

Varoufakis, G. (2007). *Political economy: The economy in the light of criticism*. Gutenberg Publications.

Yueh, L. (2018). *What would the great economists do?* Picador.

Karl Marx (1818–1883)

3

▶ **Learning Objectives**

After having studied this chapter, the reader should be able to:

- Analyse Karl Marx's views on the 'capitalist mode of production'.
- Explain Karl Marx's concept of 'class struggle'.
- Analyse Karl Marx's ideas on the functions of money.
- Give examples on the 'absolute' and the 'relative surplus value'.
- Distinguish 'simple reproduction' from 'expanded reproduction'.
- Present briefly Karl Marx's contribution to *Economics*.

▶ **Summary**

There is no doubt that Karl Marx was one of the most radical economists, sociologists and philosophers in human history, with great global influence. A fundamental principle of his philosophy is Hegel's notion that every force inevitably creates its opposite and that change is an element inherent to social life. Marx argues that social classes are constantly involved in a struggle to determine how to distribute the wealth produced in society, and this is the basis for the creation of history. Furthermore, in order to be able to reproduce over time, the ruling class must appropriate the surplus value produced by the working class. There are two forms of surplus value for Marx, one is the 'absolute surplus value' which increases as the working time is increased and the other is the 'relative surplus value' which increases as the amount of work needed to maintain employees decreases. Capitalist production serves the purpose of increasing surplus value and the rate of exploitation of workers by the ruling class. Technology-driven mechanisation of production may lead to a fall in the profit rate in the long run. In capitalism, overproduction and overaccumulation of capital, as well as the falling tendency of the profit rate, are manifestations of the economic crisis. The crisis is also attributed, in Marx's work, to the establishment of large monopolies that concentrate production in the hands of a few capitalists and cause a constant decline in total production as well as an increase in the misery of workers.

3.1 Introduction

Karl Marx was born in 1818 in Trier, Germany, to a wealthy Jewish family. As with Ricardo, he lived while the Industrial Revolution was developing, although in Germany this happened more slowly than in Britain.[1] His father, Heinrich, was a distinguished lawyer and was able to practise his profession, hitherto forbidden to Jews, thanks to the French Revolution which put an end to these inequalities. However, he was later forced to convert to Christianity in order to be able to continue his profession, as despite the French Revolution's proclamations of equality, the government again began to prohibit Jews from practising their profession in private.[2]

Heinrich Marx introduced young Karl early on to the ideas of Locke, Voltaire and Diderot. At a time when few could enrol in secondary school, Marx continued at his town's gymnasium. There he opted to learn French instead of Hebrew as a third language (after Latin and Greek), which helped him come into contact with French culture. While his grades in Latin and German were high, the same was not the case with Mathematics.[3]

The young Marx received a private education and secured a place to study *Law* at the University of Bonn. However, because of his low grades, his father transferred him to the more conservative University of Berlin where he eventually received his *Law*[4] degree. Despite his father's desire to pursue a career in *Law*, Karl Marx came into contact with *Philosophy* at the universities of Bonn and Berlin and was intrigued by the philosophy of Hegel, who taught that change is an integral part of life, and therefore history is created by the constant movement of ideas and conflicting[5] forces.[6]

In 1841, Marx received his doctorate from the University of Ienna on Ancient Greek Philosophy,[7] and in 1843, he married Jenny von Westphalen, daughter of a wealthy aristocrat, who broke off her engagement to a man of her social class to marry the socially inferior Karl Marx.[8] However, Jenny never renounced the title of nobility she held. Nevertheless, the couple's living conditions were not characterised by affluence and wealth, and their engagement could be described as an unconventional act against the established norms of the nineteenth-century aristocracy.[9]

Marx was unable to work at the University of Bonn, as his professor Bruno Bauer was fired because of his ideas in favour of the Constitution and against religion.[10] Instead, he was employed by newspapers in Germany and Paris as a journalist and editor-in-chief. Because of his radical activities, he was expelled several times and fled as a political refugee to Paris, Brussels and London. In Paris, where he had the opportunity to study the ideas of French Socialism, Marx's collaboration with Engels began in 1844. Earlier, one of Engels' treatises had made an impression on the then young Marx, who was at that time editing a radical publication with philosophical content. In general, this treatise, was intended to show that the eminent English economists were nothing more than defenders of the *status*[11] *quo*.

Engels, who was the son of a wealthy German industrialist, took over the family business in Manchester and was the person who would support Marx financially for life. However, after moving to London in 1849, where he lived until the end of his life, Marx experienced conditions of great poverty and any income he received for the articles he wrote, Engels's[12] financial assistance, and a small inheritance from a friend from the old[13] days was never enough.

Indeed, a government spy describes the Marx household in 1852 as vivid, where the friendliness of the host made the lack of amenities[14] tolerable. Unfortunately, three out of five of their[15] children could not endure the hardships and died[16] of the ensuing hardships. Marx died in 1883 at the age of 64,[17] having seen his wife die, in addition to his three children, 2 years before him.[18]

Marx's most important economic work is *Das Kapital*, the first volume of which was published in 1867. The other two volumes were published after his death, as he was unable to organise them into one edition and many chapters consist of a collection of notes,[19] while Karl Kautsky published some more manuscripts of Marx in his third work, *Theories of Surplus Value*.[20] Apart from this, Marx wrote other works of political, sociological and philosophical content, which played an important role in the social and economic development of humanity and were ideologically influential.[21] Despite Marx's appeal to an international audience, his work was initially better known to German readers as it was published primarily in German, followed by English.[22]

Marx developed his economic theory mainly in the period 1857–1867, and its existence was closely linked to the formation of different theoretical strands. A key element that contributed to the existence of different strands within Marxist theory is the fact that Marx's work displays many internal contradictions and 'readings'. Thus, Marx's work has been perceived differently by different versions of Marxism. Besides, it is so extensive, and sometimes contradictory, that different kinds of interpretations are bound to prevail.

Many consider that Marx was a classical economist, while others consider that Marx's work founded a new theoretical subject. However, the differentiation of Marxian theory from the classical approach is particularly crucial, since, according to many, it allows for the interpretation of key elements of modern capitalism, such as money and, by extension, credit and the functioning of capital[23] markets.

3.2 The Rejection of 'Human Nature'

The philosophical approach of Marx and Engels derives from Hegel's view that every force inevitably creates its opposite and that change is an element inherent in society. At the same time, Marx and Engels emphasise the fact that their philosophical positions have as their central focus the physical and social, that is, materialist context rather than the world of ideas.[24]

An important element of society, according to Marx, is the way in which people act in order to produce the goods and services they need. The way in which production is organised can vary radically according to the time and society.[25] For example, if one wants to analyse the economic system of capitalism, one can take as a starting point the commodity which is the final result of the production process.[26]

The cornerstone of Marxist theory is the rejection of the view that the individual is the driving force of the evolution of society. 'Human nature' is not seen as the essence (nature) of man, but as the result of historical evolution, the result of a particular way of organising society that arises from the battle between social classes, that is, the class struggles.[27]

Marx held that ideas are influenced by the environment in which they are produced, even when they aim to change it, and that the ideas prevailing in a period play an important role in changing the existing situation of which they are a creation. Moreover, people do create their history, but not in the way that is most desirable to them but on the basis of the circumstances in which they find themselves or under the conditions bequeathed to them by the past.[28]

Marx wrote that society does not consist of individuals, but expresses the totality of the relations, the relations of these individuals to each other.[29] Thus, the history of all societies is the history of their class struggles.[30] In this regard, it represents a departure from the principles of classical *Political Economy*, which regarded the commodity nature of the economy and its corresponding division of labour as a consequence of 'human nature'.[31]

3.3 Class Struggle

Production has been an important process in all societies, historically. But in the capitalist system, in particular, it acquires a systematic and generalised character, because the basic aim of the production of goods and services is no longer simply the satisfaction of social needs, as in previous historical periods, but rather the sale of these products in order to achieve the maximum possible profit.[32]

Thus, the radical changes that occurred in the mode of production, after the so-called Industrial Revolution, required the creation of a new social environment.[33] In this context, Marx accepted the division of society into classes according to Classical Political Economy and emphasised the element of conflicting interests between the main classes of capitalist society, that is between capitalists and workers.[34] He argued that the social classes are constantly fighting over how to distribute the wealth produced in society and this is the way history[35] is created, and in order for the ruling class to reproduce over time, it must appropriate the surplus produced by the working class.[36] Also, according to Marx, there is a huge contradiction in capitalism: The economic basis of capitalism, namely production, was based on a process of interaction between many individuals, and therefore, production had a collective character. On the other hand, society and its legal, political and ideological framework had an individualistic[37] character.

Thus, Marx seeks and identifies the elements of social relations that constitute the defining characteristic of capitalism and in this way, a new theoretical concept emerges: The *capitalist mode of production* which describes the relations that characterise every capitalist society. The capitalist mode of production is based both on the separation of the worker from the means of production and on the complete ownership of the means of production by the capitalist, that is, the power to put them into operation and the power to appropriate the surplus[38] value produced. Hence, capitalism itself would create the conditions that would lead to its[39] destruction. The capitalist system exploits labour,[40] but Marx argued that capital is more than just the means of production, but also the power to use those means of production in order to earn profit.[41] As a consequence, Marx was required to formulate a 'theory of value' in order to provide a scientific basis for his theory of 'exploitation'.[42]

3.4 Ricardian Influence, Value and Money

Marx held Ricardo in high esteem, whom he regarded as a very important economist of the nineteenth century.[43] Marx recognised right from the beginning that Ricardo's conclusion below was a fundamental characteristic of capitalism itself.[44] According to the main conclusion of Ricardian theory, the value of a commodity arises from labour and is proportional to the time spent on its production (labour expended). Therefore, value is a property of all commodities, which derives from the fact that they are products of labour, as was Smith's. Therefore, labour ensures the comparability of commodities because they are products of labour. Exchange value, as a relation of exchange of commodities, expresses the value inherent in commodities.

The capitalist's income is derived from the value of all the commodities produced by the worker during a period. Consequently, the capitalist owns the product of labour, that is, the total sum of the goods produced by the use of the labour of the worker.[45] Thus, the capitalist class appropriates part of the value produced by the worker, while the workers trade their labour power on the market against the capitalists, who seek accumulation and profitability in competition with other capitalists in order to survive.[46]

Those who argue that Marx is a *classical* economist believe that the above classical positions encapsulate the Marxian theory of value. According to these views, Marx simply added the following:[47]

(a) the clarification that these positions are valid only in the context of specific historical periods that have emerged from the process of class struggle,
(b) the assessment that the incomes of the ruling classes come from an 'exploitation relation' which will be abolished under socialism,
(c) the clarification that the worker's remuneration and what the worker sells on the labour market is not 'labour' itself, but his labour power.

However, Marx also developed extensive theoretical analysis on money[48], and thus in contrast to the Classical School, the Marxian theory of value is a monetary theory. By money, we mean a medium of exchange used by society in exchange for any good or service. Although there are various formal definitions depending on the breadth of what money includes, we would say that it consists of coins, banknotes, bank deposits and other financial assets.

▶ In this context, in the Marxian system, the value of a commodity is not expressed *per se*, but through its forms of appearance, that is, prices. Moreover, it cannot be determined in isolation, but exclusively in relation to all other commodities in the process of exchange. This exchange value relationship is implemented by money.

By money, we mean both metallic money and banknotes, as well as deposits and credit money. Thus, the defining characteristic of capitalism is not only the exchange of commodities, as the classical theories argued, but also money.[49]

Therefore, capitalism includes money, and the basic properties of money are the three functions of the *Classical School* plus three additional ones that he added. Hence, Marx's analysis goes beyond the classical conceptual scheme, as he refers to three (3) additional functions of money: (1) as a means of hoarding, (2) as a means of payment and (3) as a universal money. All three of these functions are, according to Marx, subsumed within the same type of function and, in particular, the function of money 'as money'. By this expression, Marx means that money functions in all three cases as an *end in itself* and no longer as a *means* of commodity circulation.[50]

Thus, in *hoarding*, the commodity is sold not to buy another commodity but to replace the form of the commodity with the form of money. From being a simple link, money becomes an end in itself.[51]

As a *means of payment*, money functions in all those cases where a purchase of goods takes place not by direct payment of money but on the basis of an agreement (a contract) to pay for them at a specific future time. Of course, at the specified time, the means of payment enters into circulation, but after the commodity has previously been withdrawn from it.[52] And in this case, the money becomes an end in itself.[53]

In addition, money functions as a means of payment of international bills[54] and for the transfer of wealth from one country to another[55] which prevails.

3.5 Capital and Credit

Marx considered *Classical Political Economy* as an expression of the capitalist class, during the period when the modern capitalist system was imposed, that is after the English Industrial Revolution.[56] Thus, he formulated and developed the theory of 'capital' based on the concept of value. 'Capital' is value which, although created by the working class, has been appropriated by the capitalists. In brief, the worker is paid exactly as much as those who work need to be paid in order for the latter to be able to survive.[57]

3.5 Capital and Credit

▶ Precisely 'capital' is value, and its forms of appearance are (i) money and (ii) commodity. Certain commodities function as 'capital': the means of production (fixed capital), on the one hand, and labour power (variable capital), on the other.[58]

The 'use value' of the labour power that the capitalist buys consists in the fact that it produces commodities that contain more value than its own value. If we denote by (v) the value of a unit of labour power, that is the variable capital (pre) paid by the capitalist, then the new (net) value produced by it will be (v + s), where (s) is surplus value, the part of the value produced which is appropriated by the capitalist. Whereas, if (c) is the value of the means of production worn out in the production process (or amortisation), then the (gross) value of the produced output will be (c+v+s).

The labour process is, therefore, at the same time a process of (1) value production and (2) surplus value production. Thus, the working day is also divided into the (1) necessary labour time, during which the worker produces a value equal to that of his labour power and (2) surplus labour time, during which surplus value[59] is produced.

For example, a worker works for eight hours a day, that is, more than the four hours required to produce goods whose value corresponds (equals) to the value of the goods necessary for his own maintenance. His daily wage, however, corresponds to the value of products of four hours' work. It is this difference between the value produced by the worker in all the hours he works and the value required to enable the worker to reproduce himself (which constitutes his daily wage) that the capitalist reaps. It is precisely this value resulting from 'unpaid' labour that Marx calls 'surplus value'.[60] Surplus value therefore arises because the worker produces more value than the equivalent of the wage he receives from the capitalist.[61]

The surplus value can be divided into two forms: 'absolute surplus value', which increases when the working time is extended, and 'relative surplus value', which increases when the time needed to maintain workers[62] is reduced.

In the above example, if the capitalist can force the worker to increase his daily work by two hours without increasing his daily wage, then the surplus value reaped by the capitalist increases by two hours. This increase is considered to be the result of 'absolute surplus value'. On the other hand, if labour becomes more efficient, then the maintenance of the worker can be covered by a wage corresponding, for example, to two hours less work. Thus, due to the increase in 'relative surplus value', overtime increases by two hours.[63]

On the other hand, the capitalist appears on the market as the owner of money (M) by buying commodities, which consist of means of production and labour power. In the production process, he consumes productively to create a new outflow of commodities, whose value must be greater than that of the original commodities. Finally, he sells this commodity outflow to receive an amount of money (M′) higher than (M).[64] Thus, money circulation leads to capital[65], while at the same time, money appears to possess the property of generating value.[66]

Surplus value, which is equal to $v = M'-M$, is the product of the 'exploitation' of the working class by the capitalist class and is transformed: (a) partly into the means of private consumption for the capitalists themselves and (b) partly into additional fixed and variable capital for the expansion of production.

The second process, that is the transformation of surplus value into capital, is defined as 'accumulation'. Through accumulation, the capitalist economy is reproduced on an expanded scale, so we say, in Marxian terms, that we have 'expanded reproduction'. When all surplus value goes to the capitalist's private consumption, that is when there is no accumulation, we say, in Marxian terms, that we have 'simple reproduction'. In the second volume of *Capital*, Marx formulates the conditions of simple and expanded reproduction in a capitalist economy.

Workers are forced to work longer hours than they need for their self-sustenance and are therefore exploited by capitalists.[67] The purpose of capitalist production is to increase the surplus value and the rate of exploitation. This shapes the will and decisions of the capitalist.[68]

As for the question of why a maintenance wage is established, Marx answers that it is for two reasons: First, because due to their stronger bargaining power, capitalists can determine the hours of work. And, second, because of the creation of a 'reserve army of unemployed', the supply of labour will be greater than the demand and, thus, the wage will be set at the basic subsistence level.[69]

3.6 Falling Tendency of the Profit Rate

As we have seen, the capitalist mode of production aims at achieving the maximum possible profit and, in this context, the further expansion of production is an end in itself.[70] Competition between capitalists, in their attempt to accumulate and increase their production in order to make profits at the expense of competitors, leads to an increased demand for workers and, therefore, to an increase in wages and a decrease in surplus value.

Marx, unlike Smith, did not believe that this would be overcome by improving the standard of living of the workers. He thought that capitalists would deal with the problem of rising wages by using in their production process machinery that required less use of labour and thus leaving some workers unemployed.[71]

In short, as the capitalist tries to overcome the contraction of profits brought about by the increase in wages due to increased demand for labour, he uses labour-saving[72] machinery. Only the first capitalist to use labour-saving machines can earn more than the others, but not for long, since the others will do the same by laying off workers and replacing them with machines.[73] However, as Marx wrote, competition generalises it and subordinates it to the general law, and the rate of profit begins to fall.[74]

Reducing the participation of workers in the production process deprives workers of income that could be used to buy the product produced. Consequently, as output falls, firms go bankrupt and are absorbed by larger ones that buy their

3.6 Falling Tendency of the Profit Rate

machinery at prices below its real value. The workers, being unemployed, agree to work for wages lower than their value and so surplus value reappears.[75]

So, as we have seen, on the basis of Marx, the process of the capitalist mode of production is oriented towards the extraction on the part of capitalists of more and more surplus value, either through an increase in absolute surplus value or in relative surplus value expressed through a higher rate of exploitation. In this context, the capitalist seeks to reduce the cost of his goods in order to lower his selling prices even below the cost of competing firms, in order to increase his profit and thus drive them into bankruptcy. The reduction of average production costs is achieved through technological progress and mechanisation, that is the substitution of physical capital[76] for human labour.

▶ According to Marx, the rate of profit (r) is defined as the ratio of surplus value (s) to total capital, fixed (C) and variable (v).[77] That is, $r = s / (C+v)$ or $r = [s/v] / [(C/v)+1)]$. We see, then, that the rate of profit (r) is an increasing function of the 'rate of exploitation (s/v)' and a decreasing function of the 'organic (or value) composition of capital (C/v)'.

▶ The 'mechanisation' of production due to technological progress often manifests itself through the replacement of variable capital (v) by fixed capital (C), that is in the increase of the ratio (C/v), the so-called organic (or value) composition of capital, because fixed capital incorporates new technologies that increase productivity. This, only with all other factors held constant, that is *ceteris paribus*, leads to a reduction in the rate of profit, which will tend to fall in the long run, based on the above mathematical definition. This possible outcome has come to be known as the 'law of the falling tendency of the rate of profit'.

Note that the ratio (C/v) is the expression, in terms of value, of the ratio of physical capital to human labour (K/l) in physical units, for example machines and workers, respectively, or else of the 'technical composition of capital'. Thus, with the 'law of the falling tendency of the rate of profit', it could be argued that technological innovation, introduced into production by capitalists in the context of competition, could be the cause of such a phenomenon.

We can see that in all cases where the organic (value) composition (C/v) of capital increases more rapidly than the increase in the rate of exploitation (s/v), the falling tendency in the profit rate indeed prevails. However, if we take a closer and more careful look at the previous mathematical definition, we see that there can also be a tendency for the rate of profit to rise when the rate of exploitation (s/v) increases faster than the organic (value) composition of capital or when the organic composition of capital decreases faster than the rate of exploitation. From the above, it becomes obvious that the so-called law of the falling tendency in the rate of profit is characterised by the following elements:[78]

(a) It applies under specific historical conditions of production, which Marx called 'specifically capitalist methods of production', which are characterised, among

other things, by the inability of the increasing rate of exploitation to compensate for the consequences of the increase in the organic composition of capital. Nevertheless, the 'law' does not exclude the possibility of the non-existence of these conditions and thus the containment or reversal of the falling tendency in the rate of profit.
(b) It applies 'all other factors remaining constant', that is *ceteris paribus*. Thus, it provides no adequate basis for judgement on the course of evolution of the rate of profit in general, given that this is influenced just as much by 'all the other factors' apart from those having to do with technological innovation. Among the other factors are change in the length of the working day and running speed of the machinery, change in raw materials prices affecting the 'organic composition of capital', a rise in the level of skills of working people, etc.

▶ Nevertheless, many Marxists interpret the 'law of the falling tendency' of the rate of profit as a universally valid characteristic of the capitalist mode of production, which applies for as long as capitalism exists. Furthermore, they have seen it as a strict 'law' which describes the evolution of the rate of profit, no knowledge being required of 'all the other factors' which Marx considered constant, applying the scientific principle of 'ceteris paribus'.[79] This constitutes the 'fallacy of the falling tendency of the rate of profit'.

Moreover, in Marx's works, we find only fragmentary and descriptive references to economic crises, because he focuses on the permanent features of the capitalist mode of production. This is why there is no coherent theory of economic crises in Marx's[80] work, even though crises are, according to Marx, considered to be inherent in the capitalist system. [81]

Of course, in the third volume of *Capital*, Marx calls economic crises 'crises of overproduction'.[82] Overproduction of capital (overaccumulation), the other side of which is the underproduction (in terms of output) of the demand that can pay for it (underconsumption), and a fall in the rate of profit are the concepts with which Marx describes the interdependent manifestations of the economic crisis of capitalism. Also, in Marx's work, the crisis is often considered to be the result of the creation of large monopoly corporations that concentrate production in the hands of a few capitalists, leading to a continuous increase in the poverty of workers.[83]

But what is the cause of the crisis? Depending on their answer to this question, Marxists have been divided into distinct theoretical strands within Marxism, showing that the question remains open in Marxist theory.[84]

Finally, on the basis of the above, in terms of methodological approach, Marx makes it clear that in any science, it is important to construct the *concept of* each aspect of the real, beyond direct observation which is often misleading. This is also true in *Economics*, which has neither a microscope nor laboratories. The construction of concepts requires research to be carried out by the method of 'abstracting'

3.7 The Theoretical Legacy of Marx

Karl Marx was one of the most radical economists, sociologists and philosophers, with great influence worldwide.[85] Although for some, Marxist theory is still a *taboo* subject today, Marx is regarded –along with Freud and Darwin – by many historians of Western civilization amongst the three most important thinkers who changed the way we see the world.[86] Initially, there was a particular emphasis on his political writings, but undoubtedly, both economic and social life would be quite different, globally, without the existence of Marxist theory, since Marx's work has influenced it significantly. However, despite the fact that Marx's political writings have been a source of inspiration for the countries of the former Soviet Union, Eastern Europe, China, Vietnam, Cuba, and so on, this has not resulted in a social and economic system fully acceptable to all those who embrace Marxism and/or the prospect of socialism. This development is still a matter of concern for Marxist theorists and political analysts around the world.

▶ Of course, without views and considerations linked to Marxist theory, workers as well as the rising middle class would be in much worse conditions, for example if there were no institutions such as the minimum wage and the trade unions that Marxist theory instigated.[87] Moreover, both the study of socio-economic change would lack analysis from the perspective of the 'class struggle' and the theoretical study of instability and crises would lack the perspective of Marx's theory[88] and the non-neutral role of money.

It is worth noticing that Marx's *Capital*, after the financial crisis that started in 2006 and the subsequent collapse of Lehman Brothers and a large part of the modern (financial) economic system, has increased its sales exponentially and its study is in the news. As we know, one cause of the crisis was the creation of complex and sophisticated financial products that relied on the increase in the number of mortgages made to extremely high-risk and precarious financially vulnerable mortgage buyers, also called N.I.N.J.A. (No Income No Job Assets) loans.[89]

Therefore, the idea that it is impossible for the capitalist system to exist without economic crises, precisely because of the constant and unimpeded search for profit by capitalists—even through those 'toxic' products in the financial market, based on borrowers who are unable to repay, is a key feature of the Marxist perspective. Also, and this very inability to repay on the part of the borrowers was obviously linked to their low wages, which in turn were the result of the capitalists keeping workers' wages low in order to maximise their[90] profits.

Moreover, the response to the crisis, which is struggling to achieve a very slow and weak 'recovery', with the working people seeing their lives deteriorate and even suffer, could be seen as a confirmation of Marxist theory in its critique of the existing economic system and an indication that the theory is still alive and relevant. In conclusion, we would say that Marxist theory, with its peculiarities and internal contradictions, has been particularly insightful.[91]

Key Takeaways

- Capital exploits labour.
- Surplus value results from workers producing more value than their wages.
- 'Accumulation' is the transformation of surplus value into capital.
- Social classes constantly struggle over how surplus value is distributed.
- The profit rate might fall in the long run as technology advances.
- Crises are inherent to the capitalist system.

Revision Questions

- What is 'class struggle'?
- What is the 'capitalist mode of production'?
- What are the *Classical* functions of money and what are the Marxist ones?
- How is 'surplus value' formed?
- What is 'absolute surplus value' and what is 'relative surplus value'?
- What is 'simple reproduction' and what is 'expanded reproduction'?
- What is the 'profit rate' and what does it depend on?
- What is the long-term tendency of the profit rate and why?
- Is there a complete Marxist theory of crises and why?
- What is an 'overaccumulation crisis' and what causes it?
- What is Marx's main contribution to *Economics*?

Notes

1 Yueh (2018).
2 Yueh (2018).
3 Yueh (2018).
4 Thornton (2014).
5 Heilbroner (2011).
6 Thornton (2014).
7 Drakopoulos and Karagiannis (2003).
8 Thornton (2014).
9 Yueh (2018).
10 Heilbroner (2011).
11 Heilbroner (2011).

Notes

12 Tsoulfidis (2008).
13 Heilbroner (2011).
14 Thornton (2014).
15 Heilbroner (2011).
16 Thornton (2014).
17 Thornton (2014).
18 Heilbroner (2011).
19 Screpanti and Zamagni (2005).
20 Tsoulfidis (2010).
21 Varoufakis (2007).
22 Yueh (2018).
23 Milios et al. (2018).
24 Heilbroner (2011).
25 Heilbroner (2011).
26 Tsoulfidis (2010).
27 Milios et al. (2018).
28 Heilbroner (2011).
29 Marx (1993).
30 Marx and Engels (1985).
31 Milios et al. (2018).
32 Tsoulfidis (2010).
33 Heilbroner (2011).
34 Milios et al. (2018).
35 Heilbroner (2011).
36 Tsoulfidis (2010).
37 Hcilbroner (2011).
38 Milios et al. (2018).
39 Heilbroner (2011).
40 Marx and Engels (1985).
41 Screpanti and Zamagni (2005).
42 Milios et al. (2018).
43 Yueh (2018).
44 Mariolis (2010).
45 Screpanti and Zamagni (2005).
46 Heilbroner (2011).
47 Milios et al. (2018).
48 Tsoulfidis (2010).
49 Milios et al. (2018).

50 Milios et al. (2018).
51 Marx (1990).
52 Marx (1990).
53 Marx (1990).
54 Marx (1990).
55 Marx (1990).
56 Screpanti and Zamagni (2005).
57 Heilbroner (2011).
58 Milios et al. (2018).
59 Milios et al. (2018).
60 Heilbroner (2011).
61 Tsoulfidis (2010).
62 Drakopoulos and Karagiannis (2003).
63 Drakopoulos and Karagiannis (2003).
64 Milios et al. (2018).
65 Marx (1990).
66 Marx (1990).
67 Heilbroner (2011).
68 Marx (1990).
69 Drakopoulos and Karagiannis (2003).
70 Tsoulfidis (2010).
71 Heilbroner (2011).
72 Heilbroner (2011).
73 Heilbroner (2011).
74 Marx (1991).
75 Heilbroner (2011).
76 Tsoulfidis (2010).
77 Milios et al. (2018).
78 Milios et al. (2018).
79 Milios et al. (2018).
80 Milios et al. (2018).
81 van Staveren (2021).
82 Marx (1991).
83 Backhouse (2009).
84 Milios et al. (2018).
85 Yueh (2018).
86 Thornton (2014).
87 Thornton (2014).

88 Tsoulfidis (2010).
89 Thornton (2014).
90 Thornton (2014).
91 Heilbroner (2011).

References

Backhouse, R. E. (2009). *The evolution of economic thought*. Kritiki.
Drakopoulos, S., & Karagiannis, A. (2003). *History of economic thought: An overview*. Kritiki Publications.
Heilbroner, R. L. (2011). *The worldly philosophers: The lives, times and ideas of the great economic thinkers*. Simon and Schuster.
Mariolis, T. (2010). *Essays in the logical history of political economy*. Matura.
Marx, K. (1990). *Capital* (Vol. 1). Penguin Classics.
Marx, K. (1991). *Capital* (Vol. 3). Penguin Classics.
Marx, K. (1993). *Grundrisse. Foundations of the critique of political economy.* .
Marx, K., & Engels, F. (1985). *The communist manifesto*. Penguin Classics.
Milios, J., Dimoulis, D., & Economakis, G. (2018 [2002]). *Karl Marx and the classics, an essay on value, crises and the capitalist mode of production*. Routledge.
Screpanti, E., & Zamagni, S. (2005). *An outline of the history of economic thought*. OUP.
Thornton, P. (2014). *The great economists: Ten economists whose thinking changed the way we live*. Pearson UK.
Tsoulfidis, L. (2008). *History of economic theory and policy*. University of Macedonia Publications.
Tsoulfidis, L. (2010). *Competing schools of economic thought*. Springer Science & Business Media.
van Staveren, I. (2021). *Alternative ideas from 10 (almost) forgotten economists*. Springer Nature Press.
Varoufakis, G. (2007). *Political economy: The economy in the light of criticism*. Gutenberg Publications.
Yueh, L. (2018). *What would the great economists do?* Picador.

Leon Walras (1834–1910)

4

▶ **Learning Objectives**

After having studied this chapter, the reader should be able to:

- Understand the basic principles of General Equilibrium analysis.
- Analyse the key assumptions of General Equilibrium models.
- Describe the role of the 'auctioneer'.
- Name the key players in the economy.
- Analyse the key points of the neoclassical theoretical system.
- Present briefly Leon Walras's contribution to *Economics*.

▶ **Summary**

Léon Walras is considered as one of the pioneers of the Neoclassical School of *Economics*. According to his theory, the economy is composed of different actors: (a) producers, (b) consumers and (c) entrepreneurs, and economic equilibrium results from the simultaneous interaction between them in the market. Market exchange relations are developed by the various agents as a result of the pursuit of their individual interests. Through *Mathematics*, Walras attempted to answer the question of whether it would be possible to discover the prices that would make all the individual markets in the economy achieve General Equilibrium, and he found that such a discovery is indeed possible, but under certain conditions. Therefore, Walras showed in his General Equilibrium model that the various actors in the economy can reach a market equilibrium – under certain conditions – by pursuing their individual interests. Therefore, he is considered the founder of the General Equilibrium theory, which bears his name, that is also known as Walrasian Equilibrium. Lastly, Walras's and other neoclassical economists' work has led to a theory demonstrating that the market is self-regulating and results in optimal resource allocations.

4.1 Introduction

Léon Walras was born in France in 1834 and, along with Carl Menger and Stanley Jevons with whom he came to similar conclusions although they did not work together, is considered one of the pioneering economists of the so-called Neoclassical School.[1] His work is very important because he is the 'father' of the modern Neoclassical General Equilibrium theory,[2] which dominates Microeconomic Analysis and also certain fields of Macroeconomic Analysis with microeconomic foundations.

His father, Auguste Walras, was an amateur economist of his time, and it was he who encouraged the young Léon to take up the study of *Economics*. In fact, he believed that *Economics* would be transformed into *Mathematics*, and it is he who provided young Walras with a highly regarded library of *Economics* books to study.[3] Léon Walras twice failed to gain admission to the famous Ecole Polytechnique, that is, the Polytechnical School of Paris, because of inadequate preparation in Mathematics.[4] He eventually studied Engineering, but at the Ecole des Mines in Paris,[5] until his interest was attracted to Social Sciences and *Economics*, under the constant encouragement of his[6] father.

Among other professions, such as author of literary books, he was for a short time a journalist, and in 1865, he co-founded a cooperative bank which he ran. Between 1866 and 1868, he also published a monthly magazine, *Le Travail*, which was mainly devoted to the cooperative movement. During this period, Walras gave public lectures on social issues.[7] The activities of the cooperative bank were terminated in 1868, whereupon he started working for a private bank until 1870,[8] at the same time that, thanks to an important acquaintance with an influential politician,[9] he occupied the chair of *Political Economy* at the University of Lausanne. There, he remained engaged in research and teaching *Economics* until 1892 when he retired at the age of 58. Unfortunately, he was not an inspiring teacher,[10] and perhaps for this reason, he had no loyal students, combined with his frequent mental exhaustion and irritability.[11]

His life was unconventional for the time, with children in and out of marriage, one of whom died in infancy, two marriages, the first of which ended with the death of his wife and with unprecedented financial problems that caused him to experience very difficult years. Thus, in addition to his research and teaching at the university, he was forced to write for newspapers and to work as a consultant for an insurance company.[12] His second marriage was a happy one, and he inherited some considerable money that helped him to pay off the debts he had incurred from the publication of his work and the dissemination of its[13] results.

Léon Walras is considered the founding figure of the Neoclassical School of Lausanne, while his successor in the chair of *Political Economy* and the successor of his work was Vilfredo Pareto. Walras's innovative ideas on how prices are determined, transactions are conducted and General Equilibrium is achieved were published in 1874 in his work entitled *Éléments d' Économie Politique Pure*.[14] The ideas of both Walras and the other pioneers of the 'marginal revolution', Menger and Jevons, were incorporated into mainstream economic theory several decades after their formulation and gradually formed the core of what is now called 'Neoclassical Economics'.[15]

As regards the relatively late integration of Walras's work into *Economic*, this may have been due to the fact that Walras was French and, moreover, that he belonged to the area of so-called utopian socialism.[16] His work shows that he identified himself as a 'scientific socialist' and this may be indicated by the fact that he was an advocate of nationalisation of land and natural monopolies and supported the reliable operation of the capital market by the state. At the same time, his *Political Philosophy* was a mixture between liberalism and state interventionism that favoured moderate reforms in socio-economic matters,[17] while arguing that *Economics* has nothing to do with economic policy[18] making.

Today, it is characteristic that parts of Walras's work are found in many modern *Economics* textbooks, while today's economists are more familiar, even if unaware of it, with Walras's work than any other well-known economist. Typical of the influence of the concept of General Equilibrium, and of Walras's wider work in *Economics*, is the fact that Joseph Schumpeter considers him to be the most important theoretical economist.[19] In contrast, Keynes mentions him in his well-known *General Theory* only once.[20]

Walras used *Mathematics* extensively to analyse economic phenomena and was a proponent of the idea that *Economics* should make use of the methods and tools of *Physics*. This is why he finds parallels between physical phenomena (such as friction) and economic phenomena (such as free competition).[21] For instance, we argued that the market is perfectly competitive, just as in pure *Mechanics* we assume that machines operate without friction.[22] Thus, Walras, through his work, offered a different prism through which to analyse the important role that the competitive market model holds for modern neoclassical *Microeconomic Analysis*.[23]

4.2 The Functioning of the Economy

Although the issue of the interdependency between the various actors in an economy had been studied by earlier economists such as Condorcet and Cournot using *Mathematics*, no economist had been able to construct a general analytical structure linking the various economic actors in the system. It was, after all, the time when economists admired physicists and began to use *Mathematics* more widely in *Economics*. The two most important representatives were the British chemist, meteorologist and author Stanley Jevons, and the other was certainly Léon Walras.[24] Meanwhile, in addition to Jevons, Walras considered Ricardo's theory to be logically and economically flawed and, therefore, unable to contribute in a way that would provide coherence to both the determination of the relative prices of commodities and the distribution of income.[25]

For the first time, in Walras's theory, the economy consists of various economic agents participating in the market either as (a) producers, (b) consumers (c) or entrepreneurs, interacting in the market. That is, labour is transformed into (a) products, which are (b) either purchased by entrepreneurs for further use in the production of other products or (c) consumed by final consumers. The latter, having offered their labour to the entrepreneurs, buy the products produced from them, spending the income they have received from them in return for their labour. The pursuit of their individual interests leads the various actors to develop exchange relationships on the market.[26]

A key objective of Walras's theory was to analyse and demonstrate how voluntary exchanges between economic actors who are (a) well-informed, (b) aware of their own interests, (c) seeking to maximize their goals, will lead to an efficient and effective mode of production and income distribution.[27] Thus, through the General Equilibrium model constructed by Walras, he demonstrated that the agents in the economic system, through the pursuit of their self-interest, can – under certain conditions – reach a market equilibrium and for this contribution he was the founder of the theory of General Equilibrium, named in his honour 'Walrasian Equilibrium'.[28]

Walras, developing his theory after the era of the *Classical* economists, for the first time presented a theoretical model that took analytical expression and had as its basic starting point the fact that all actors in the economy interact and are fully interdependent.[29] In fact, Walras's theoretical effort to find under which mathematical conditions an economy with interdependent agents could operate efficiently and mutually beneficially had an enormous influence on modern *Neoclassical Economics*, so much so that a very large part of modern *Economics* deals with issues of Walrasian General Equilibrium.

4.3 The General Equilibrium

In order to establish, with the help of *Mathematics*, the General Equilibrium model at a given price level, Walras made the following assumptions, which to this day are dominant in modern *Neoclassical Economics*:[30]

- Consumers seek to maximise their utility, while firms seek to maximise their profits.
- The market is competitive, as the number of consumers and producers is so large and they act in an individual way, which does not allow them to influence the price level of the products.
- Firms produce homogeneous products, face the same cost conditions and have similar technological capabilities.
- Economic actors take their decisions with full knowledge of the current product prices.
- Both, inputs and outputs, have a positive price and are not unlimited.

4.3 The General Equilibrium

- Consumers' utility increases with increasing quantity, but at a decreasing rate, and their desire to consume is not subject to satiation.
- The demand for inputs and outputs depends on their price.
- The supply and demand functions in the economy do not experience unexpected jumps, that is, they are practically continuous.
- Each production function of a good corresponds to a specific and unchanging combination of factors of production, as the substitution of production factors is not possible by existing technology.
- There is a good whose price is arbitrarily chosen as a measure of the values of the other goods and factors of production (numéraire).
- Products and factors of production initially have a given distribution.

His analysis took as its starting point an exchange economy and, more specifically, a market in which auctions take place and where everyone has at their disposal some quantity of each good as an initial endowment.[31] The quantity of goods is given, and each person in the room knows how many units of each good he or she possesses. A central auctioneer, who is responsible for conducting the auctions, is responsible for announcing the relative prices of the goods on a table, based on the price of the arbitrarily chosen unit of the good.

Then, each person, based on the announced prices, states his intentions about which part of the goods he intends to sell and his intentions about the above products he intends to buy and records them on a piece of paper. The auctioneer, Walras argued, would collect these papers, and after ascertaining which goods' prices were causing *an excess demand* and which were causing *an excess supply*, he would announce new *increased* prices for the first class of goods and new *decreased* prices for the second class of goods, respectively.

Individuals will restate their intentions as to the quantities of goods they are willing to demand or offer at the new prices, the auctioneer will reassemble the cards to determine where there is *excess demand* and *excess supply*, and this auction process (tâtonnement in French and trial-and-error in English) will continue until the price at which demand equals supply is found for each good. At these prices, the famous Walrasian Equilibrium is reached, and before these prices are discovered, individuals are not allowed to buy or sell goods.[32]

Using the above assumptions, Walras showed, using systems of linear interdependent equations, that there can be prices that lead to equilibrium markets, that is ensure equality between aggregate demand and aggregate supply.[33] Moreover, as far as the General Equilibrium is concerned, it does not imply the absence of excess demand on the part of consumers or excess supply on the part of sellers. In some markets, supply may exceed demand or *vice versa*. What equals zero will be the *sum of* the values of excess demand and excess supply, which means that under this condition, Walras's law can hold even when all individual markets are out of equilibrium.[34] Thus, for Walras, the imbalance between supply and demand will be settled if the price of the good changes, while causing spillover effects in other markets in the system.

But at the same time, there is another issue. In order to show that the wishes of the individual agents lead to mutually beneficial transactions, we need to show that there exist prices which make this possible. To this end, price analysis is central to General Equilibrium theory, since prices are the parameters on the basis of which individual choices are made. This establishes a set of relationships between the prices and the quantities exchanged in relation to inputs and outputs. Indeed, this set of relationships is in a state of General Equilibrium when prices and quantities are such that all actors maximise their[35] objectives.

More precisely, an economy is in a state of General Equilibrium when there is a set of prices for which: (a) in every market supply equals demand, (b) every agent in the economy is able to buy and sell exactly what he/she planned to buy and sell, (c) all firms and consumers can exchange exactly the quantities of goods that maximize their profits and utility, respectively.[36]

In order to arrive at this result, we need to know the number of consumers, the number of firms, the initial stocks of resources, consumer preferences and the available production technologies. All the rest of the process is left free to the maximising behaviour of the economy and the competitive market[37] mechanism. In practice, however, two key elements are needed to achieve this balance. The first, as we have already seen, is the specific role of the auctioneer. The second is the equally specific role of firms.

Walras, in his analytical model, considered that in an equilibrium position, the profit of firms is zero, because of competition between them. Thus, in practice, in the Walrasian General Equilibrium approach, only one class of agents maximises its objectives, and that is the consumers. The entrepreneurs, like the auctioneer, simply coordinate and organise, taking prices and production technologies as given. Thus, the existence of profit is a sign of disequilibrium, so the entrepreneur reacts by increasing the scale of production when there is a profit and, correspondingly, reducing it when there is a loss.[38] In other words, in a state of equilibrium, entrepreneurs have neither profits nor losses.[39] That is, for Walras, a firm is in equilibrium when its profit becomes zero due to competition between firms.[40]

In this context, Walras tried to answer, with the help of *Mathematics*, the question whether it is possible to discover those prices that will lead all markets in an economy to General Equilibrium and found that this is indeed possible, but under the conditions: (a) that purchases and sales will be hidden until the central auctioneer manages to 'discover' General Equilibrium and (b) that firms make zero profits in General Equilibrium.

As we have seen, Walras constructed a system of simultaneous interdependent equations to describe the interaction between consumers and entrepreneurs. There are as many markets as there are goods, including their factors of production and services, and for each market, three equations are defined: one for demand, one for supply and one for equilibrium. However, a necessary but not sufficient condition for such a system to have a solution is that the number of unknowns equals the number of equations, a condition that has created several problems. One of these is, for example, that such a system is not always guaranteed to have a unique solution, since it may be either impossible or have infinite solutions, or even if there is a unique solution, we do not know whether it has economic significance (e.g. a negative value or quantity). The problem in question took almost a century to be addressed by neoclassical economists[41] with the famous Arrow-Debreu (1954) model which showed that under certain restrictive conditions there can be a unique solution in the General Equilibrium of the market.[42]

▶   In conclusion, thanks to Walras's work, one has the opportunity to reflect both on the complexity of all the economic interdependencies and transactions that take place and on the difficulty of achieving the Walrasian General Equilibrium in a real economy in order to solve problems such as unemployment or economic fluctuations and crises.[43]

4.4 The Theoretical Legacy of Walras

There are several key features of the neoclassical theoretical system that prevailed in economic thought and are present in Walras's[44] work. Thus, a first key to such point is the abandonment of economic development and other socio-economic aggregates. In their place, emphasis was put on the allocation of the limited resources between alternative uses, and especially the analysis of the conditions that ensure optimal such allocation. As Samuelson[45] informed us, at the heart of all economic problems is now the maximisation of a mathematical function under constraints, for example, the maximisation of utility under a budget constraint.

A second feature that has to do with the 'methodology' is that of using the calculus of variations to search for the conditions under which the optimal solution is chosen.[46] Thus, there is the concept and the dominance of 'marginal utility'[47] in terms of the calculus of variations, that is 'extra utility', seen as a measured quantity, that an 'extra unit' of a good provides.[48]

A third characteristic element that runs through the analysis of neoclassical economists and Walras's work is the acceptance of the utilitarian approach as a pillar of the neoclassical synthesis, the best-known representative of which is Bentham. The adoption of this approach means that man is no longer by his 'nature', for example a merchant as in Smith, but a subject who acts according to the principle of maximum utility, that is directs his actions towards increasing the pleasures from the use of goods,[49] since nature has placed mankind under the dominion of pain and pleasure.[50]

This leads us to a fourth element which implies the replacement of the 'objective' theory of value with a 'subjective' theory of value derived from the utility of the object. Thus, an object now has value only if a subject[51] desires it, as opposed for instance to the labour theory of value, where its value exists independently of individual choice and is due to the labour expended to produce it. Therefore, labour is no longer seen as the intrinsic, quantitative characteristic of commodities.[52]

A fifth element that is pervasive in Walras's work as a neoclassical economist has to do with the individualistic status of all actors in the economy and the maximisation of the interests of individual actors maximising their own individual interest.

Thus, we have, for example, the individual as consumer, as producer, as entrepreneur and the 'minimal' possible social actors, such as households and firms, eliminating the total economy and the large social classes. That is, it does not require or imply any social concept or theory. Consequently, the individual or agent is considered to be sufficiently representative of the whole society. The neoclassical approach does just that. It applies the principle of the 'substitution' of the individual[53] for society, since society is seen as an abstract theoretical concept and it is considered meaningless to speak of the interest of society without understanding the interest of the individual.[54]

Finally, a sixth and last basic element related to the previous one in the work of Walras, as one of the main representatives of the neoclassical school, is the attempt to transform *Economics* into *Physics*, with strict laws in *Physics* and theorems in *Mathematics* which are, in Platonic terms, absolute, objective, indestructible and eternal. Thus, we must remove social relations from the field of *Economics* in order to establish the universal validity of their 'laws'.[55] Thus, Walras, redesigned *Economics* on the lines of the *Natural Sciences*, while being hostile to those who resisted the process of its transformation into a *Mathematical Science*.[56]

In conclusion, through the neoclassical approach, Microeconomic Theory emerged as a theory of individual choice, as opposed to the *Classical* approach of Macroeconomic Theory as a theory of aggregate, social quantities.[57] Of course, both approaches share a love of the *laissez-faire* free market. However, in the classical school, this was focused on aggregate accumulation, while in the neoclassical school, it is oriented towards individual maximisation. Consequently, a theory emerged through the work of Walras, as well as other neoclassical economists, which argued that the market is 'self-regulating', leading to the optimal allocation of resources for the agents within it.[58]

The next turning point in the dominance of the Neoclassical School in *Economics* was the work of Keynes, who refocused on the laws of the total economy and questioned the 'automatic' tendency of a market economy to return to equilibrium, thus creating a new Keynesian theory of macroeconomics.

Key Takeaways

- The economy is composed of a variety of market participants.
- Economic activity arises from the interaction of all market participants.
- Market participants pursue their own interests in exchange relations.
- Under certain conditions, an equilibrium can be achieved in the market.
- Markets are 'self-regulated' to distribute resources efficiently.

Revision Questions

- How would you define 'Neoclassical Economics'?
- What are the key players in the economy?
- What are the main assumptions behind General Equilibrium analysis?
- What is the 'auctioneer's' role?
- When does a firm experience zero profits in the economy?
- Does the General Equilibrium problem have a solution?
- What is Walras's main contribution to *Economics*?

Notes

1 Tsoulfidis (2010).
2 Varoufakis and Theocharakis (2005).
3 Walker (1987).
4 Britannica (2021).
5 Walker (1987).
6 Jaffe (1965).
7 Walker (1987).
8 Jaffe (1965).
9 Walker (1987).
10 Jaffe (1965).
11 Walker (1987).
12 Walker (1987).
13 Walker (1987).
14 Drakopoulos and Karagiannis (2003).
15 Tsoulfidis (2010).
16 Varoufakis and Theocharakis (2005).
17 Screpanti and Zamagni (2005).
18 Screpanti and Zamagni (2005).
19 Drakopoulos and Karagiannis (2003).
20 Tsoulfidis (2010).
21 Drakopoulos and Karagiannis (2003).
22 Walras (1954).
23 Varoufakis and Theocharakis (2005).
24 Backhouse (2009).
25 Mariolis (2010).
26 Screpanti and Zamagni (2005).
27 Screpanti and Zamagni (2005).
28 Varoufakis and Theocharakis (2005).
29 Drakopoulos and Karagiannis (2003).
30 Varoufakis and Theocharakis (2005).
31 Varoufakis and Theocharakis (2005).
32 Varoufakis and Theocharakis (2005).
33 Drakopoulos and Karagiannis (2003).
34 Tsoulfidis (2010).
35 Screpanti and Zamagni (2005).
36 Screpanti and Zamagni (2005).
37 Screpanti and Zamagni (2005).
38 Screpanti and Zamagni (2005).

39 Walras (1954).
40 Screpanti and Zamagni (2005)
41 Screpanti and Zamagni (2005)
42 Arrow and Debreu (1954)
43 Varoufakis and Theocharakis (2005).
44 Screpanti and Zamagni (2005).
45 Samuelson (1947).
46 Screpanti and Zamagni (2005).
47 Milios et al. (2018).
48 Milios et al. (2018).
49 Milios et al. (2018).
50 Bentham (1948).
51 Screpanti and Zamagni (2005).
52 Milios et al. (2018).
53 Milios et al. (2018).
54 Bentham (1948).
55 Screpanti and Zamagni (2005).
56 Varoufakis (2007).
57 Screpanti and Zamagni (2005).
58 Screpanti and Zamagni (2005).

References

Arrow, K. J., & Debreu, G. (1954). Existence of an equilibrium for a competitive economy. *Econometrica, 22*, 265–290.
Backhouse, R. E. (2009). *The evolution of economic thought*. Kritiki.
Bentham, J. (1948). *The principles of morals and legislation*. Hafner Press.
Drakopoulos, S., & Karagiannis, A. (2003). *History of economic thought: An overview*. Kritiki Publications.
Encyclopedia Britannica. (2021). Leon Walras. https://www.britannica.com/biography/Leon-Walras
Jaffe, W. (Ed.). (1965). *Correspondence of Leon Walras and related papers* (3 vols.). North-Holland Publishing Company.
Mariolis, T. (2010). *Essays in the logical history of political economy*. Matura.
Milios, J., Dimoulis, D., & Economakis, G. (2018 [2002]). *Karl Marx and the classics, an essay on value, crises and the capitalist mode of production*. Routledge.
Samuelson, P. (1947). *Foundations of economic analysis*. Harvard University Press.
Screpanti, E., & Zamagni, S. (2005). *An outline of the history of economic thought*. OUP.
Tsoulfidis, L. (2010). *Competing schools of economic thought*. Springer Science & Business Media.
Varoufakis, G. (2007). *Political economy: The economy in the light of criticism*. Gutenberg Publications.
Varoufakis, G., & Theocharakis, N. (2005). *Microeconomic models of partial and general equilibrium*. Typotheo—GiorgosDardanos.
Walker, D. A. (1987). Walras, Leon. In J. Eatwell, M. Milgate, & P. Newman (Eds.), *The new Palgrave: A dictionary of economics* (Vol. 4 (Q to Z)). Macmillan Press.
Walras, L. (1954). *Elements of pure economics* (W. Jaffe, Trans.). Allen and Unwin.

John Maynard Keynes (1883–1946) 5

▶ **Learning Objectives**

After having studied this chapter, the reader should be able to:

- Present Keynes's point of view on the role of the state.
- Analyse Keynes's ideas on money demand.
- Compare Keynes's ideas to those of the neoclassical economists.
- Describe Keynes's view of the financial system.
- Present briefly John Keynes's contribution to *Economics*.

▶ **Summary**

It is widely recognised that John Maynard Keynes is one of the most important economists of the twentieth century, and his influence on most Western governments' policies is considerable. His views were strongly influenced by the conditions that prevailed after World War I and the Great Depression, when, unlike the Classical School, Keynes considered the reaction of economies to be extremely slow. As a result of the Great Depression following the Crash of 1929, Keynes argues that the economy can remain in recession for a long period of time, below the level of full-time employment, and thus output will fall below its potential. As a result of declining economic activity, and consequently unemployment, entrepreneurs are reluctant to invest, and individuals are unable to save as a result of economic difficulties. In his work, Keynes supported private initiative and proposed measures to save the economy. To help the economy recover from the recession, the government will need to make public expenditures, but it will be up to private sector initiatives to drive economic growth. Keynes's main contribution to *Economics* is both his focus on macroeconomic factors in analysing a social and economic formation versus a microeconomic perspective of the individual entity and his rejection of the idea that free markets resolve recessions on their own since prices and wages are adjusted automatically.

5.1 Introduction

John Maynard Keynes was born in Cambridge, England, in 1883, the year Marx died. He is considered by many to be the greatest economist of the twentieth century, and his influence on the policies of most Western governments is tremendous. His father, John Naville Keynes, was also a prominent academic at Cambridge[1] University. The young John had a particular affinity as a student for *Mathematics*, and was also interested in *Classical Studies* and *Philosophy*. He even received many prizes for his performance in subjects such as *Mathematics, History, English* and *Chemistry*.[2]

He went on to Cambridge University where he studied *Mathematics*.[3] He was a student of Alfred Marshall, who persuaded him to take up *Economics*, and it was Marshal who secured for him in 1908 a lectureship at Cambridge[4] University, sponsored by Pigou, successor to the Marshall[5] Chair. He was a member of high society with a particular interest in art, served as a civil servant, met politicians such as Roosevelt and Churchill, and other personalities such as Picasso and George Bernard Shaw. Keynes's wife was the ballerina Lydia Lopokova, whom he fell in love with at a performance in which she participated in 1921,[6] and the couple were separated by his death in 1946.[7] Keynes was a great investor just like Ricardo[8] and made a considerable fortune from his activities in the foreign exchange[9] market. When he died, his fortune was still at a high level, although it was almost wiped out by the Depression, and he had to borrow to invest in the stock[10] market. Keynes was the editor-in-chief for 33 years of the *Economic Journal*, perhaps the most influential scholarly journal in Britain.[11] He believed that to be an economist required a mixture of skills and personality traits. He also considered it essential to have knowledge in the fields of *Philosophy, Political Science, Mathematics* and *History*.[12] His views on *Economics* were particularly influenced by the conditions that prevailed after World War I and the Great Depression, where, unlike the Classical School, Keynes believed that the reaction of economies was extremely slow.[13]

Following the end of World War I, he was a member of the British delegation to the Treaty of Versailles in 1919. Despite the terms of the Treaty, Keynes disagreed with them,[14] as he believed they would lead to unfair international trade practices and result in the resurgence of German militarism and authoritarianism.[15] In his book *The Economic Consequences of the Peace,* he articulated his polemic against the Treaty of Versailles.[16]

Another book by Keynes, but one whose main theme was the search for the causes that make the economy prosper for a period and then experience a recession, was published in 1930 under the title *A Treatise on Money*.[17] There, Keynes reached his theoretical conclusions based, on the one hand, on Marshall and Wicksell's theories and, on the other hand, on Hobson's and Tugan-Baranovsky's views. As a result, he borrowed the idea of analysing the economy in the context of two subsectors, consumption and investment expenditures, and particularly the idea of studying economic dynamic behaviour as a result of supply and demand imbalances.[18]

5.2 Macroeconomic Aggregates

His book *A Treatise on Money* was, in a way, a precursor to Keynes's most important work, published in 1936, entitled *The General Theory of Employment, Interest and Money*. In it, influenced by the Great Depression that followed the 1929 crash, Keynes argued that the economy could remain in recession for a long time, that is a level below the level of full employment and thus produce output below what it potentially could. This reduced economic activity, which translates into unemployment, is due to the reluctance of entrepreneurs to invest and the simultaneous inability of individuals to save in a period of economic hardship.[19]

▶ It is important to note that prior to the emergence of Keynes and despite Marx's opposition, the foundation of macroeconomic theory was based on the so-called Say's Law, according to which long-term voluntary unemployment is theoretically impossible as long as the macroeconomic balancing mechanisms of supply and demand exist.[20] In this context, a first important contribution of Keynes's work is exactly his criticism of Say's Law.[21]

However, the world economy went through a period of crisis, culminating in the crash of 1929 with unemployment rates of between 20 per cent and 30 per cent, roughly, in Britain and the United States in the 1930s, respectively, which showed that it was indeed possible to have long-term unemployment, despite analyses to the contrary. The need to study and address the phenomenon of unemployment was urgent.[22]

The General Theory raised new questions and turned the focus to the overall sizes of the economy and unemployment. These are the total output produced in the economy, total employment, the unemployment rate, etc. Most of Keynes's predecessor economists had not dealt extensively with similar issues, and concepts such as the aggregate supply and demand function were absent from their work. They were concerned not with aggregate quantities, but with quantities such as the price level and the supply and demand of individual goods or industries. The well-known neoclassical economist Paul Samuelson, a student at Harvard when the book was published, compared Keynesianism to a microbe that had infected those who were under 40 years of age, while the older ones had become immune.[23]

Keynes in his *The General Theory* focused his attention on the short term. He identified the cause of the Great Recession as insufficient demand, the components of which are the low level of household consumption and insufficient investment by firms. As the incentive to invest is weak even in normal times and the tendency to hold on to money is strong, when investment is low the result is that the economy operates below the level of full employment. If this is even accompanied by a stock market crash, the result is a major recession with widespread unemployment and low output. Governments in this case need to stimulate the economy in order to bring it back to the level of full employment, even if this means that they have to shoulder the needs of debt repayment. Indeed, as the economy is operating below the level of full employment, this will not cause inflation.[24]

In the work of other great economists, there are analyses of the economy as a whole, but the focus on macro rather than microeconomic variables was consolidated with the publication of the *The General Theory*. This is why Keynes considered by many to be the founder of Macroeconomic Theory. In this context, a contribution of Keynes to *Economics* also consists in the creation of the system of national accounts. Thus, he was influential in getting countries to collect economic data in a systematic way, as the prevailing view against government intervention until Keynes made this unnecessary, at least in most countries.[25]

According to Keynes, the level of income determines, more than any other factor, consumption and therefore savings, while it is the entrepreneurial initiative to invest that will put the economy on a growth path and create wealth.[26] When investment in capital goods and equipment declines, the consequence is economic contraction. Inherent in the economic system, according to Keynes, is uncertainty, and the possibility of recession is always possible, without the entrepreneurs[27] being responsible for it.

In this context, Keynes argued that if everyone took steps to save money, this would eventually lead to lower savings as reduced economic activity would create a recession. Therefore, if projected savings exceeded a critical level, downward pressure on growth would be caused, while the potential excess of investment would stimulate it.[28]

Finally, an important element in Keynes's work is his critique of *Say's law* with an emphasis on the causal relationship between production and consumption. In contrast, Keynes believed that it is not production that creates expenditure, and therefore demand. But, it is the desires and spending decisions of individuals in the economy that create demand, and therefore an increase in output follows. In this context, he studied the determinants of demand which, in turn, determine the level of employment.

5.3   State Intervention

Keynes supported private initiative, and the proposals he made in his work were directed towards the rescue of economies. The government would have to undertake public spending in order to assist the economy out of the recessionary situation, but economic activity would have to have private initiative at its core. It is true that Keynes argued that government intervention in the economy in a prolonged recession may not be the most ideal solution, but he believed that the consequences of non-intervention would be more severe.[29]

5.3 State Intervention

▶ An ironic response to the claims of the classical economists who argued that in the long run the private sector would recover after wage cuts: 'In the long run, we are all dead'.[30] Instead, we need something short term and highly effective. This is nothing but state interventionism.[31]

Keynes's calls for the government to take the initiative in order to halt the recession were in harmony with the New Deal policy that had begun to be implemented even before the publication of *The General Theory* in the United States. The New Deal was a set of measures on the part of the government aimed at solving the socio-economic problems that had arisen. Although these actions were seen as urgent solutions and were not fully implemented, they yielded positive results, but they were viewed with suspicion by the business community.[32]

Keynes argued that there are certain activities in which private initiative plays an essential role and in which the state should not intervene, as well as other activities in which the state operates more effectively than the private sector.[33] Moreover, Keynes did not have much confidence in the ability of markets to coordinate economic activity during times of uncertainty due to the inherent uncertainty of people operating within the framework of a free market.[34] As an investor himself, he was convinced that investments are influenced by human emotion, such as expectation, hope, fear, envy, etc.[35] Market psychology can have a significant impact on the economic cycle, deepening its phases as a result.

Keynes's observations that the economy was unable to regulate itself in case of a prolonged recession and therefore the state had to take systematic measures to solve the problem were not new. Other economists before him, such as the Swedes Myrdal and Wicksell amongst others, had come to similar conclusions, but without the same influence as Keynes. Moreover, government interventions to stimulate the economy had already been implemented, for example in the Nordic countries. Such practices were to be advocated by *The General Theory*.[36]

The central idea in Keynes's work is that public works can create even more jobs in the economy. His reasoning is as follows: workers in public works will earn income, which they will want to spend on consumer goods, thus increasing the demand for them and thus their production, which, in order to increase, will need more workers. However, Keynes did not explain precisely the mechanism by which this would happen nor did he express it mathematically.[37]

As we have seen, Keynes formulated the view that it is demand that determines the amount of output that will be produced in the economy and further argued that it is expected profitability, not current profitability, that determines the amount of investment that will be made by entrepreneurs.

The acquisition of capital goods (buildings, machinery, tools, equipment, etc.) is a means by which one secures the right to some future income that one may receive from the sale of the goods produced by these assets.[38] However, there is no guarantee when and to what extent investments will be made by businesses, and therefore the state must take on this role temporarily, by spending public money and implementing public projects, helping the economic system to recover until private entrepreneurial initiative increases.[39]

On the other hand, the state should also intervene in the distribution of income. More specifically, Keynes pointed out that the natural tendency of a free-market regime is to create a distribution of income that is unfair, and he believed that large amounts of savings generated by the large inequality in income distribution would result in keeping expenditure and aggregate demand low and the state would have to intervene in this case as well. It is the view of Keynes that intervention in the economic system should be conducted in a manner that respects private ownership of the means of production. Based on the above, one would be tempted to say that Keynes was an economist who defended state interventionism as well as the state expression of Adam Smith's *invisible hand*.[40]

5.4 Profits and Capitalism

Keynes, like other great economists before him, such as Adam Smith and Karl Marx, argued that in the long run the profitability of firms, under certain conditions, may show a downward trend.[41] He put forward two main arguments to support this position: a short-term and a long-term one. The short-term argument is based on supply and, according to this argument, when a firm increases its investment, in the short term, it will have to compete with other firms in order to obtain the necessary factors of production (labour, capital, raw materials, etc.) on its behalf. This will lead to an increase in their price and thus to a reduction in profits, assuming that the selling price of the product remains constant. This fall in profits affects not only the firm but also the whole economy. There is a possibility that the growth of the population and the development of improved production methods could act to slow the downward trend in profitability of firms.[42]

The long-run argument starts from demand: as the firm grows and increases the quantity it produces, if it wants to remain competitive and maintain the same level of sales, it will have to reduce the price of the product, which implies a reduction in its profit. Consequently, Keynes considered that, in the short term, reasons originating on the supply side and, in the long term, causes rooted on the demand side, can reduce the profits of firms.[43] Keynes, however, seems to have contributed little to the debate initiated by earlier great economists concerning the downward trend in profit.[44]

Keynes's *The General Theory* was published after the Great Depression, which was a strong indication of the inability of the economic system to ensure prosperity. However, as far as the future prospects of the economic system are concerned, Keynes believed that the long-term survival of capitalism is feasible.[45] Of course, although he did not agree with the prospect of capitalism being replaced by another economic system, he did support the necessity of an 'alternative' policy which would provide full employment within the economic system.

5.5 Financial Sector

▶ According to Keynes, the amount of money demanded for transactions (*transactions motive*) and precautionary purposes (*precautionary motive*) is positively related to income, while the demand for money for speculation (*speculative motive*) is negatively related to the interest[46] rate.

More specifically, the *transactions motive* is due to transaction needs, since economic actors need liquidity. In this context, the main factor influencing the demand for money is the level of income. The *precautionary motive* refers to meeting unforeseen needs and again the main factor is the level of income. Finally, the *speculative motive* is related to the interest rate, since when the interest rate on bonds is high, it is in the individual's interest not to retain cash in his/her possession but to invest in bonds. Conversely, when the interest rate on bonds is low, then cash is retained since it is not advantageous to take on risk at the low interest rate that bonds[47] have.

In this context, Keynes considered that the basic cause of the problems associated with speculation in capitalism is the absence from the production process of the owner of capital (rentier).[48] Thus, the absent owner of capital enjoys high returns, slowing down the growth potential of the firm (i.e. the 'real economy') as he simply can obtain interest because capital is scarce, just as the owner of land can obtain rent because land is scarce.[49] Consequently, Keynes advocates gradual reduction of the financial system by eliminating the 'rentiers'.[50]

Moreover, Keynes considered that uncertainty plays a very important role in decisions, especially regarding the volatility of investments and the stock market. Unlike classical and neoclassical economists who believed in a 'certain' return of the market to equilibrium, Keynes argued that this was uncertain, since the precarious nature of markets was due to the ever-changing expectations and assessments of investors, especially when investors were trying to estimate returns over long periods of time.[51]

Therefore, for Keynes, *Economics* is a science related to psychological and sociological variables such as motivation, expectations and uncertainty, and therefore should include moral evaluations.[52] While he does not reject the use of *Mathematics* in his analysis, he considers its excessive use inappropriate since increased mathematisation can obscure the many-faceted interdependencies of reality and the analysis may be reduced to a cloud of outdated and meaningless symbols. Finally, economic models can be empirically tested using *Statistics* and *Econometrics*.[53]

Immediately after the publication of *The General Theory*, several studies dealing with Keynes's work were published and led to the formation of modern Macroeconomic Analysis. One of the most important such studies is the one that developed the well-known IS-LM model.

5.6 The Theoretical Legacy of Keynes

During World War II, Keynes played an important role in the formulation of economic policy, serving in the Treasury Department, and had a decisive influence on the formation of the international monetary system. In addition, he envisioned the creation of the International Monetary Fund (IMF) and the World Bank (WB) and believed that economic problems were universal in nature and should be treated as such.[54]

After the financial crisis of the last decade, many economists, politicians, bankers, businessmen, analysts and journalists turned to both Marx's work, which showed a sharp increase in sales,[55] and Keynes's work to imbibe their teachings. In fact, as the then Federal Reserve Central Banker Alan Greenspan[56] admitted in 2008, he was wrong to believe that the private interests of institutions, especially banks, were capable of protecting their shareholders and their capital during a deep recession.

The theories of classical and neoclassical economists did not seem to be able to predict or explain why the market did not 'self-regulate' during the financial crisis of the previous decade. Perhaps the mispricing of uncertainty highlighted by Keynesian theory was a critical element in the development of the crisis, especially after nearly three decades of economic 'liberalisation'.

In any case, Keynes's 'return' after the crisis was impressive. A coordinated package of measures emerged in order to prevent a complete collapse of the global economic system, by stimulating the total economy.[57] Several analysts believe that this prevented the worst from happening to the global economy, which began to recover slowly after 2010. However, the debt crisis in various countries like Greece, with the cutting of public spending and the raising of taxes to reduce deficits, led to harsh austerity measures and proved the short-lived nature of the Keynesian parenthesis.[58]

Overall, we could say that Keynes's contribution to *Economics* is both his emphasis on the macroeconomic aggregates in the analysis of a social and economic formation as opposed to the microeconomic perspective of the individual economic unit and his rejection of the thesis that the free market alone resolves recessions, as prices and wages are 'automatically' adjusted. Instead, he introduced the idea, which has become widely accepted, that to a greater or lesser extent, state intervention is needed in order to smooth out the fluctuations in the economy but also to enable poorer countries to pursue higher levels of growth. In the same context, the idea that full employment could only be maintained through government spending was particularly important.[59] Therefore, Keynes's work continues to be relevant through the ongoing crises and recessions experienced by the global economy.

Key Takeaways

- There could be a long-term recession below full employment.
- Individuals' desires create demand, which leads to increased production.
- Smoothing out economic fluctuations requires state intervention.
- The free market tends to create an unfair distribution of income.

- Economic decisions are affected by uncertainty.
- Psychology and sociology are part of *Economics*.
- In order to shrink the financial system, speculators should be removed.
- Mathematical and statistical models can be reasonably used in *Economics*.

Revision Questions

- How is Keynesian Theory related to the 'Great Depression'?
- What is 'Say's law'?
- What is Keynes's position on public spending?
- What is the New Deal and what is Keynes's role?
- Which position does Keynes take on profitability?
- What is Keynes's view of the financial system?
- What is Keynes's main contribution to *Economics*?

Notes

1 Thornton (2014).
2 Yueh (2018).
3 Thornton (2014).
4 Tsoulfidis (2008).
5 Thornton (2014).
6 Yueh (2018).
7 Heilbroner (2011).
8 Yueh (2018).
9 Tsoulfidis (2010).
10 Yueh (2018).
11 Heilbroner (2011).
12 Heilbroner (2011).
13 Yueh (2018).
14 Tsoulfidis (2010).
15 Heilbroner (2011).
16 Tsoulfidis (2010).
17 Heilbroner (2011).
18 Screpanti and Zamagni (2005).
19 Heilbroner (2011).
20 Drakopoulos and Karagiannis (2003).
21 Mariolis (2010).
22 Drakopoulos and Karagiannis (2003).
23 Backhouse (2009).

24. Yueh (2018).
25. Tsoulfidis (2010).
26. Heilbroner (2011).
27. Heilbroner (2011).
28. Thornton (2014).
29. Heilbroner (2011).
30. John Maynard Keynes in Beranek and Kamerschen (2016).
31. Thornton (2014).
32. Heilbroner (2011).
33. Screpanti and Zamagni (2005).
34. Varoufakis (2007).
35. van Staveren (2021).
36. Tsoulfidis (2010).
37. Tsoulfidis (2010).
38. Tsoulfidis (2010).
39. Heilbroner (2011).
40. Screpanti and Zamagni (2005).
41. Tsoulfidis (2010).
42. Tsoulfidis (2010).
43. Tsoulfidis (2010).
44. Tsoulfidis (2010) and Tsoulfidis (2008).
45. Tsoulfidis (2010).
46. Tsoulfidis (2010).
47. Drakopoulos and Karagiannis (2003).
48. Keynes (2009).
49. Keynes (2009).
50. Keynes (2009).
51. Thornton (2014).
52. Karagiannis (2001).
53. Karagiannis (2001).
54. Tsoulfidis (2008).
55. Thornton (2014).
56. Alan Greenspan in Thornton (2014).
57. Thornton (2014).
58. Robert Skidelsky in Thornton (2014).
59. Thornton (2014).

References

Backhouse, R. E. (2009). *The evolution of economic thought*. Kritiki.
Beranek, W., & Kamerschen, D. (2016). Examining two of Keynes's most popular statements-wasteful public spending can be acceptable, and, in the long run we are all dead-yields some surprising implications. *The American Economist, 612*, 263–267.
Drakopoulos, S., & Karagiannis, A. (2003). *History of economic thought: An overview*. Kritiki Publications.
Heilbroner, R. L. (2011). *The worldly philosophers: The lives, times and ideas of the great economic thinkers*. Simon and Schuster.
Karagiannis, A. (2001). *Economic methodology*. Kritiki Publications.
Keynes J. M. (2009). *The general theory of employment, interest and money, management laboratory press*. Unabridged Edition.
Mariolis, T. (2010). *Essays in the logical history of political economy*. Matura.
Screpanti, E., & Zamagni, S. (2005). *An outline of the history of economic thought*. OUP.
Thornton, P. (2014). *The great economists: Ten economists whose thinking changed the way we live*. Pearson UK.
Tsoulfidis, L. (2008). *History of economic theory and policy*. University of Macedonia Publications.
Tsoulfidis, L. (2010). *Competing schools of economic thought*. Springer Science & Business Media.
van Staveren, I. (2021). *Alternative ideas from 10 (almost) forgotten economists*. Springer Nature Press.
Varoufakis, G. (2007). *Political economy: The economy in the light of criticism*. Gutenberg Publications.
Yueh, L. (2018). *What would the great economists do?* Picador.

Joseph Schumpeter (1883–1950)

▶ **Learning Objectives**

After having studied this chapter, the reader should be able to:

- Define 'economic development' according to Schumpeter.
- Analyse the meaning of 'creative destruction' in the economy.
- Formulate the 'Schumpeterian hypothesis'.
- Analyse Schumpeter's view on entrepreneurial activity.
- Describe Schumpeter's ideas on the future of capitalism.
- Present briefly Joseph Schumpeter's contribution to *Economics*.

▶ **Summary**

Joseph Alois Schumpeter was an influential economist of the twentieth century who was involved actively in business and economic policymaking. He investigated the activities of innovative companies and their relationship to the economic development and prosperity of society. Technological innovations are considered by Schumpeter to be the force that may have the potential to lead the economy to a dynamic flow, thus allowing profits to be formed. Profits, Schumpeter argues, do not come from the 'exploitation' of labour, but are the result of a completely different process. Entrepreneurship for Schumpeter is the starting point of the growth process, which cannot be understood without innovation. Furthermore, the economic system cannot be boosted without entrepreneurial activity. Schumpeter defines development as follows: the introduction of a new commodity; the introduction of a new method of production; the opening of a new market, the conquest of a new source of raw materials or semi-processed goods; the execution of a new organisational structure of any industry. Furthermore, he believed that capitalism was doomed to failure. There is no reason to believe that this is a result of the system's inability to control successive crises nor is it related to the uprising of the working class, but rather to a change in the general economic climate. According to Schumpeterian theory, monopoly and oligopoly market structures, as well as a large economic unit, are positively related to technological progress and innovation. As a result, Schumpeter considered capitalism to be a form or method of economic change, while this process of 'creative destruction' is an essential feature of capitalism.

6.1 Introduction

Joseph Alois Schumpeter was born in 1883, that is the year Karl Marx died and John Maynard Keynes was born, in Triesch, a small town in the Austrian province of Moravia, then the Habsburg Empire and now part of the Czech Republic. His grandfather owned a textile factory, which was taken over by his father, who passed away when Joseph, the only child in the family, was 4 years old. His mother married, 7 years after his father's death, a prominent general. Young Joseph went to a private school where children belonging to aristocratic circles usually went. The aristocratic manners and habits he acquired in his childhood were something that would follow him for life.[1]

In 1901, Schumpeter enrolled at the Faculty of Law of the University of Vienna, and in 1906 he received the title *Doctor utriusque iuris* (*Doctor of Law*) because in Vienna, as in other European cities, *Economics* was taught at the Faculty of Law. Schumpeter stood out for his academic achievements from an early age at the University of Vienna, which was an important centre for the study of *Economics*.[2]

In 1905, he took part in the seminar of Boehm-Bawerk, Professor at the University of Vienna, when he returned to his academic career after serving as Minister of Finance. During his studies as an undergraduate student, he published three articles, and his ambition was to pursue a career as a professor and civil servant. Schumpeter married in 1907, at the age of 24, Gladys Ricarde-Seaver, 12 years his senior, and the daughter of a Church of England official. This marriage actually ended with the end of World War I, and Schumpeter declared himself 'unmarried'.[3]

In 1909, Schumpeter was appointed assistant professor at the University of Czernowitz, the easternmost province of Austria, now part of Ukraine. Between 1911 and 1919, he taught *Political Economy* as a first-rank professor at Graz. In 1913, at the age of 30, he worked as a visiting professor at Columbia University in the United States.

In 1908, at the age of 25, he published his first important book, *Das Wesen und Hauptinhalt der theoretischenNationaloekonomie*, and in 1912, his well-known *Theorie der wirtschaftlichen Entwicklung* (*Theory of Economic Development*), while every year he published a series of important and particularly long articles in scientific journals. By the end of his university studies, he had studied in-depth much of the economic literature, both classical and modern, especially

6.1 Introduction

Anglo-Saxon. The two most important intellectual influences on Schumpeter's work probably come from Leon Walras and Karl Marx.[4] From the former, he was taught the emphasis on the interdependence between economic variables, while with regard to Karl Marx, Schumpeter admired his understanding of the process of economic change.

In 1918, Schumpeter, after retiring from the university, was a member of the German Socialisation Commission, signing the report that suggested the socialist course as the only way to increase economic efficiency, and his participation was often used as 'proof' of his socialist convictions.[5] In fact, when asked how a proponent of private initiative could be a member of such a committee, Schumpeter famously replied that 'if someone wants to commit suicide, it is good that a doctor is present'.[6]

The following year, the Social Democrats emerged as the strongest party in Austria and Joseph Schumpeter served as Minister of Finance in that government. In 1921, after leaving the University of Graz, he was appointed president of a historic banking house (Biederman Bank) and when the bank went bankrupt (1924) as a result of hyperinflation in Germany, Schumpeter returned to academia. Schumpeter refused to protect himself under the umbrella of bankruptcy laws. Instead, he repaid his creditors in full, losing all his capital and part of his income for the next 10 years.[7]

In 1925, he accepted an academic position at the University of Bonn in Germany, after having spent a very brief period as a visiting professor in Japan. In the same year, at the age of 42, he married Anna Josefina Reisingero who was then 22 years old and whom he had known since childhood, despite his mother's objections to her 'humble origins' and her parents' objections to the age difference that separated them. The following year, Schumpeter's wife died in childbirth, as did the infant. During this period, he also lost his mother. Although obviously affected by these losses, he devoted himself to hard work, and his stay in Bonn proved to be extremely fruitful and productive with sixty-five publications. Schumpeter sent part of his financial earnings to his late wife's parents, which he continued to do until the end of his[8] life.

In 1931, after a semester at Harvard, he visited Japan for lectures, as well as Germany, and left Bonn in 1932. From 1932 until his death in 1950, he taught at Harvard University in the United States, receiving the highest possible return provided for professors, with which he supported friends and former students and paid off his remaining debts from his time in Vienna. Although he was a distinguished and successful professor, Schumpeter suffered from anxiety and melancholy, and indicative of this was that he measured his work productivity on a daily basis.[9]

Finally, Schumpeter was one of the founders of the Econometric Society, and its president (1937–1941), as well as the first non-American economist to serve as president of the American Economic Association since 1948. In 1937, at the age of 54, he married Elizabeth Boody Firuski, 15 years his junior, with whom he lived for the rest of his[10] life. Schumpeter died in his sleep on 8 January 1950.[11]

6.2 The Creation of Profit

In his *Theory of Economic Development*, Schumpeter presents his version of how the capitalist system develops and is reproduced. Schumpeter introduces us to a completely stationary capitalist world in which the element of change and evolution is non-existent, in which stagnation is the norm of economic reality.[12] As a first point, Schumpeter's analysis of the capitalist system is devoid of capital accumulation, the element that is responsible for growth in Smith, Marx and Keynes. Thus, Schumpeter believed that stagnation provided the ideal environment for capitalism to flourish.[13] According to Schumpeter, the automatic repetition of our actions results from the cumulative experience of man and his nature.[14] Economic life lacks the element of challenge, as people tend to repeat the economic course that they have empirically found to be in their best interest.[15]

This stagnant state is characterised by perfect competition, full adjustment to equilibrium, and no net saving or credit. Income is spent on consumer goods produced in the previous period. But given that production processes are synchronised, each supply is matched to its own demand at expected prices, which barely cover unit costs. Money may be committed without losing something important that is happening in the economy. The economic situation can only change under certain circumstances (e.g. situations such as population growth, wars, etc.), but Schumpeter's interest does not lie there. By the term development, he refers to those changes in economic life which are not imposed from outside but come from within.[16] He was therefore suggesting that there was a source of energy internal to the system which would in itself disrupt any equilibrium that could be achieved. On the basis of the above, one could say that Schumpeter focused on 'endogenous' changes.

Schumpeter defines innovation as follows: (1) The introduction of a new good or a new quality of good. (2) The introduction of a new method of production. (3) The opening of a new market. (4) The acquisition of a new source of supply of materials. (5) The execution of a new organisational scheme.[17]

▶   An important feature of this stagnant flow in the economy is the fact that competition will have eliminated all profits in excess of the 'value' of one's contribution to production, since it argues that competition between the big capitalists leads the race and forces them to pay workers the full value of the product they produce.

In this context, the capitalist receives nothing beyond his salary as a manager. Therefore, the contribution to production derived from capital goods that he owns will have been absorbed by the value of the labour and resources expended in production. Consequently, Schumpeter argues that in a stagnant, non-evolving economy, there is no room for profit.

But, according to Schumpeter, the force that could lead outside this stagnant flow to a dynamic flow, which would allow the formation of profits, is the introduction of technological innovations. Profits, Schumpeter argues, do not come from the 'exploitation' of labour power, but are the result of an entirely different process. More precisely, only the force of the introduction of new technological innovations can break the 'routine'. Thus, as a result of these innovations, a new income flow is created that is not attributable either to the contribution of labour or to the contribution of capital. Instead, it requires a new production process, which enables the innovative capitalist either to produce and market exactly the same products at lower costs or to introduce completely new products and to outperform his competitors by dominating the market.[18]

6.3 The Innovative Entrepreneur

The new income stream resulting from the introduction of innovation, as shown in the previous analysis, is not a continuous and permanent income stream. It is an entirely temporary gain, unless this advantage is systematically 'cultivated'. Innovation therefore requires the existence of an (innovative) person who implements the combination of factors of production in an innovative way. These innovative people within the firm, that is the 'revolutionaries of production', Schumpeter called them entrepreneurs and made it clear that these entrepreneurs are not ordinary capitalists, but people who constantly bring about change and who do not belong to a particular social class.[19]

Schumpeter believes that innovations are the work of pioneers and believes that behind the new business innovation follows a series of would-be imitators, so the discovery becomes more widely known and 'copied'. Thus, it is deprived of its comparative advantage even though, at the same time, the investments made to disseminate and copy it had led to economic growth. Thus, the dynamics of the capitalist system, according to Schumpeter, contrary to what, for example, Marx would have believed, rests not on the class struggle but on the innovative entrepreneur.[20]

In Schumpeter's work, the innovative entrepreneur is not necessarily the same person as the profit maker, despite the fact that he created the profits. Rather, the profits go to the owner of the firm, who has also taken the risk of financing these new innovations, possibly assisted by the granting of credit inherent in the Schumpeterian system.[21] Moreover, entrepreneurship is not a profession, a skill or a title that can be passed down from generation to generation. Rather, it is a distinct form with leadership skills related to identifying and exploiting business opportunities and for which society as a whole does not seem to have much respect or even appreciation.

Therefore, given the lack of direct entitlement to profits and the lack of social recognition, why does the innovative entrepreneur undertake this task? Schumpeter explains that first of all there is the dream and the desire to establish a private kingdom and then there is the desire for conquest, that is the impulse to compete, to prove himself superior to others, to succeed not for the fruits of his success but for success itself. Finally, there is the joy of creating, of achieving goals or simply of exercising one's energy and imagination.[22]

Therefore, the dynamics of the system is in the hands of a non-capitalist elite and the historical evolution of the system is based on the influence of this leading elite on the 'static' economy. However, the interpretation of the gaps in the 'cyclical' behaviour of technological innovations remained a question to be explored.

6.4   Innovations and Business Cycles

According to Schumpeter, technological change in the capitalist process is incessant and discontinuous. It is fuelled by the introduction of new combinations of factors of production or by the discovery of new ways of producing commodities by the entrepreneur. Thus, innovations are defined simply as either 'other things' or 'the same thing by a different method'. They are 'new combinations' introduced by 'new people' through the creation of 'new enterprises'. Entrepreneurship for Schumpeter is the starting point of the growth process, which cannot be understood without innovation. Similarly, without entrepreneurship, there can be no economic efficiency to the capitalist process.[23]

What needs to be interpreted is the 'discontinuity' of innovations and growth in capitalism. We have seen that entrepreneurs are the 'revolutionaries' of the production process. Their motivation to innovate is consistent with their strong desire to become members of the capitalist class, since being an entrepreneur is the way to become a member of the capitalist class.[24] However, every time they achieve this, they lose their 'revolutionary' spirit.

Future inventors do not independently have the purchasing power to control the productive forces needed to introduce new innovations. In a social organisation where private ownership of the means of production and individual production are given, the basic function of banks is to grant credit in favour of entrepreneurs to overcome the barriers to innovation. The inflow of new purchasing power increases the demand for labour and land and thus creates upward pressure on wages, incomes and income.

Credit is granted to entrepreneurs before they contribute to the new flow of goods. The financing of entrepreneurs, however, is hindered by a short-term money rate. New firms will be able to pay the interest rate, which is perceived as a tax on entrepreneurial profit, if and when their new supply is introduced to the market and they start to make a profit. Old firms are replaced by new firms unless they manage to 'copy' competitors. As long as the first innovative firms help to reduce social resistance to innovation and lead to reorganisation of old firms, they introduce a second wave of innovation.

▶   The economic system fails to adapt automatically to these changes and moves away from equilibrium. The partial imbalance, introduced endogenously by entrepreneurs, can only decompose into a generalised imbalance characterised by a change in prices and quantities. As traditional entrepreneurial activity declines, adaptive behaviour and competition settle in. The economic system approaches, once again, a new cyclical flow in which profit disappears. This is the fundamental two-phase cycle of growth and recession. This simple biphasic cycle is the basic core of the capitalist process, according to Schumpeter.

Schumpeter goes on to describe a second approach, the four-phase cycle, in which recovery leads to growth and decline leads to recession. Here, credit is used as an explanatory factor, not only for financing innovation but also for the general accumulation of capital, and over-financing through credit leads the cycle to uncertainty and instability, followed by decline and recession.

▶ Schumpeter introduced as an explanatory scheme the large-scale innovation processes that feed the 45–60 year Kondratieff cycle, medium-sized innovations that feed the 8–11 year Juglar cycle and the 3–5 year Kitchin cycle based on changes in stocks. Large innovations and inventions associated with the first cycle are those that cause fundamental changes and effects, such as the automobile and the steam engine. Still, regarding the generalised recession, Schumpeter argued that this was the result of the unfortunate coincidence of three different types of business cycles reaching their lowest point simultaneously.[25]

6.5 The Future of Capitalism

For Schumpeter, capitalism's survival was dependent on the values and morals it embodied. However, this faith seemed to be eroding despite the fact that the system was enjoying economic prosperity.[26] For Schumpeter, the capitalist system, just like a machine, needed fuel to keep itself alive, and this translated into the necessity of active entrepreneurship.[27] As the economic basis of the capitalist system gives it a rational and critical sign, it is ultimately the very mentality of capitalism that will be the cause of its[28] end.

Schumpeter saw the fall of capitalism and the rise of socialism as inevitable.[29] He argued that when we speak of capitalism, we mean an evolutionary process.[30] The process of 'creative destruction' has been the basic characteristic of capitalism historically. He believes that capitalism is by nature prone to economic change and, in this spirit, the process of entrepreneurial change brings about a revolution in the economic structure from within, destroying the old and creating something new. This process of 'creative destruction' is the basic characteristic about capitalism.[31] That is, he sees as the most important element of capitalism the 'process of creative destruction' and the constant change and evolution, the invention and creation of new products, new technologies and new markets. In other words, the economy is in a state of flux, fuelled by technological innovation. To Schumpeter, the concepts of 'capitalism' and 'stability' are contradictory to each other.[32]

Schumpeter also advocates a person-centered rather than a class-centered system, which implies that he deconstructs the class system and introduces a different type of individuality. In summary, entrepreneurship consists of exploiting new discoveries or, more generally, untested technological possibilities in order to manufacture new products or to rework old products in a more efficient manner, to open up new markets or sources of raw materials, to reorganize industries, etc.[33]

Schumpeter begins an attempt to demonstrate that capitalism is doomed with his question 'Can capitalism survive?'.[34] The question remains, however, what ultimately contributes to the collapse of the system? The capitalist process has, as we have seen, reduced the importance of the function through which the capitalist order is aspired to. As we have seen, capitalism creates a critical mentality that, after destroying the moral authority of so many other institutions, now turns against itself.

In this way, the end of the capitalist life cycle is coming. The 'bureaucratised' gigantic unit 'expels' the small and medium-sized enterprise and 'expropriates' its owners. And, in the end, it also expels the entrepreneur and expropriates the bourgeoisie, which in its development will lose not only its income, but something infinitely more important, its function. In this way, the capitalist life cycle is coming to an end. Consequently, bureaucracy will predominate over personality and character, and innovation will become a routine effort. Therefore, the end of capitalism will be brought about by the change of climate and atmosphere, not by the inability of capitalism to control successive crises following one another or by the uprising of workers.[35]

6.6 The Schumpeterian Hypothesis

The analysis of the market structure, the size of the economic unit and the conditions conducive to technological progress led to the so-called 'Schumpeterian hypothesis', which can be summarised as follows: 'the monopolistic/oligopolistic market structure and the large size of the economic unit are positively related with technological progress and innovation'. In *Capitalism, Socialism and Democracy*, Schumpeter rejected perfect competition and argued that full competition cannot promote technological progress. In particular, he argued that monopolies have a very important ability that makes them superior to competitive capitalism. More specifically, the monopoly has at its disposal superior methods which are not at all or not so easily available to the competitors.[36] According to Schumpeter, innovations were creators of 'temporary monopolies'. He believed that the main difference between them is that innovations are temporary and last until other firms catch up, whereas oligopoly power lasts longer as it is based on a barrier (usually economic or legal) that excludes the entry of other firms.[37]

The periodisation of competitive capitalism is based, first and foremost, on the knowledge that has been accumulated historically about the course of capitalism. In this respect, Schumpeter distinguished two major periods:[38]

(a) The period of competition dominated by small businesses lasting until about the year 1880.
(b) The period of oligopolistic competition dominated by large firms and mono/oligopolistic structures. This period lasts from 1880 to the period of writing his book.

Moreover, according to Schumpeter, the superiority of monopolistic capitalism rests upon another factor, namely its ability to increase the sphere of influence of the best and to reduce the sphere of influence of the worst.[39] Thus, Schumpeter argued that competition is not able to promote technological change and development[40] since a perfectly competitive enterprise is inferior in technological productivity[41], and hence perfect competition is both inferior and lacks the credentials to be considered an ideal model of productivity. This rejection is mainly based on the following reason: The system of perfect competition cannot lead to excess profits and thus fails to create real incentives for the development of innovative activity and risk-taking on the part of the economic unit.[42]

We note that Schumpeter contrasts the competitive firm with the large firm implying that the monopolistic character of a firm is consistent with the large size of the firm.[43] He wrote that the monopoly has been practically identified with the large-scale enterprise. Hence, the second key element of Schumpeter's hypothesis is that it is the large firms in the industry that lead the race of technological progress and innovation. He argued that only large firms have sufficient resources to undertake innovative actions and technological improvements.[44] Lastly, he concluded[45] that we must accept that the large enterprise has necessarily happened to be the most powerful engine of progress and especially of the long-term development of total production.

6.7   The Theoretical Legacy of Schumpeter

As we have seen, Joseph Schumpeter's often unconventional positions, combined with his historical approach, have caused a lot of controversy about his theoretical classification. Schumpeter was also concerned with presenting his work in a purely analytical manner, free from ideological influence. Schumpeter attempted to investigate the activity of innovative enterprises and their relations with the well-being of society and economic growth.[46]

In light of the above, it is particularly difficult to categorise Schumpeter's work within a single school of thought. Accordingly, Schumpeter abandons Adam Smith's view of the individual as a 'trader', and instead treats him as a rational thinking individual guided by psychological motives. Moreover, he is not in agreement with the neoclassical view of the market as being competitive and accepts the existence of equilibrium, but not as a general principle.[47]

Schumpeter's analysis is based on the implicit principle of satisfying individual motives without implying that society is substituted for the individual; he simply emphasises the importance of the individual motives (methodological individualism). Furthermore, Schumpeter disregards the central importance of the concept of labour, one of the defining characteristics of Classical Political Economy.

As for methodology, he argued that historical and abstract methods do not contradict each other, and he rejected methodological absolutism by advocating a twofold approach to *Economics* involving both qualitative and quantitative research. Moreover, he suggested that theories should be developed to describe economic phenomena, often based on empirical evidence, as the complexity of economic phenomena makes it difficult for theories to predict economic phenomena in the future.[48]

▶ Due to Schumpeter's use of dynamic approaches to general equilibrium, the emphasis that he places on individual psychological motivation, and his incorporation of mathematical and econometric techniques, as well as eliminating the central role of the concept of work, he shows similarities to neoclassical Walrasian approaches, whose principles he frequently modifies.

▶ In the 1930s–1950s, the Keynesian Revolution completely eclipsed Schumpeter's theory of growth and innovation, followed in the 1950s–1960s by Solow's growth theories, which were, in turn, replaced by the New Growth Theory. Since the 1980s, however, Schumpeterian issues have been the subject of renewed debate, as industrialised countries are facing major development challenges, innovation has been elevated to a social problem, and the economic fluctuations associated with capitalist growth have been the subject of intense debate and sustained analysis.

Due to the revival of interest in Schumpeter's work, what is now referred to as the (neo)Schumpeterian Political Economy[49] and other similar approaches friendly to the Schumpeterian tradition came into existence, such as *Evolutionary Economics* and *Institutional Economics*. As a result, one can examine the structures, institutions and processes that determine the extent to which innovations are created over time, as well as the contribution these innovations make to economic growth. A strategic, cognitive and organisational approach is taken in order to understand entrepreneurial behaviour.

Key Takeaways

- Technological innovation could lead the economy to a dynamic flow.
- Entrepreneurship is the starting point of the growth process.
- A socialist society will eventually replace capitalism.
- The process of 'creative destruction' is a basic characteristic of capitalism.
- Large firms and monopolies/oligopolies promote technological change.

Revision Questions

- How are profits created in the economy?
- What causes business cycles in the economy?
- According to Schumpeter, what is the future of capitalism?
- What is the 'Schumpeterian Hypothesis'?
- What is the mechanism of Schumpeter's 'creative destruction'?
- What school of economic thought does Schumpeter belong to?
- What is Schumpeter's main contribution to *Economics*?

Notes

1 Heilbroner (2011).
2 Heilbroner (2011).
3 Yueh (2018).
4 Oser and Blanchfield (1975).
5 Haberler (1950).
6 Heilbroner (2011).
7 Heilbroner (2011).
8 Yueh (2018).
9 Yueh (2018).
10 Yueh (2018).
11 The following analysis is based on Schumpeter's student Heilbroner (2000), but also on Andersen (1991), Screpanti and Zamagni (2005), Papadogonas (1996) and Reppas (2002).
12 Scott (1989).
13 Heilbroner (2011).
14 Schumpeter (1949).
15 Heilbroner (2011).
16 Schumpeter (1934).
17 Schumpeter (1934).
18 Heilbroner (2011).
19 Heilbroner (2011).
20 Heilbroner (2011).
21 Heilbroner (2011).
22 Schumpeter (1949).
23 Yueh (2018).
24 Schumpeter (2010).
25 Heilbroner (2011).
26 Heilbroner (2011).
27 Yueh (2018).
28 Heilbroner (2011).
29 Schumpeter (2010).
30 Schumpeter (2010).
31 Schumpeter (2010).
32 Yueh (2018).
33 Schumpeter (2010).
34 Schumpeter (2010).
35 Heilbroner (2011).

36 Schumpeter (2010).
37 Bowles and Edwards (2005).
38 Screpanti and Zamagni (2005).
39 Schumpeter (2010).
40 Schumpeter (2010).
41 Schumpeter (2010).
42 Schumpeter (2010).
43 Schumpeter (2010).
44 Varoufakis (2007).
45 Schumpeter (2010).
46 Yueh (2018).
47 Screpanti and Zamagni (2005).
48 Karagiannis (2001).
49 Hanusch and Pyka (2007).

References

Andersen, E. (1991). *Schumpeter's Vienna and the Schools of Thought*. Smaskrift No. 70, August, Aalborg University.

Bowles, S., & Edwards, R. (2005). *Understanding capitalism: Competition, command, and change* (3rd ed.). Oxford University Press.

Haberler, G. (1950). Joseph Alois Schumpeter: 1883–1950. *Quarterly Journal of Economics, 64*, 333–372.

Hanusch, H., & Pyka, A. (2007). Principles of Neo-Schumpeterian Economics. *Cambridge Journal of Economics, 31*, 275–289.

Heilbroner, R. L. (2011). *The worldly philosophers: The lives, times and ideas of the great economic thinkers*. Simon and Schuster.

Karagiannis, A. (2001). *Economic methodology*. Kritiki Publications.

Oser, J., & Blanchfield, W. 1975. *The evolution of economic thought*. New York: Harcourt Brace Jovanovich.

Papadogonas, Th. (1996). *Research and development expenditure in Greek industry*. Department of International and European Economic Studies, Athens, Athens University of Economics and Business.

Reppas, P. (2002). *Economic development: Theories and strategies (vol. A)*. Papazisis Publications.

Schumpeter, J. A. (1934). *1912*. Harvard University Press.

Schumpeter, J. A. (1949). Economic history and entrepreneurial history. In R. Clemence (Ed.), *Essays: Joseph Schumpeter*. Transaction Publishers.

Schumpeter, J. A. (2010). *Capitalism, socialism and democracy*. Routledge.

Scott, M. F. (1989 [1998]). *A new view of economic growth*. New York and Oxford: Oxford University Press.

Screpanti, E., & Zamagni, S. (2005). *An outline of the history of economic thought*. OUP.

Varoufakis, G. (2007). *Political economy: The economy in the light of criticism*. Gutenberg Publications.

Yueh, L. (2018). *What would the great economists do?* Picador.

Friedrich Hayek (1899–1992) 7

▶ **Learning Objectives**

After having studied this chapter, the reader should be able to:

- Present Hayek's views on the dissemination of knowledge.
- Analyse his approach regarding the business cycle.
- Explain Hayek's ideas on the role of credit money and interest rates.
- Formulate his ideas on 'market socialism'.
- Analyse Hayek's point of view on the role of the state.
- Present briefly Friedrich Hayek's contribution to *Economics*.

▶ **Summary**

Hayek is an economist whose work is fully compatible with today's dominant economic and political system. According to Hayek, the free market is the best way to organise economic life and society. As such, he rejected both Keynesianism and Socialism as well as any other theory that allows the state to play a significant role in the functioning of economic life and society. One of Hayek's most enduring contributions to *Economics* and *Political Philosophy* is his position that free choices by individuals lead to a better distribution of resources, while the involvement of the state in economic activity tends to distort it, leading to undesirable results. Given that monetary quantities, and in particular money, play a very important role in economic fluctuations, Hayek sought to adapt the neoclassical analysis of General Equilibrium to his theory of dynamic business cycles. It is possible for the economy at times to slow down, to move between ascending and descending phases without apparent periodicity, as if it were oscillating. An economy based on monetary policy should maintain a 'neutral' stance in order not to disrupt the market's real exchange relations. According to Hayek, the authorities are aggravating the operation of the economic system. The theory of Hayek was that long-term large-scale projects, because of the large amount of time required for completion, become less profitable over time, leading to increased unemployment once they are cut, suspended or even cancelled. The 'socialist' idea that all knowledge can be concentrated within the minds of one or at best only a very small number of individuals who formulate the equations to be solved is non-reasonable, according to Hayek. Finally, in contrast to other neoclassical economists, Hayek strongly disagreed with the idea that *Economics* should be directly comparable to *Physics*.

7.1 Introduction

Friedrich von Hayek was born in 1899 in Vienna, into a noble family. His father was a doctor and taught as a lecturer at the University of Vienna,[1] and his mother the daughter of wealthy landlords. Friedrich became friends with the philosopher Ludwig Wittgenstein, who was a distant cousin. At the age of 15, he decided to take up *Political Philosophy* and *Economics*, although he was not a very good student at school. It is indicative that at the age of 14 he failed his *Latin*, *Greek* and *Mathematics* classes and was forced to repeat his class.[2]

In 1917, just before he turned 18, he joined the Army and fought in World War I in Italy in an artillery battalion. As he later stated, this was a particularly defining experience that led him to pursue an academic career in order to help avoid the mistakes that led to war. During the war, he studied all the Schools of Economic Thought and Political Philosophy that had existed up to that time. In 1918, he studied Law at the University of Vienna, receiving his B.A. in 1921.[3] In the summer of 1922, he began a thesis on productivity, which he successfully completed in the spring of 1923.[4] During his studies, he was primarily interested in *Political Science*, *Philosophy* and *Economics,* and he was affiliated to the (neo-)liberal school of thought.[5]

Vienna at that time was experiencing a particularly difficult period with food and fuel shortages, hyperinflation and an atmosphere in favour of Marxism, Socialism, centrally managed economy and the welfare state. However, Hayek never embraced these approaches.[6] Carl Menger was then the dominant figure of the *Austrian School of Thought* in *Economics* at the University of Vienna, which promoted private property and full freedom of action for individuals, in contrast to the revolutionary climate of the time. In fact, it was Menger who first described the concept of a 'spontaneous' order derived from the application of laws that allows individuals to prosper in society. Later, as we shall see, Hayek adopted this very concept in his theoretical system.[7] At the same time, he attended the famous private seminars of the prominent member of the *Austrian School*, Ludwig von Mises, where both the dominant role of individuals in the economy and the theory of business cycles[8] were discussed.

In 1921, he began working on National Accounts, while also teaching at the University of Vienna. Two years later, he went, on Joseph Schumpeter's recommendation, to New York University to continue his studies and also to work as a research associate. However, he never completed the Ph.D. he started there in business cycle[9] theory. At the same time, hyperinflation in Austria was driving his family into poverty, and he returned home. In 1927, he began to write systematically against both monetary and fiscal policies in the economy.

Thus, while Keynes was developing his economic theory at Cambridge, the Austrian political philosopher and economist was formulating his own theoretical approach and preparing to move to London to later receive the Nobel Prize in *Economics* for ideas that rejected both Keynesianism and Socialism, as well as any other theory that allowed the state to play an important role in the functioning of economic life and society. For, as we shall see later, he considered the free market to be the best way of organising the economy.[10]

In 1931, he moved to the prestigious London School of Economics (LSE) at the invitation of Lionel Robbins, Keynes's theoretical rival and chairman of the Economics Department, who was cultivating liberalism at LSE,[11] as opposed to Cambridge Keynesianism. Hayek's move to London contributed to the spread of the Austrian theory of the business cycle, which had been formulated in 1912.[12] Because of Nazism, he was unable to return to Austria, so in 1950 he moved to the famous Chicago School, the American centre of (neo-)liberalism. Hayek, however, did not join the Economics Department due to its dominance by the Neoclassical School which favoured the modelling of *Economics* after *Physics*, an idea which Hayek opposed.[13]

In 1962, he left America to return to Germany, and to the University of Freiburg, where he stayed until 1969. He then moved again to America (U.C.L.A.), then to Austria (University of Salzburg) and finally back to Freiburg in 1977.[14] There, he stayed until the end of his life in 1992 at the age of 92, having received the Nobel Prize in *Economics* in 1974, and having witnessed the collapse of the centrally planned Soviet Union and the fall of the Berlin Wall.

7.2 Business Cycle

Hayek was a supporter of the free market ideology and subscribed to the view of—among others—Smith and Walras that the total power of the myriad transactions in an economy is what 'drives' the market.[15] Hayek tried to adapt the neoclassical analysis of General Equilibrium to his theory of business cycles with a dynamic character, given that monetary variables, especially money, played a very important role in economic fluctuations. However, this could not easily happen since in the theoretical model that Walras had developed, money[16] was not included. Moreover, he believed that for the purposes of the dynamic analysis of economic fluctuations, the concept of equilibrium and the theoretical implications arising from it would have to be revised.[17]

In this context, he argued that in some periods, the economy slows down and may move between upward and downward phases with or without periodicity, as if it were oscillating. His theory of the business cycle was based on the concept of 'natural prices', and more specifically on the concept of the 'natural rate of interest', that is, the price at which savings equal investment, so that we are in 'equilibrium'. At certain stages, as we shall see, the interest rate deviates from the natural rate in equilibrium, in which case it is either higher or lower and is therefore 'out of equilibrium'.[18]

Thus, periods of excessive credit and over-investment mean that investment will continue to increase as firms look to further increase their profits. This increase in economic activity beyond the 'normal' path due to the desire to increase firms' profits eventually leads to recession, through two mechanisms, which we will see below, and for which the central authorities[19] are responsible.

Under one mechanism, the banks reduce the lending rate, which expands the supply of money, resulting in an explosion of investment as individuals and firms benefit from 'cheap' money. In the second mechanism, when expectations about the future of the economy are positive, firms wish to borrow more money to anticipate an increase in interest rates due to the upcoming increase in demand for loans. So, the central bank, in a 'liquidity injection', increases the amount of money to commercial banks and so they now increase liquidity, thus keeping the interest rate low to attract new loans.

In other words, in both of the above cases, there is credit expansion that keeps the interest rate low, resulting in overinvestment and overborrowing that often results in both inefficient uses or inability to repay loans and high interest rates due to increased demand. The central bank then intervenes by providing liquidity in order to reduce the interest rate. Thus, according to Hayek, the opposite should have been allowed to happen, that is, the interest rate should have been allowed to rise in order to keep lending under control.[20]

He wrote that these facts make money a kind of loose link in the otherwise self-directing mechanism of the market, a loose link that can hamper the adjustment mechanism and cause, on a recurrent basis, the orientation of production in the wrong direction.[21] Thus, for Hayek,[22] the central management of the quantity of money does not allow the formation of those prices that are necessary for equilibrium in a production[23] economy. Therefore, monetary policy should remain 'neutral' in order not to disturb the real exchange relations that are formed in the market.[24] Consequently, the authorities act as a burden on the functioning of the economy, according to Hayek.

Another of his main reservations about the role of the central bank stemmed from the fact that he believed that a monopoly on money issuance, even if it were necessary in times of financial constraint, would result in non-'neutral' economic interventions as we have seen before, and for this reason he proposed the issuance of private money.[25] However, in the end, Hayek eventually accepted the necessity of a central bank, as is nowadays a common practice.[26]

7.3 The Role of Time

Among Hayek's most important factors in the business cycle is time, as it plays an important role in the allocation of physical capital, such as machinery, buildings and other assets. Because long-term major projects require sustained investment over time, they lead to a rise in the prices of materials, equipment and labour. This, in turn, leads to an increase in the interest rate in order to offset the increased demand for loans. Thus, an increase in the credit money will lead to a very large rise in the interest rate which will result in the end of the growth phase. Consequently, long-term large projects, because of the time it takes to implement them, are now becoming less profitable.[27]

Thus, given that in the aforementioned analysis, time plays an important role, two quantities of goods at different times should, in essence, be considered as two different goods. Precisely because of the introduction of time as a parameter in the study of economic phenomena, they become 'dynamic', and thus the 'expectations' of the economic conditions that will prevail in the future play an important role. That is, in order for General Equilibrium to be achieved, individuals must be able to continuously produce correct predictions about future conditions of the economic system, which formed the basis for the so-called *Rational Expectations Theory*, but also for other approaches adopted and further developed by the economist John Hicks and others. However, Hayek never fully adopted this approach by Hicks as well as by other economists, such as Nicholas Kaldor, because it led to 'disequilibrium theories'.[28]

7.4 A Critique of Socialism

Hayek's most important contribution to *Economics* and *Political Philosophy*, for which he is remembered, is his view that the 'free' decisions of individuals lead to a better allocation of resources, while the participation of the state in economic activity 'distorts' the economy, that is, leads to sub-optimal results.[29] He even used the Greek terms *cosmos* and *taxis* to describe the free economy and the centrally planned economy, respectively.[30]

Thus, the first step was to challenge the idea that market socialism can lead to better economic outcomes than the free market. In this context, Hayek had to challenge the popular idea that socialism, with the help of the market, could achieve good economic results.[31] The idea of 'market socialism' referred to a society with state ownership of the means of production and all other elements of the economic system as they were.[32]

▶ Thus, in a famous article entitled *Economics and Knowledge*, he developed his interpretation of the operation of the free market as a process of discovery, whereby information is dispersed among many economic agents, and within the market the various pieces of information are collected, exchanged and used efficiently. In other words, 'the market generates knowledge'.[33]

In more detail, each individual is the sole owner of specific knowledge and only through the free exchange of knowledge and information between economic agents can this knowledge be disseminated for the benefit of society as a whole. In contrast, in market socialism, he argued that there would be only one central authority, with insufficient information and authority over the sphere of individual actions. And this situation could only be consciously achieved by someone who possessed the combined knowledge of all individuals.[34] So, he questions this by arguing that all the knowledge of the market cannot possibly be possessed by a single individual.[35]

Moreover, in his famous book, *The Road to Slavery*, Hayek states that free markets not only ensure better economic outcomes and thus greater prosperity but also help to ensure individual freedom. He recommends the least possible interference by the state and suggests that we should avoid delegating power and authority to permanent public bodies.[36] He was of the view that the role of the state should only be concerned with establishing general rules, for example, free trade, infrastructure projects and anti-crime, while the rest should be left to the full freedom of the individual. Moreover, the role of government is to support the individual in order to improve their[37] knowledge, skills and talents.

Hayek also argued that across the whole spectrum of social action, free interaction between individuals leads to rules that contribute to the progress of society. And this progress is not the result of a conscious plan constructed and implemented for collective purposes by a central authority, as in market socialism, but has arisen as a 'spontaneous' result of free, individual will and action.[38]

7.5 The Financial System

We saw that 'market socialism' referred to a society with state ownership of the means of production and all the other elements as we know them. Therefore, one could say that market socialism is a variant of capitalism, with the only difference being the ownership of capital, since the means of production are now state-owned or 'nationalised'. This corresponds to a capitalism without a capital market, that is, practically without a financial system.[39]

In the above context, market socialists argued that a central authority can implement the Walrasian auction or trial-and-error procedure[40] as in the free market mechanism. Therefore, this could be achieved after some series of successive auctions (tâtonnement, or trial and error). Hence, accounting prices in a socialist economy can be determined by the same trial-and-error process by which prices in a competitive market are determined'.[41]

Perhaps the most interesting point of this argument is that since the financial system has little or no importance in the Neoclassical, Walrasian system of General Equilibrium where we have seen that it is absent, then socialism as a regime of state ownership of the means of production without a financial system can be an equally 'realistic' alternative.[42]

On the other hand, Hayek may have differed in some respects from the neoclassical conception of perfect competition and static equilibrium, but he never rejected the free market system. The free market system may not be perfect, but for Hayek, it is the only 'recipe', since no economic regime can come close to the success of competitive free market[43] capitalism. Thus, he set out to highlight the role and importance of the financial system.

In this context, the required knowledge corresponding to the productive potential of the economy cannot be available to anyone without competitive capital markets, even if one could collect and aggregate all the decentralised information scattered in the economy, because it is through the mechanism of the competitive market that knowledge is produced, as we saw earlier ('the market generates knowledge').[44] At the same time, no economic regime ever reaches a 'static' equilibrium. The character of any economic organisation is 'dynamic', not 'static'.[45]

According to Hayek, contrary to the 'theoretical utopia' of the neoclassical system, decisions in the real world are made on the basis of expected but *unknown* future outcomes. We can attribute to the latter a subjective, for each of us, measure of probability. This fact poses a challenging economic problem because it is very difficult for central authorities[46] to collect the vast amount of information that exists in the economy as a whole in order to direct production according to plan.

▶ Also, according to Hayek, it is absurd to assume that all knowledge can be concentrated in the heads of one or at best a very few people.[47] But even if there were a way to concentrate all this knowledge in a single brain, the fundamental economic problem would be different: most of the knowledge used in practice 'does not exist' already, since it will be produced by the market.[48]

Therefore, no economic action can be taken without capital pricing and risk assessment without being subject to interventions, changes and revisions by a central authority. Thus, the entrepreneur's subjective decisions regarding investment and risk-taking will be made on the basis of existing market prices for capital and risk, which, despite their imperfections, are still the best information available.[49]

In other words, prices in the context of competitive markets mobilise the production process of the economy. If markets are abolished, the entire rest of the economy is undermined. In this case, it would be useless to even find a way to collect and aggregate existing information at any given point in time, as the abolition of competition would undermine the actual content of existing information or knowledge.[50]

For Hayek, it is precisely this point that market socialists overlooked when they adopted the concept of equilibrium under central planning. The restriction of competitive markets, and especially the capital market, creates obstacles to the development of the economic system.[51] In this sense, Hayek's argument may well be seen as a defence of the thesis that the modern capitalist economic system cannot exist without the financial system, that is, without a market for pricing capital and evaluating risk. This is because, as we have seen, the free market system provides the incentives for economic agents to create and discover knowledge in order, among other things, to devise their economic plans.[52] Ultimately, any drastic restriction of capital markets jeopardises the reproduction of the economic system.

A first critical analysis within the Austrian school can also be found in Mises's work under the German title *Die Gemeinwirtschaft* (1922), translated as *Socialism* (1924).[53]

7.6 Economics as a Science

As a genuine descendant of the Austrian School, Hayek follows their own theoretical principles which often differ from the dominant neoclassical school with which he nevertheless shows enough theoretical relevance, especially with regard to methodological individualism. More specifically, first, he attempts to demonstrate that individual economic decisions taken in an economy are 'combined' with each other, producing thus the best possible outcomes. Second, he seeks to highlight the inferiority of the socialist system, compared to the free market system. Third, he introduces the concept of uncertainty in long-term economic decisions, as well as the time factor to explain behaviours in the economy. Fourth, he openly argues that only a liberal economic system could lead to an increase in the welfare of individuals. Finally, fifth, he emphasises the substitution of society for the individual in the way economic decisions are made.[54]

Moreover, as a political philosopher, Hayek expressed many interesting views on *Economics*, often differing from the mainstream. Thus, Hayek strongly opposes the view that physical and social phenomena can be treated with the same methodological approach, as we have seen in Walras. Precisely to describe this situation, he developed the term 'scientism', that is, the inappropriate use of the assumptions and methodological tools of the *Physical Sciences* in the *Social Sciences* that can lead to erroneous conclusions.[55]

There are many reasons why such a practice is completely inappropriate.[56] First, in *Economics*, we seek to explain human behaviour, whereas in the *Physical Sciences*, we study physical objects, which means that the research subject is different. Second, economic phenomena are 'subjective', that is, they are related to the opinions, desires and intentions of the individuals who then shape[57] them, whereas in the *Physical Sciences*, the various phenomena are not dependent on the human factor and therefore have an objective substance, that is, they are 'objective'. Third, in the *Physical Sciences*, we rely on hypotheses derived from systematic empirical observations and generalisations in order to proceed with our analysis, whereas in *Economics*, the hypotheses cannot be determined in an absolute way through systematic empirical observation, due to the enormous complexity of phenomena and, of course, the subjectivism of the researcher who formulates the hypotheses. Fourth, in the *Physical Sciences*, phenomena are traced back to a few known and strictly defined causes, whereas in *Economics*, on the contrary, phenomena are often traced back to many unknown and often indeterminate or vague causes. Fifth, a phenomenon, for example, in Physics, if it is monitored and interpreted appropriately, its development can usually be accurately predicted, unlike in *Economics* where this is very difficult or even impossible.[58]

Indeed, in his Nobel Prize speech, Hayek attacks those who claim that the assumptions and conclusions in *Economics* should be measurable, and thus opposes empiricist approaches, arguing that they create the well-founded fallacy that the factors that could be 'identified' and 'measured' are indeed the most important[59] ones. Indeed, he goes further by arguing that the most important element through which empirical support can be given to analytical economic propositions is the development of an appropriate explanatory theory to explain the causal relationship between different economic phenomena.[60]

Also, Hayek argued that usually the economic, social and institutional environment in which theoretical hypotheses are made to explain the choices and decisions of individuals differs from the one in which the analysis is carried out, resulting in the questionable validity of the conclusions reached.[61] Indeed, Hayek believed that the models of Neoclassical Economists taught in *Economics* textbooks, which start from the analysis of perfect competition, serve in reality the aims of those who are against the free market. The reason for this is that these models describe a perfect situation which no one can or has an incentive to influence. They therefore end up distorting the true picture of capitalism which is characterised by constant movement and uncertainty.[62]

▶ Finally, he does not support the historical approach as a means of discovering knowledge since he believes that the theoretical framework within which the phenomena[63] took place must first be established. Consequently, the historical evidence, he claims, is nothing more than theories about how certain phenomena[64] took place in the past.

7.7 The Theoretical Legacy of Hayek

Certain aspects of Hayek's work are structural elements of the contemporary dominant economic and political system. Thus, the idea that excessive credit expansion is the cause of the business cycle is found in many modern analyses and practices dominated by austerity policies. Meanwhile, his view that the system is spontaneously driven to order through myriad complex transactions continued to prevail and dominated many conceptions of the functioning of the economy and the financial market. However, perhaps the most fundamental idea adopted by the economic system is that of the primacy of market freedom without interference from the state or any other central authority in the management of the economy and society. Indeed, Hayek and the Austrians' analysis is perhaps the strongest defence of the market system that can be found within modern *Economics*. For when defending the free market system, it was not only 'market socialism' that was the opponent but also any intermediate attempt to curtail the market system through, for example, Keynesian-style interventions.[65]

We have also seen that perhaps the most important consequence of Hayek's critique of market socialism is that the modern capitalist economic system cannot exist without the financial system, that is, without a market for pricing capital and evaluating risk because this does not allow economic agents to devise their economic plans. Moreover, we have seen that he sought to adapt the Neoclassical General Equilibrium analysis to his theory of business cycles with a dynamic character, given that both money and time played an important role in economic fluctuations, which, in the theoretical scheme that Walras had developed, was not included. Thus, he believed that for the purposes of dynamic analysis of economic fluctuations, the concept of equilibrium and the theoretical implications arising from it would have to be revised.

At the end of the 1930s, Hayek, as had happened earlier with Schumpeter, was pushed aside by Keynes, at a time when the world economy was in crisis and thus the free economies were ready to receive help from state governments to deal with rising unemployment and inflation. The debates between Keynes and Hayek were particularly intense. However, despite the confrontations and tensions, there was, to a large extent, mutual respect between the two men, and in 1944 Keynes nominated Hayek for a major recognition within the British Academy, at the expense of Keynesian economists Joan Robinson. Indeed, Hayek returned the acknowledgement in a letter to Keynes's widow in 1946, in which he expressed his[66] respect.

Hayek, by all accounts, was a teacher without communicative power, lacking charisma and with a heavy accent, and his writing was, at times, complex.[67] Thus, after the dominance of Keynes and the state interventions in the economy that became standard practice, Hayek and his debates with Keynes were forgotten.[68] Indeed, it is indicative of the Keynesian dominance that even Hayek's previously neoliberal ideological centre in Britain, the famous London School of Economics (LSE), had become 'Keynesian'.[69]

However, the story about Hayek does not stop there. When the various economies entered periods of deep recession in the 1970s due to stagflation, the popularity of Keynesian policies had begun to wane, as it became apparent that they were not a panacea. On this occasion, many liberal economists and conservative politicians pulled Hayek out of the closet to advocate a neoliberal path away from state involvement and closer to free markets, at a time when Keynesianism and the state machine were unable to effectively deal with the chronic problems of inflation and unemployment, So, indeed, Hayek, in 1974, received the Nobel Prize in *Economics* at a time when many well-known Harvard and MIT economists did not even know his name, as the well-known Nobel Prize-winning economist Samuelson[70] admitted.

The influence of Hayek's doctrine was particularly strong, since both Margaret Thatcher in the United Kingdom and Ronald Reagan in the United States pursued a programme that would have been the envy of even Hayek himself, with public sector cuts, numerous privatisations, and support for big business, and both of them praised him for his work.[71] Indeed, the collapse of the Soviet Union in the 1980s was seen as a confirmation of Hayek's prophecy of the weaknesses of the socialist market system and his claims of reduced economic efficiency and curtailment of individual freedom. In fact, his books were sold on the 'black market' in many Eastern European countries and 'inspired' many of their[72] leaders at the time.

However, despite the collapse of the former Eastern bloc, the current picture of the global economy includes many states with a strong public sector, with a dominant presence in the health, education and national security sectors, while interventions continue to take place centrally, for example, by the European Central Bank and the Federal Reserve. Finally, many economies have introduced, among other simum wages, social benefits and taxes on pollutants, while actions against unemployment and inequality are welcomed by society.[73]

Meanwhile, modern *Economics* continues to operate by studying and pursuing 'equilibrium' and largely ignoring profitability, instability and recurrent crises, economic cycles, downplaying the role of money and the financial system, while adopting the assumptions and methods of the *Physical Sciences*, ignoring the social substance of economic phenomena. Consequently, if Hayek were alive today, he might not be as happy as he would have wished.

> **Key Takeaways**
> - The 'free market' is the best way to organise the economy.
> - State's involvement 'distorts' the economy.
> - The economy faces instability and business cycles.
> - Monetary policy should remain 'neutral' in the market.
> - A few people can't hold all the knowledge.
> - *Physics* assumptions and methods should not be used in *Economics*.

> **Revision Questions**
> - What is the role of credit money and interest rate in the business cycle?
> - What is the role of the Central Bank and what does Hayek think?
> - How does time affect the financial system?
> - What is Hayek's position on (market) 'socialism'?
> - According to Hayek, how is knowledge produced and disseminated?
> - What methodological principles did Hayek follow?
> - According to Hayek, are the physical and social sciences related?
> - What is Hayek's main contribution to *Economics*?

Notes

1 Yueh (2018).
2 Yueh (2018).
3 Caldwell (2004).
4 Caldwell (2004).
5 Thornton (2014).
6 Yueh (2018).
7 Yueh (2018).
8 Thornton (2014).
9 Yueh (2018).
10 Thornton (2014).
11 Screpanti and Zamagni (2005).
12 Screpanti and Zamagni (2005).
13 Klein (2007).
14 Thornton (2014).
15 Screpanti and Zamagni (2005).
16 Screpanti and Zamagni (2005).
17 Screpanti and Zamagni (2005).
18 Thornton (2014).
19 Thornton (2014).
20 Thornton (2014).

21 Hayek (1960).
22 Hayek (1968).
23 White (1999).
24 Sotiropoulos et al. (2013).
25 Sotiropoulos et al. (2013).
26 Goodheart (1988).
27 Thornton (2014).
28 Screpanti and Zamagni (2005).
29 Thornton (2014).
30 Hayek (1968).
31 Thornton (2014).
32 Sotiropoulos et al. (2013).
33 Screpanti and Zamagni (2005).
34 Screpanti and Zamagni (2005).
35 Hayek (1937).
36 Thornton (2014).
37 Yueh (2018).
38 Screpanti and Zamagni (2005).
39 Sotiropoulos et al. (2013).
40 Lange (1936).
41 Lange (1936).
42 Sotiropoulos et al. (2013).
43 Sotiropoulos et al. (2013).
44 Screpanti and Zamagni (2005).
45 Sotiropoulos et al. (2013).
46 Sotiropoulos et al. (2013).
47 Hayek (1935).
48 Hayek (1935).
49 Sotiropoulos et al. (2013).
50 Sotiropoulos et al. (2013).
51 Hayek (1940).
52 Kirzner (1992).
53 Klein (2007).
54 Karagiannis (2001).
55 Hayek (1942).
56 Karagiannis (2001).
57 Hayek (1953).
58 Hayek (1942).
59 Karagiannis (2001).
60 Barry (1979).

61 Karagiannis (2001).
62 Varoufakis (2007).
63 Hayek (1942).
64 Karagiannis (2001).
65 Sotiropoulos et al. (2013).
   Karagiannis (2001).
66 Yueh (2018).
67 Yueh (2018).
68 Thornton (2014).
69 Thornton (2014).
70 Thornton (2014).
71 Thornton (2014).
72 Thornton (2014).
73 Thornton (2014).

References

Barry, N. P. (1979). *Hayek's social and economic philosophy*. Macmillan.
Caldwell, B. (2004). *Hayek's challenge: An intellectual biography of F.A. Hayek*. University of Chicago Press.
Goodhart, C. (1988). *The evolution of central banks*. MIT Press.
Hayek, F. A. (1935). The present state of the debate. In F. A. Hayek (Ed.), *Collectivist economic planning: Critical studies on the possibilities of socialism*. Routledge & Kegan Paul Ltd.
Hayek, F. A. (1937). Economics and knowledge. *Economica, 4*, 33–54.
Hayek, F. A. (1940). Socialist calculation III: The competitive solution. In F. A. Hayek (Ed.), *Individualism and economic order*. The University of Chicago Press.
Hayek, F. A. (1942). The facts of the social sciences. In F. A. Hayek (Ed.), (1949), *Individualism and economic order*. Routledge & Kegan Paul Ltd.
Hayek, F. A. (1953). *The counter-revolution of science*. Collier-Macmillan.
Hayek, F. A. (1960). *The constitution of liberty*. University of Chicago Press.
Hayek, F. A. (1968). Competition as a discovery procedure. In F. A. Hayek (Ed.), *New studies in philosophy, politics, economics and the history of ideas*. Routledge [1978].
Karagiannis, A. (2001). *Economic methodology*. Kritiki Publications.
Kirzner, I. M. (1992). *The meaning of market process: Essays in the development of modern Austrian economics*. Routledge.
Klein, P. (2007). *Biography of F. A. Hayek (1899–1992)*. Articles of Interest, Mises Institute. Retrieved March 17, 2021, from https://mises.org/library/biography-f-hayek-1899-1992
Lange, O. (1936). On the economic theory of socialism: Part one. *The Review of Economic Studies, 4*(1), 53–71.
Screpanti, E., & Zamagni, S. (2005). *An outline of the history of economic thought*. OUP.
Sotiropoulos, D. P., Milios, J., & Lapatsioras, S. (2013). *A political economy of contemporary capitalism and its crisis: Demystifying finance*. Routledge.
Thornton, P. (2014). *The great economists: Ten economists whose thinking changed the way we live*. Pearson UK.
Varoufakis, G. (2007). *Political economy: The economy in the light of criticism*. Gutenberg Publications.
White, L. H. (1999). Hayek's Monetary theory and policy: A critical reconstruction. *Journal of Money, Credit, and Banking, 31*(1), 109–120.
Yueh, L. (2018). *What would the great economists do?* Picador.

Milton Friedman (1912–2006)

8

▶ **Learning Objectives**

After having studied this chapter, the reader should be able to:

- Understand if Friedman's theory of money is exogenous and why.
- Explain Friedman's monetaristic rule.
- Analyse Friedman's ideas on the NAIRU.
- Formulate the 'Quantity Theory of Money'.
- Analyse Friedman's point of view on the role of the state.
- Present briefly Friedman's contribution to *Economics*.

▶ **Summary**

Milton Friedman, winner of the Nobel Prize in *Economics* in 1976, is well known for his liberal views on various economic and social issues. Friedman defined 'permanent' income as what a person expects to earn throughout his lifetime. Still, in stark contrast to Keynes, he was a proponent of the idea that the Great Depression was not due to excessive savings. Friedman reformulated the quantity theory of money in an attempt to show that Monetarism can offer satisfactory analysis and policy proposals in key economic problems. For Friedman, inflation is a monetary phenomenon, and the appropriate policy to keep inflation low is to increase the money supply at a steadily low, annual rate. Friedman has shown remarkable scientific work on the subject of unemployment and contributed to the design of public policy. He argued that there is a rate beyond which unemployment cannot be reduced without leading to higher inflation. This is the 'natural' unemployment rate, known as the NAIRU (non-accelerating inflation rate of unemployment). Friedman has shown remarkable scientific work on the subject of unemployment and contributed to the design of public policy. He believed that government intervention led to temporary results and chronic irreversible negative situations, preventing the economy from finding its 'natural' percentage. He also proposed the introduction of a basic income, subject to the abolition of other social benefits. In relation to money, Friedman believed that it simply facilitated trading and only affected the price level.

8.1   Introduction

Milton Friedman was born in 1912 in Brooklyn, New York, to Jewish parents who had emigrated to the United States at an early age from an area of Europe that was then part of the Austria-Hungarian empire, later Czechoslovakia and now Ukraine.[1] His father, Saul Friedman, was engaged in small business ventures that were not particularly successful,[2] while his mother, Sarah Ethel, was in charge of a small store in New Jersey, where the family moved when Milton was one year old. As a result, the income of the family, which consisted of Milton and his three sisters, was limited and unstable due to the extremely uncertain economic conditions at the time.

After he graduated from school, he received a scholarship to continue his studies at Rutgers University, a small private university with limited government funding, covering the rest of his expenses with the money he earned doing various odd jobs. His initial desire was to study *Mathematics* and he specialised in it, but his interest was also attracted to *Economics*, and in 1932, at the age of 20, he received his first degree in *Mathematics and Economics*, having finished school at 16.[3]

In fact, he received a scholarship from the prestigious Economics Department of the University of Chicago, which he chose over a second scholarship in Applied Mathematics from Brown University, as *Economics* had become his sole interest. His first year at the University of Chicago, 1932–1933, although accompanied by financial difficulties, opened up new horizons for him as he found himself among distinguished professors from around the world. In fact, in the Department of *Economics* at the University of Chicago, from its inception in 1969–2018, there have been 29 Nobel Prize winners in *Economics* associated with it.[4]

That year, 1932–1933, in Chicago, he met his Jewish, Russian-born classmate Rose Director,[5] with whom they were to marry six years later and work closely together in academia. Chicago became his intellectual home and the place where he developed his free market theories. The following year he received his MA in *Economics* from Chicago[6] and went to Columbia on a fellowship for a year, where he was exposed to new approaches and introduced to *Mathematical Economics*. He then returned to Chicago where he was employed as a research[7] assistant.

As early as 1935, Milton Friedman embarked on a study of consumption, which he exploited some 20 years[8] later, by publishing *The Theory of the Consumption Function*, based on the research Friedman did alongside Nobel Prize-winning economist Simon Kuznets.[9] Friedman published a study together with Kuznets which argued that the incomes of some professions (e.g. dentists) had increased due to the monopoly forces prevailing in their profession[10] and was published in 1945,

8.1 Introduction

forming the basis for the introduction of the concepts of 'permanent' (anticipated and planned income) and 'transitory' (unexpected and surprising) income in *Economics*.[11]

The period between 1941 and 1943 found Friedman at the U.S. Treasury Department working on tax policy, while in 1943–1945 he returned to Columbia University, working on *Statistics*. He then joined George Stigler at the University of Minnesota and the following year accepted an offer from the University of Chicago to teach the subject of *Economic Theory*. During the same period, he worked at the National Bureau of Economic Research, assuming responsibility for investigating the role of money in economic fluctuations. His work, both there and at the University of Chicago, was highly productive and resulted in the establishment of a strong basis for the support of Monetary Theory.[12] As a teacher, he was particularly strict and demanding, while outside the lecture halls, he was very kind, polite and generous.[13]

In 1948, Friedman began to study with Anna Schwartz the role of the money supply in the economy.[14] In 1950, he went to Paris responsible for administering the Marshall Plan for the U.S. government. There, he was invited to study the Schumann Plan, which was the forerunner of European unification. At the time, Friedman concluded that the establishment of a common market would also entail the elimination of exchange rate fluctuations. In 1953–1954, Friedman was visiting professor at Cambridge University, where academics were divided into two camps: those who were against Keynes's policies and those who were in favour of them.[15] In 1956, he published the edited volume *Studies in the Quantity Theory of Money*, which was the cause for the ideas of Monetarism[16] to become widely known.

The 1960s found Friedman actively involved in the public sphere, commenting on current affairs in *Newsweek* magazine, while, with his scholarly work as his first priority, he declined offers to provide his services exclusively to the White House.[17] In 1963, he even published the conclusions of his research with Anna Schwartz in *A Monetary History of the United States, 1867–1960*, which presented, in a popularised manner, the idea of the effect of the money supply on the functioning of the economy. And that book turned the interest of economists to the monetarist[18] approaches and prompted the Federal Reserve to start tracking some key monetary indicators.[19]

In 1975, Milton Friedman travelled to Chile at the invitation of Dictator Augusto Pinochet to advise him after the preceding coup d'état, for which he was publicly condemned by public opinion, even at the 1976[20] Nobel Prize for *Economic Sciences* ceremony.

Thus, towards the end of the 1970s, Friedman became the new prophet of capitalism who warned that state intervention will lead to economic and social disaster.[21] In 1977, at the age of 65, Friedman stopped actively teaching at the University of Chicago and transferred his research activities to Stanford University. Friedman expounded his liberal views regarding various economic and social issues in a programme on television in the United States and other countries on a serial basis entitled *Free to choose*. In 1982, his *Monetary Trends in the United States and the United Kingdom*, the product of his long collaboration with Anna Schwartz, was published, and he continued to write in newspapers and magazines about his views and served as an advisor to President Ronald Reagan.[22] He also found strong support for his ideas in the British Prime Minister, Margaret Thatcher.[23] He died on 16 November 2006.

8.2 Income and Economic Recession

In general, Friedman's views were based on his concerns about the Great Depression, while the solutions he proposed were completely opposite to those proposed by Keynes and his[24] supporters.

Friedman considered 'permanent' income to be what a person expects to earn during his or her lifetime, while 'transitory' income is what a person earns without expecting it.[25] He believed that individuals can accurately estimate the amount of income they will have on average over the long term ('permanent income'). Starting from this estimate, individuals seek to 'smooth consumption' by saving some of their money in times of normality in order to meet their expenses in difficult times.

Friedman argued that even in a recession, individuals spend on the basis of their permanent income rather than their temporary or transitory income, which they see declining. This means that in times of recession, they will not reduce their consumption as much in relation to their income and therefore their savings will not change much. Therefore, the Great Recession was not due to excessive saving. This was in direct contradiction to Keynes, who believed that restraint in consumption exacerbated the recession, and therefore the state should take measures to stimulate the economy.[26]

As for the causes of the Great Depression of the 1930s, Friedman rejected the idea that it was due to the reckless actions of greedy investors.[27] According to Friedman and Schwartz, in their book *A Monetary History of the United States, 1867–1960*, the U.S. data show that the cause of the Great Depression, simply put, was the misguided pursuit of monetary policy on the part of the Federal Reserve, which restricted the money supply by raising interest rates rather than supplying the market with liquidity, as it was eventually forced to do in 1932.[28]

8.3 Money and Monetarism

The so-called Quantity Theory of Money concerns the understanding of how the quantity of money in the economy can affect or is affected by the price level and other variables in the economy.[29] It is one of the oldest economic theories, since Bodin was probably the first to[30] formulate an incomplete expression of the Quantity Theory of Money in 1568 and was also the first theory of macroeconomic stability.[31]

In his *Studies in the Quantity Theory of Money*, Friedman reformulated the quantity theory of money in an attempt to show that *Monetarism* can offer satisfactory proposals for addressing key economic problems, such as inflation and recession,[32] which is summed up in the famous expression: 'money matters'. In fact, in a famous statement about the usefulness of injecting money in the form of liquid cash into the economy, he became famous for the idea of helicopter money: 'Let us suppose now that one day a helicopter flies over this community and drops an additional $1000 in bills from the sky'.[33] Recall that money consists of currencies, banknotes, bank deposits and reserves, bills and cheques, cards (debit and credit) and instruments issued by financial institutions.

According to the Quantity Theory of Money, the product of the quantity of money circulating in the economy (M), times the velocity of circulation (V), equals the price level (P) times the volume of transactions (T), that is, $MV = PT$. Friedman held that the velocity of circulation of money remains relatively constant like the volume of transactions.[34] Therefore, with the velocity of circulation and the volume of transactions constant, the remaining relationship is that between the variables of the quantity of money and the general price level, with causality being in the direction *from* the quantity of money *to* the general price level, and not vice versa. This means that inflation is a monetary phenomenon.[35] Therefore, the appropriate policy to keep inflation low is to increase the money supply at a constant low, annual[36] rate.

At the same time, fiscal policy on the part of the government is ineffective or even incapable of influencing economic activity,[37] in contrast to monetary policy which is beneficial under certain conditions.[38] An increase in the money supply, for example, leads to an increase in the demand for consumer goods, positively affecting the economy.[39] Of course, the positive effects in the long-run context fade away. However, according to Friedman, the only certainty is that wrong choices in monetary policy are disastrous.[40]

In general, according to Friedman, governments and central banks must create a stable monetary framework in order to support the proper functioning of the private sector of the economy. He formulated the so-called monetarist rule, according to which the money supply increases at a constant rate each year to keep pace with the growth of output and population, in general. He estimated this rate at around 1–3 per cent per year.[41] Therefore, the best that could be done on the part of the monetary authorities would be to increase the money supply at the rate required by long-term real growth and leave the market alone to deal with short-term adjustments.[42]

8.4 Unemployment and 'Natural' Rate

Friedman showed remarkable scientific work on the topic of unemployment, and his contribution to the design of public policy was significant. He argued that unemployment fluctuates and that there is a rate beyond which unemployment cannot be reduced without leading to higher inflation.[43] That is, there is a rate of unemployment even at the 'full employment' level. Full employment does not imply zero unemployment, as there will always be a rate of unemployment, which is expected and normal.[44] This is the so-called natural unemployment rate, known as the NAIRU (non-accelerating inflation rate of unemployment).[45] Unemployment that exists in an economy is therefore considered a serious problem when the unemployment rate is higher than the 'natural' rate.[46]

Unlike some economists who believed that there is a negative relationship between unemployment and inflation and therefore governments should choose through fiscal policy the desired ratio between the unemployment rate and inflation rate, Friedman believed that government interventions lead to temporary effects and chronic irreversible negative situations, preventing the economy from finding its[47] 'natural' rate.

▶ Of course, the natural rate of unemployment is not a constant, but is affected by the situation in the labour[48] market and, according to Friedman, is never zero, for various reasons. For example, there are people who register as unemployed until they find the employment they want or who switch from one job to another, while others seek to register as unemployed to take advantage of some favourable welfare[49] state arrangements, or who enter the labour market for the first time (women, young people), or who, in addition, have skills different from those required by the market.

Friedman also stressed the inability of individuals to adapt to the new demands of the labour market and highlighted the importance of training in order for workers to be able to meet them.[50] With regard to education, Friedman regarded it as a key factor in the creation of human capital, which in turn is a component of an individual's wealth, along with cash, bonds, stocks and other durable consumer or capital goods in his possession. In fact, the value of human capital is derived by calculating the present value of the income that the individual is expected to earn because of the skills acquired and the knowledge gained through his[51] or her education.

8.5 State Intervention

Friedman, like Hayek, considered the absolute freedom of the market to be a necessary condition for the proper functioning of a society and set out his views on this in his books *Free to Choose* and *Tyranny of the Status Quo,* which he co-authored with his wife, and in *Capitalism and Freedom*. State interventionism for Friedman, apart from undermining the economic well-being of citizens, is a coercive and manipulative factor in their[52] behaviour.

▶ Friedman, like other economists we have known, thought that the role of the state should be limited to matters of, for example, defence against internal and external risks, and the provision of certain public goods which cannot, for various reasons, be produced by private actors, such as infrastructure and education. It should also establish laws and rules that support the proper functioning of society and markets.[53]

Moreover, Friedman believed that since the economic system has inherent mechanisms that can bring it back to equilibrium after strong external shocks, the state should take care to formulate and ensure a regulatory framework within which the market will operate freely and smoothly. The state should intervene to remove obstacles that discourage the free functioning of the market. Any excesses or mismanagement, especially in relation to the money supply by the government, risks plunging the economy into prolonged periods of recession.[54]

In addition, government interventions could become the cause of a diversion of the democratic constitution and its transformation into a dictatorship that restricts the individual freedoms of citizens, granting privileges only to those who support and maintain the system. In this way, Friedman believed, the fundamental political and economic rights of individuals (e.g. freedom of movement, the ability to choose the products they consume, the work they do or even their place of residence) are violated, and the free expression and circulation of ideas[55] is impeded.

▶ Friedman also expressed another view in favour of the free market, arguing that particularly 'powerful' governments will not allow free expression since this could lead to ideas and opinions that are in conflict with the government regime, whereas, on the contrary, in a free market economy, all different opinions will be allowed, since the primary motive will be to make money and not to support certain ideas or opinions.[56]

▶ His strong belief in individual liberty led Friedman to oppose both discrimination against homosexuals and compulsory conscription in the United States, as this would probably deter individuals from participating in the market, and he supported the libertarian ideas of legalising prostitution and drugs. Furthermore, he proposed the introduction of a basic income, subject to the abolition of other social benefits. According to this idea, people whose income falls below a minimum threshold should be financially supported by the state, while those whose income exceeds this threshold should be subject to a higher tax.[57]

8.6 The Theoretical Legacy of Friedman

Friedman's basic thesis that money is 'neutral', in the sense that it merely facilitates transactions and has an impact only on the price level (with all other factors constant) expresses a basic position of neoclassical *Economics*. Of course, Friedman's views on the Quantity Theory of Money are not without serious criticism. For example, the basic equation of the theory tells us nothing in itself about the direction of causality, that is, whether the price level depends on the quantity of money or, conversely, whether the quantity of money depends on the price level. However, Friedman, under the assumption of constant velocity of money and volume of transactions, implicitly assumed that causality is directed *from* the quantity of money (M) *to* the price level (P), and not *vice versa*.

▶ This means that the increase in the quantity of the money stock is 'exogenous' to the economic system, since it is regulated by the decisions of a public authority, the Central Bank (exogeneity of money). Similarly, the reverse view of causality holds that the quantity of money changes according to demand conditions that lead to price increases, and is considered 'endogenous' to an economy since it originates within it (endogeneity of money).

In fact, on this issue, a huge debate on the 'exogeneity' or 'endogeneity' of money has been developed since the nineteenth century, which continues even today, and which shows empirical results that sometimes support or contradict both theories. The exogenous view is supported by the monetarists and neoclassical economists.

At the same time, the endogenous view was adopted, amongst others, by the so-called Post-Keynesian economists, who adopted the Keynesian theoretical system, considering it incompatible with the neoclassical[58] one and arguing that it is the creation of credit money in response to the demand for investment that leads the Central Bank to increase the money[59] supply. That is, in the Post-Keynesian perspective, the money supply is understood as a response to the demand for money in the economy. Also, the endogenous view is supported by Marxist economists, who believe that money is not simply endogenous to the economic process, but that it is the result of the very expression of the commodity production process that leads to the creation of more money. After all, money is the form of the appearance of value and, therefore, of capital.[60]

Friedman's view, even if it sounds strange, was also criticised 'internally', that is, within the neoclassical approach by the so-called[61] Neo-Keynesian economists, since Friedman's arguments against the Neo-Keynesian system always provoked intense controversy.[62] In short, the Neo-Keynesians argue that (a) quantity theory can only be applied in the case where there is only one type of money (e.g. banknotes), (b) it does not give us information about the adjustment of the economy after a monetary disturbance, (c) it completely ignores the effect of prices, output and interest rate on the quantity of money and, finally, (d) empirical analyses do not seem to support[63] it. We might perhaps be tempted to accept Friedman's view that empirical research will provide definite answers to these questions. However, this has not[64] happened.

Consequently, the attempt to apply Friedman's ideas to the economic and social sphere has met with strong obstacles, although some of his ideas have been widely accepted. For example, the Federal Reserve Bank of the United States in 2009 applied the 'prescription' proposed by Friedman retroactively, as did other countries in the case of the CoVid-19 recession. Indeed, in the latter case, in an alternative and unconventional variant of 'helicopter money', there was a direct and immediate transfer of liquid money from central authorities to households rather than to banking institutions, in the form of grants, subsidies and subsidies intended to stimulate aggregate consumption.

It would not be an exaggeration to claim that Milton Friedman was among the most influential economist of the late twentieth century and one of the foremost academics to become a media star around the world,[65] as he helped popularise

8.6 The Theoretical Legacy of Friedman

Economic Theory, challenged the validity of Keynesian theory, and his policy proposals were implemented by influential politicians around the world.[66] One could even say that he had two careers. During the first half as an academic economist and during the second half as a political figure and ardent supporter of neoliberalism.[67]

▶ Friedman's theories have played an important role, both in the practice of economic policies and in teaching and academic textbooks. For example, the 'permanent income hypothesis' is widely used in the study of household spending and saving by various institutions. The natural rate of unemployment is used to set interest rates by central banks. Also, the relationship between money, prices and output and the quantity theory of money are key chapters in many textbooks.[68]

His writings and his theories against Keynesianism appeared at the right time, that is, before and immediately after the collapse of the Soviet Union and the Berlin Wall, causing worldwide interest, and his books to sell millions of copies even in countries of the former Soviet Union. As a result, his media appearances influenced everyone from Ronald Reagan to Queen Elizabeth II and Prince Philip.[69] Indeed, as Friedman himself and his wife wrote: 'Once in power, Reagan faithfully followed our advice'.[70] Similarly, in Britain, Margaret Thatcher, like Hayek, fervently embraced Friedman's views, while the academic centre for both was the famous London School of Economics (LSE), where Friedman presented his famous lecture entitled *The Counter-Revolution in Monetary Theory*.

From an ideological point of view, the main contribution of Friedman is the establishment of Monetarism. As the famous economist John Kenneth Galbraith put it, the age of John Maynard Keynes gave way to the age of Milton Friedman, and as the Nobel Prize-winning economist Paul Samuelson once wrote in a book, in the future, stabilisation policies will be executed by the monetary policy of the Federal Reserve.[71]

▶ Friedman's theoretical work, like that of the other economists we have studied who shared a strong belief in the absolute freedom of markets and an aversion to state interventionism, has strong implications at the level of policy making, since it expresses the fact that the economic system presupposes the 'free' market and the unimpeded movement of individuals and private capital, precisely because it allows it to set in motion the mechanisms of pricing, risk assessment and business development that guarantee its reproduction and development.

One recognition of Friedman's work during the crisis that started in 2006–2007 was the reduction of interest rates to near zero, but also the "injection" of liquidity into the economy based on the principles of monetarism. In simple terms, central banks 'printed' money and used it to buy bonds, which constitute public or private sector debt. This created money on the balance sheets of companies that sold bonds in exchange for cash, which the central authorities hoped would lead to new investment, stimulating the total economy.[72]

Nevertheless, Friedman's theoretical prediction of inflationary pressures due to the huge liquidity injections in the 2006–2007 crisis, in line with his own 'endogenous' view of quantitative theory that we saw earlier, does not seem to have been confirmed. On the contrary, expansionary monetary policies in response to economic crisis contexts *did not* lead to an increase in inflation, as his theory predicted. Rather, the approaches of Post-Keynesian economists who, in their own 'endogenous' view, remind us that Keynes repeatedly rejects the idea that the price level will vary directly with the change in the quantity of money[73] were confirmed. Moreover, 'bailing out' the banks was a policy that Friedman never directly advocated and would probably have disagreed, arguing for a prescription for a greater supply of liquidity.[74]

Therefore, Friedman's ideas were not a panacea. For example, attempts to apply his ideas on liquidity provision to the U.S. economy in the periods 1953–1957 and 1971–1975 were accompanied by great instability, as well as in Britain in 1980. Yet, the public sector, as a percentage of the total economy, has remained stable in recent decades, while voices of general acceptance are calling for an end to the excesses of the free market, such as in the financial sector, and the 'exogenous' view of money in quantitative theory is both theoretical and empirically challenged. It is possible that Friedman has begun to lose some of his influence on economic theory and policy analysis.[75]

Key Takeaways

- 'Permanent' income is what a person expects to earn throughout his life.
- The Great Recession was not due to excessive savings.
- Inflation is primarily a monetary phenomenon.
- Over time, unemployment cannot be reduced without causing inflation.
- State intervention leads to temporary results and negative situations.

Revision Questions

- What is Friedman's 'permanent income' hypothesis?
- What is the basic equation of the 'Quantity Theory of Money'?
- What is Friedman's monetarist rule?
- What is NAIRU?
- What is the role of state intervention in Friedman's view?
- Is Friedman's theory of money 'exogenous' and why?
- What are the criticisms of Friedman's view of money?
- What is Friedman's main contribution to *Economics*?

Notes

1 Friedman (1992).
2 Thornton (2014).
3 Thornton (2014).
4 Yueh (2018).
5 Yueh (2018).
6 Yueh (2018).
7 Friedman (1992).
8 Yueh (2018).
9 Friedman (1992).
10 Thornton (2014).
11 Friedman (1992).
12 Friedman (1992).
13 Yueh (2018).
14 Thornton (2014).
15 Friedman (1992).
16 Tsoulfidis (2010).
17 Friedman (1992).
18 Tsoulfidis (2010).
19 Thornton (2014).
20 Thornton (2014).
21 Varoufakis (2007).
22 Friedman (1992).
23 Thornton (2014).
24 Thornton (2014).
25 Thornton (2014).
26 Thornton (2014).
27 Thornton (2014).
28 Thornton (2014).
29 Blaug (1995).
30 Bodin (1578).
31 Skidelsky (1995).
32 Johnson (1971).
33 Friedman (1969).
34 Tsoulfidis (2010).
35 Thornton (2014).
36 Tsoulfidis (2010).

37 Tsoulfidis (2010).
38 Thornton (2014).
39 Tsoulfidis (2010).
40 Tsoulfidis (2010).
41 Thornton (2014).
42 Screpanti and Zamagni (2005).
43 Thornton (2014).
44 Tsoulfidis (2010).
45 Thornton (2014).
46 Tsoulfidis (2010).
47 Thornton (2014).
48 Thornton (2014).
49 Tsoulfidis (2010).
50 Thornton (2014).
51 Tsoulfidis (2010).
52 Tsoulfidis (2010).
53 Thornton (2014).
54 Tsoulfidis (2010).
55 Thornton (2014).
56 Thornton (2014).
57 Thornton (2014).
58 Screpanti and Zamagni (2005).
59 Lavoie (1984), Itoh and Lapavitsas (1999), Mollo (1999).
60 Milios et al. (2018).
61 Screpanti and Zamagni (2005).
62 Screpanti and Zamagni (2005).
63 Tobin (1972).
64 Screpanti and Zamagni (2005).
65 Thornton (2014).
66 Thornton (2014).
67 Yueh (2018).
68 Thornton (2014).
69 Thornton (2014).
70 Thornton (2014).
71 Thornton (2014).
72 Yueh (2018).
73 Moore (1994).
74 Thornton (2014).
75 Thornton (2014).

References

Blaug, M. (1995), Why is the quantity theory of money the oldest surviving theory in economics. In: *The quantity theory of money, from Locke to Keynes and Friedman*. Edward Elgar Publication Company.

Bodin, J. (1578). *Discours sur le rehaussement et diminution des monnoyes*. Dupuys.

Friedman, M. (1969). *The optimum quantity of money*. In: The optimum quantity of money and other Essays. Aldine Press: Chicago, IL.

Friedman, M. (1992). In A. Lindbeck (Ed.), *Nobel lectures, economics 1969–1980*. World Scientific Publishing Co..

Itoh, M., & Lapavitsas, C. (1999). *Political economy of money and finance*. Macmillan.

Johnson, H. G. (1971). The Keynesian Revolution and the monetarist counter-revolution. *American Economic Review, 61*(2), 1–14.

Lavoie, M. (1984). The endogenous flow of credit and the post Keynesian theory of money. *Journal of Economic Issues, 18*, 771–797.

Milios, J., Dimoulis, D., & Economakis, G. (2018 [2002]). *Karl Marx and the classics, an essay on value, crises and the capitalist mode of production*. Routledge.

Mollo, M. L. R. (1999). The endogeneity of money: Post-Keynesian and Marxian concepts compared. In P. Zarembka (Ed.), *Economic theory of capitalism and its crises, research in political economy* (Vol. 17, pp. 3–26). Jai Press.

Moore, B. J. (1994, September). *The demise of the Keynesian multiplier: A reply to cottrell*. *Journal of Post Keynesian Economics, 17*(1), 121–133.

Screpanti, E., & Zamagni, S. (2005). *An outline of the history of economic thought*. OUP.

Skidelsky, R. (1995). J. M. Keynes and the quantity theory of money. In *The quantity theory of money, from Locke to Keynes and Friedman*. Edward Elgar Publication Company.

Thornton, P. (2014). *The great economists: Ten economists whose thinking changed the way we live*. Pearson UK.

Tobin, J. (1972, September/October). Friedman's theoretical framework. *Journal of Political Economy, 80*, 852–863.

Tsoulfidis, L. (2010). *Competing schools of economic thought*. Springer Science & Business Media.

Varoufakis, G. (2007). *Political economy: The economy in the light of criticism*. Gutenberg Publications.

Yueh, L. (2018). *What would the great economists do?* Picador.

Robert Solow (1924–…)   9

▶ **Learning Objectives**

After having studied this chapter, the reader should be able to:

- Understand the meaning of the 'production function'.
- Explain briefly what the 'Solow Residual' is.
- Analyse how technological progress is expressed.
- Explain the Solow Growth model and its assumptions.
- Name the factors on which long-term growth depends.
- Present briefly Robert Solow's contribution to *Economics*.

▶ **Summary**

The production function is a technical relationship between the output produced and the factors of production or inputs, in the sense that it expresses the way in which the various inputs, in the typical case physical capital and labour, combined in a certain way are transformed into output. Solow is well known for his work on long-term growth in equilibrium and the role of technological change. He showed that a very significant percentage of the per capita output growth of any economy is not due to the traditional production factors such as capital and labour, but to what he called 'Total Factor Productivity' (TFP) and it turns out to be equal to the remainder of the production function, known as the Solow residual, when evaluated econometrically. Solow, through his model, studied the economic growth of the United States during the period 1909–1949 and came to the striking conclusion that a very high percentage of output growth per hour was due to technological progress, that is, to factors beyond capital and labour inputs. Solow's famous model of economic growth was based on the fact that in the short run there are significant fluctuations in output, labour, investment and consumption. However, in the long run, per capita output and per capita physical capital increase at a steady rate, while the capital–output ratio remains almost constant. Much of the branch of modern Macroeconomics as well as the whole field of Economic Growth has relied on Solow's model, as it was shown that the economic system, despite its instability, can lead to growth with a positive trend. Actually, it has the tendency to return to a sustainable balanced growth trajectory after a disturbance or crisis. In addition, the model showed that countries with completely different levels of economic growth can at some point 'converge' to similar levels of balanced growth.

9.1 Introduction

Robert (Bob) Solow was born in Brooklyn, New York, on 23 August 1924, the eldest of three children of an immigrant family. His parents, who had no college education, had to earn a living as soon as they finished school. Robert grew up in Brooklyn, where his father was a fur trader.[1] He received a very good education in the New York City public schools and was awarded a scholarship to Harvard, where he enrolled in September 1940 at the age of 16.[2]

His basic studies were in *Sociology* and *Anthropology*, and it was there that he acquired his first introductory knowledge of *Economics*.[3] At the end of 1942, when he was 18 years old, he joined the U.S. Army. He served in North Africa, and then from the beginning to the end of the war, he served in Italy until he was discharged in August 1945. As he claims, these three years as a soldier greatly shaped his character, as he was part of a close group, worked hard with faith in his strength and was led by a very remarkable man.[4]

In 1945, Solow returned to Harvard and married Barbara Lewis, who later became a student of economic history, while he chose to major in *Economics*. Fortunately for him, the famous Nobel Prize-winning economist Wassily Leontief, and founder of the discipline of Input–Output analysis, became his teacher, mentor and friend. It was from him that he learned modern *Economics,* and it was he who introduced him to empirical research with statistical data.[5]

In 1949–1950, he spent a year on a fellowship at Columbia, and shortly before he went there, MIT hired him to teach *Statistics* and *Econometrics*, since he had begun to work on probabilistic models. So, in 1949, he finally moved from Harvard to MIT. Faculty relations in the Department were very good, there were no conflicts and a policy of 'open doors' was in force.[6]

At first, Solow thought that throughout his later career, he would be exclusively involved in the field of *Statistics* and *Econometrics*. However, he was given an office next to the Nobel Prize-winning economist and student of Schumpeter, Paul Samuelson, which was to change his research career.[7] Samuelson was, at the time, one of the best economists in the world and interacted with everyone. So for six decades, they shared the same space as well as many deep discussions about *Economics*.

Meanwhile, the team of economists that was formed at MIT produced creative research, based on mathematical models framed by statistical data and empirical analyses. This was a turning point in Solow's[8] professional life.

In 1956, Solow published his famous article 'A Contribution to the Theory of Economic Growth' in the *Quarterly Journal of Economics* and, in 1957, in an equally famous article entitled 'Technical Change and the Aggregate Production Function' in *The Review of Economics and Statistics*, Solow provided the related empirical analysis for the American economy.

Thus, at the age of 37, Solow was recognised by the American Economic Association as one of the leading American economists under 40,[9] and this recognition placed him at the centre of public debate since he moved to Washington in 1961 as economic advisor. In collaboration with James Tobin, Kermit Gordon and Arthur Okun,[10] he helped draft the Keynesian economic policy framework that dominated American politics during the Kennedy and Johnson administrations.[11]

The highlight of his scientific career was the Nobel Prize in *Economics* awarded to him in 1987 'for his contribution to the theory of economic growth'. His work has had a decisive influence on the field of Economic Growth in the context of modern Macroeconomic Theory. Today, Solow, as Professor Emeritus, still works on technology and productivity, monitors international events and political debates, associations and continues to reflect alone, as both his MIT partner of six decades, Paul Samuelson, and his precious wife Barbara[12] have passed away. At the same time, he has had the satisfaction of proudly watching several of his students' progress, and some of them have even been awarded the Nobel Prize in *Economics* as well.

9.2 The Solow Growth Model

From Solow's Keynesian-inspired emphasis on Macroeconomic aggregates[13] and from the Keynesian theory he was familiar with,[14] we know that the 'equilibrium' income of an economy is defined at the point where Total Demand, as expressed by Total Expenditure, is equal to Total Supply, as expressed by Total Output. In this context, the key question of all Economic Growth models has been to find the growth rate that ensures that the change in Total Expenditure over time is equal to the change in Total Output over time.

A key finding of the economic growth models of the time, such as the one by Harrod-Domar, was the dependence of long-term growth on a number of economic variables and parameters that could not be controlled. Thus, there is uncertainty about the macroeconomic equilibrium level of the economy, with the possibility that equilibrium may not be achieved. Consequently, an important finding for the various economies has been the persistence over time of severe macroeconomic problems such as inflation, unemployment and economic fluctuations. As a result, instability has often appeared to make government intervention possible to keep the economy within acceptable levels of inflation and unemployment.[15] This situation is in sharp contrast, for example, to the theoretical positions of neoclassical economists on the self-regulating character of the market.

As we have seen in Smith's 'invisible hand' and in the 'Walrasian Equilibrium', through the operation of the competitive market and the balancing of countervailing forces, the market is 'self-regulating' due to both the maximisation of consumer utility and the maximisation of firm profits. Thus, the acceptance of the concept of 'equilibrium', without judgements and fluctuations, is one of the dominant ideological principles, especially of the neoclassical school. For this reason, models such as Solow's began to be constructed that were close to these concepts that dominated economic science[16] and also took into account the particularly important role of technology highlighted earlier by Schumpeter. It was precisely at this point that Solow's two seminal articles appeared which studied the stability of long-term growth in equilibrium and the role of technological change, thus reflecting some of the theoretical and/or methodological views of various schools of economic thought, primarily dominated by the neoclassical school.

▶ Thus, Solow's famous economic growth model was based on the observation that in the short run there are significant fluctuations in output, labour, investment and consumption. However, at the long-run level, per capita output and per capita physical capital increase at a constant rate, while the capital–output ratio remains almost constant. This model, published in 1957 by Solow, uses a neoclassical Cobb–Douglas-type production function with two inputs (physical capital and labour), is based on a standard first-order differential equation and studies the economy in a long-run equilibrium.

The production function is a technical relationship between the output produced and the factors of production, in the sense that it expresses how the various factors of production or inputs, in the simplified case physical capital and labour, combined in a certain way are transformed into output. Although it has been widely applied, the Neoclassical Cobb–Douglas production function has been heavily criticised in the past on various issues, mainly of a theoretical nature.

The basic assumptions of Solow's model are: (a) the existence of a Keynesian equilibrium in terms of aggregate supply and aggregate demand, (b) the use of two factors of production, (c) the existence of a constant production technology, (d) the existence of constant returns to scale, (e) the first partial derivatives of the production function with respect to the factors of production are positive and the second are negative, and there is (f) a constant rate of saving in the economy and (g) a constant rate of depreciation.

▶ The differential equation of the model on which the analysis is based studies the accumulation of capital and reflects the fact that the rate of change of physical capital is equal to new investment minus the depreciation of a percentage of the existing capital. Solving the resulting Bernoulli-type first-order differential equation yields the solution, namely, the value of per capita natural capital as a function of time.

9.2 The Solow Growth Model

From the solution equation, it follows that the long-run equilibrium level of capital per capita and income per capita depends positively (i.e. it is an increasing function) on the level of technology and the propensity to save, while it depends negatively (i.e. it is a decreasing function) on the rate of capital depreciation and the rate of labour growth.

▶ Moreover, the long-run equilibrium is 'asymptotically stable', that is, in a very long period of time, theoretically ('asymptotically') infinite, the price of physical capital per capita will reach a certain, stable level. 'Stable' means that if the economy finds itself with a per capita capital different from that of the long-run equilibrium, forces are created, none other than new investment, which will bring it back to the level of the long-run equilibrium.[17]

▶ Indeed, the level of this long-term equilibrium does not depend on the level of per capita physical capital from which the economy started to grow. This gave rise to the formulation of a theory of 'convergence' between countries at different levels of development (e.g. 'poor' and 'rich'), which led to a discussion on its relatively limited empirical verification.

One of the basic features of the model is that, based on the production function, the continuous increase in capital per capita causes smaller and smaller increases in output per capita, with the consequence that the smaller output per capita created results in a lower level of savings—investment, and from a certain point onwards, these are barely sufficient to replace the capital consumed and depreciated. The above situation is expressed by the assumption that the second partial derivative of the production function with respect to the factors of production is negative.

However, several empirical findings have led to the questioning of some of the assumptions of Solow's model, such as the one above. Thus, for example, the existence of growth is based on the above process of capital accumulation at a decreasing rate, while technology is considered an 'exogenous' variable. In this context, the per capita physical capital is increasing over time, leading the economy to a steady state, while one solution to overcome this state is a high level of technology, which, however, is defined exogenously in the original model.

Consequently, the questioning of some of the initial assumptions of Solow's model,[18] mainly due to certain empirical results, led to the consideration of technology as an 'endogenous' variable as well as to the abandonment of the declining rate of accumulation of the per capita capital.[19] The so-called 'New Growth Theory',[20] in contrast to Solow's[21] original model, assumes that the rate of growth is 'endogenously' determined and that the rate of accumulation of physical capital is not decreasing. The idea that technological progress is determined by forces internal to the economic system[22] often leads to a focus on Research and Development (R&D) expenditures, because it is considered to be a crucial factor in the growth path of economies and the expression of the intensity and speed with which it is diffused within an economic system.

However, despite the acceptance of this theory,[23] the evaluation of the results showed that some of the ideas developed, and especially the endogeneity criterion, were already known.[24] This criterion practically requires that long-term growth be determined from within the system, that is endogenously, rather than from outside the system, that is exogenously.[25] The theory of endogenous growth was mainly associated with the following sources of economic growth: (a) natural capital, (b) human capital, (c) technological progress, (d) infrastructure and (e) the institutional environment.

Thus, in some models of economic growth, such as Romer (1990),[26] technology is no longer an 'exogenous' variable, but one of the variables in the production function. In order to consider the stock of knowledge as an 'endogenous' variable in the model, its change over time is determined endogenously and not by an exogenously given rate. According to this model, the production of knowledge and its change over time depends on the existing stock of knowledge and on the human capital employed in the production of new knowledge. Thus, under this model, knowledge production becomes an incentive for new investment, which in turn, and in combination with the stock of knowledge, increases output and economic growth, in general.

On the other hand, a low level of investment has always been an obstacle to technological change.[27] Much of the technological change, perhaps most of it, can only find its way into actual production through the use of new and different capital equipment.[28]

9.3 Total Factor Productivity (TFP)

At the same time, technology was regarded as a driving force for economic growth and was often associated with the emergence of economic fluctuations, at least since the time of Schumpeter, of whom Solow was a student.[29] Thus, the positive result of the application of technology in the economy, which is technological progress, can mean that:[30] (a) a larger quantity of a product/service can be produced with the same quantities of inputs; (b) the same quantity of a product/service can be produced with smaller quantities of inputs; (c) the available inputs are improved in quality; (d) entirely new products/services are produced.

Solow again used the method of describing the production process by means of a Cobb–Douglas production function, for the study of the growth process in the economy. Then, by applying basic calculus to the Cobb–Douglas production function, Solow showed that a very significant proportion of the growth in the per capita output of any economy is due not to the factors of production of capital and labour, but to what he called 'Total Factor Productivity' or simply TFP, and is equal to the residual of the production function, known as the 'Solow residual', when estimated econometrically. Total Factor Productivity (TFP) is considered to reflect primarily technological change, as well as any other factors contributing to economic growth not explicitly included in the production function. The above methodology was applied, in its complete form, for the first time by Solow,[31] and became widely known as Growth Accounting, while another version of the methodology was also presented by Abramovitz.[32]

In an alternative formulation, according to the Growth Accounting methodology, the difference between the rate of change of output and the rates of change of appropriately weighted inputs is equal to the rate of change of a factor called, as we have seen, Total Factor Productivity or TFP, which expresses technological change. That is, growth in an economy is decomposed over time, with the help of a production function, into a part that is interpreted by the factors of production and another part that is attributed to technological change.[33]

In that article Solow, based on his model, studied the economic growth in the United States during the period 1909–1949 and came to the striking conclusion that a very high percentage of the increase in output per hour was due to technological progress, that is, to factors beyond capital and labour[34] inputs. The high proportion of growth explained by technological progress also includes other factors not explicitly taken into account in the production function.

It is characteristic that the application of the above framework to the member countries of the Organisation for Economic Co-operation and Development (OECD) has shown that about 50 per cent of the increase in the output of these countries is due neither to the increase in labour nor to the increase in physical capital, but to the increase in TFP, or otherwise, to the additional output produced by these economies, with the quantity of their[35] factors of production constant.

▶ The Growth Accounting methodology is particularly popular as it requires the use of reasonable statistical data, no arbitrary assumptions are required, and empirical estimates and calculations are checked at every step.[36] Some attempts have been made to extend the methodological framework,[37] but the Growth Accounting methodology continues to be widely used even today.

9.4　The Theoretical Legacy of Solow

In summary, Solow developed the so-called neoclassical model of economic growth, in an attempt to extend earlier models such as the Keynesian-inspired Harrod–Domar model that led to worrying conclusions for the economic system, on the one hand, because of its inability to lead unambiguously to economic growth and, on the other hand, to sustain it. On Solow's model, much of the discipline of modern Macroeconomic Theory has been built upon, through the field of Economic Growth, since it demonstrated that the economic system, despite its instability, can be driven on a growth path with a positive trend, and even has the tendency to return to a sustainable balanced growth path after a disturbance.[38] Moreover, the model has shown that countries with completely different levels of economic growth can at some point 'converge' to similar levels.

▶ In addition, he developed the Growth Accounting methodology which is still very popular today, where growth in an economy is decomposed over time, with the help of a production function, into a part interpreted by the factors of production and another part attributed to technological change.[39]

One could say that the Solow model inherited a fundamental issue in modern *Economics*, that of the exogenous view of technology.[40] Its exogeneity implied that in an economy where the rate of change in technology is determined exogenously, state intervention is meaningless or at best may be existent but extremely limited and only involves corrective measures aimed at accelerating the rate of growth. At this point, the 'New Growth Theory' emerged, which has flourished in the past decades since it 'endogenised' technology, while highlighting other critical variables and factors such as education, infrastructure projects, institutional environment, etc. This has now provided the theoretical foundation for the implementation of government interventions and policies.[41]

However, for all of the above, the individual economic unit still functions as a 'black box' and a multitude of factors have not yet been fully explored. Thus, the firm very often enters the market seeking 'equilibrium' with the other firms.

Key Takeaways

- There are fluctuations in output, labour, investment and consumption.
- In the long run, the capital–output ratio remains almost constant.
- The production function is a relationship between inputs and outputs.
- A high percentage of output growth is due to technological progress.
- The economic system, despite its instability, can lead to growth.
- Countries with different initial levels of wealth could 'converge' to similar levels of growth.

Revision Questions

- How is the Neoclassical School related to Solow's work?
- On what theoretical assumptions is Solow's growth model based?
- What does it mean that the equilibrium is 'asymptotically stable'?
- On what factors does long-term growth depend?
- What is the key element of the New Growth Theory?
- What is a 'production function'?
- What is the 'Solow Residual'?
- How is technological progress expressed?
- What is the Total Factor Productivity (TFP)?
- What is Solow's main contribution to *Economics*?

Notes

1 Dizikes (2019).
2 Solow (1988).
3 Solow (1988).
4 Solow (1988).
5 Solow (1988).
6 Dizikes (2019).
7 Solow (1988).
8 Dizikes (2011).
9 INFORMS (2021).
10 Solow (1988).
11 Henderson (2008).
12 Dizikes (2019).
13 Ballandonne and Rubin (2020).
14 Henderson (2008).
15 Tsoulfidis (2008).
16 Tsoulfidis (2008).
17 Reppas (2002).
18 Tsoulfidis (2008).
19 Reppas (2002).
20 Barro and Sala-i-Martin (1995), and Aghion and Howitt (1998).
21 Solow (1956).
22 Jones (1993).
23 Romer (1986), and Lucas (1988).
24 Kurz and Salvadori (2000).
25 Barro and Sala-i-Martin (1995).
26 Romer (1990).
27 Yueh (2018).
28 Solow (1988).
29 Boianovsky and Hoover (2014).
30 Jones (1993).
31 Solow (1957).
32 Abramovitz (1956).
33 Yueh (2018).
34 Dornbusch and Fischer (1990).
35 O.E.C.D. (1996).
36 Thirlwall (2001).

37 Denison (1967).
38 Tsoulfidis (2008).
39 Yueh (2018).
40 Yueh (2018).
41 Tsoulfidis (2008).

References

Abramovitz, M. (1956). Resource and Output Trends in the United States since 1980. *American Economic Review, 46*(2), 5–23.
Aghion, P., & Howitt, P. (1998). *Endogenous growth theory*. Cambridge, MA: MIT Press.
Ballandonne, M., & Rubin, G. (2020). Robert Solow's Non-Walrasian conception of economics. *History of Political Economy, 52*, 827–861.
Barro, R. J., & Sala-i-Martin, X. (1995). *Economic growth*. McGraw-Hill.
Boianovsky, M., & Hoover, K. (2014). In the kingdom of Solovia: The rise of growth economics at MIT: 1956–70. *History of Political Economy, 46*, 198–228.
Denison, E. (1967). *Why growth rates differ*. The Brookings Institution.
Dizikes, P. (2011, October 25). The office next door. *MIT Technology Review*. Retrieved April 8, 2021, from https://www.technologyreview.com/2011/10/25/21338/the-office-next-door/
Dizikes, P. (2019, December 27). The productive career of Robert Solow. *MIT Technology Review*. Retrieved April 8, 2021, from https://www.technologyreview.com/2019/12/27/131259/the-productive-career-of-robert-solow/
Dornbusch, R., & Fischer, S. (1990). *Macroeconomics*. McGraw-Hill.
Henderson, D. (2008). Robert Merton Solow. In D. Henderson (Ed.), *The concise encyclopedia of economics*. Library of Economics and Liberty. Retrieved March 3, 2021, from https://www.econlib.org/library/Enc/bios/Solow.html
INFORMS. (2021). Robert Solow. Retrieved March 3, 2021, from https://www.informs.org/Explore/History-of-O.R.-Excellence/Biographical-Profiles/Solow-Robert
Jones, H. (1993). *Introduction to modern theories of economic growth*. Kritiki Publications.
Kurz, H., & Salvadori, N. (2000). The dynamic Leontief Model and the theory of endogenous growth. *Economic Systems Research, 12*(2), 255–265.
O.E.C.D. (1996). *Research and development expenditures in industry*.
Reppas, P. (2002). *Economic development: Theories and strategies (vol. A)*. Papazisis Publications.
Romer, P. (1986). Increasing Returns and Long-Run Growth. *Journal of Political Economy, 94*, 1002–1037.
Romer, P. (1990). Endogenous technological change. *Journal of Political Economy, 98*, 71–102.
Solow, R. (1956). A contribution to the theory of economic growth. *Quarterly Journal of Economics, LXX*, 65–94.
Solow, R. (1957, August). Technical change and the aggregate production function. *Review of Economics and Statistics, 39*(3), 312–320.
Solow, R. (1988). *The Nobel Prizes 1987* (W. Odelberg, Ed.). Nobel Foundation.
Thirlwall, A. (2001). *Growth and development*. Papazisis Publications.
Tsoulfidis, L. (2008). *History of economic theory and policy*. University of Macedonia Publications.
Yueh, L. (2018). *What would the great economists do?* Picador.

John Nash (1928–2015) 10

▶ **Learning Objectives**

After having studied this chapter, the reader should be able to:

- Understand the meaning of 'Nash equilibrium'.
- Analyse the assumptions behind the 'Nash equilibrium'.
- Describe in a few words the so-called Prisoner's Dilemma.
- Describe the limitations of 'Nash equilibrium'.
- Present briefly John Nash's contribution to *Economics*.

▶ **Summary**

Based on a very broad definition of *Economics* as being the science that focuses on the behaviour of individuals related to economic decisions within a social context, Nash's theory plays an important role. One of Nash's most important contributions to *Economics* was his theory of two-person negotiations. In addition to the normal form of von Neumann's games and the non-cooperative notion of equilibrium, Nash argued that both provide a complete general methodological framework for the analysis of games. Therefore, the so-called Nash equilibrium is a state that no player wishes to leave when all players behave rationally. It should be noted that the 'Nash equilibrium' does not necessarily result in the best outcome for all members or for individuals. In fact, it can even prove to be a sub-optimal, even a catastrophic decision for all members, since there is a possibility that all of them could benefit if they worked together. Based on Game Theory, rational actors are seen as key players in the economy who act in accordance with their individual preferences, to achieve their best possible result, maximising their utility, while also being aware of other people's possible strategies. As a result, the primary objective is to obtain the best possible result, regardless of whether it is desirable on a collective level or not. In

Economics, Nash's work is of great importance because it demonstrated yet another issue: that some types of behaviour lead to situations which are not beneficial to the whole and, consequently, to the individual.

10.1 Introduction

John Forbes Nash Jr was born in 1928 in Bluefield, West Virginia, USA. His father was a World War I veteran and electrical engineer who had come to Bluefield from Texas to work for a power company, while his mother Virginia was a native of Bluefield and was an English and Latin teacher. John showed an early interest in science and letters, studying books in his family home. In high school, he was introduced to *Mathematics* and engaged in experiments in *Chemistry* and *Physics* (*Electricity*), and his goal was to follow his father's major as an electrical engineer.[1]

He began his studies as a chemical engineer on a scholarship at Carnegie Institute of Technology, only to switch briefly to pure *Chemistry* and eventually to concentrate on *Mathematics*, in which he had a passion, and was awarded both an MSc and a BSc[2] from Carnegie Institute of Technology. He then accepted offers to continue his studies at Harvard and Princeton on scholarship, choosing the most generous one, that of Princeton University, which had the key advantage of being closer to Bluefield.

The elective course in *International Economics* during his studies at Carnegie Institute of Technology gave Nash the opportunity to further explore problems of an economic nature.[3] It also provided the impetus, while studying at Princeton, to conceive the ideas that prompted him to develop his theory.[4]

At Princeton, John Nash began working on Game Theory with John von Neumann and Harold Kuhn, while his supervisor was Albert Tucker.[5] Kuhn was by his side even during the most difficult periods of his life, and he was also the person who informed him that he was awarded the Swedish Academy Prize in memory of Alfred Nobel.[6]

As a PhD student, Nash made important discoveries, and his ideas on Game Theory, based on those of von Neumann and Morgenstern, formed the basis of his 27-page PhD thesis[7] entitled *Non-cooperative Games*.[8] In 1950, the first year after receiving his PhD from Princeton, he taught at the same university, and between 1951 and 1959 he worked at the Massachusetts Institute of Technology (MIT), with a one-year break (1956–1957) when he was back at Princeton. In addition, prompted by a scientific discussion that had begun at MIT concerning a classical problem on *Differential Geometry* that had remained unsolved until then, Nash zealously devoted himself to trying to solve it and finally succeeded.[9]

As a character, according to those who knew him there, Nash was considered a strange one.[10] In 1956–1957, he married his partner Alicia, whom he had met as a *Physics* student at MIT[11] and, in 1958, *Fortune* magazine made special mention of Nash, calling him the most brilliant representative of the new generation of mathematicians. Indeed, in the eyes of many, his work revolutionised *Economics*, similar to what was brought about by, for example, Newton, Mendel and Darwin in the scientific fields in which they were active.[12]

In 1959, when his wife became pregnant, John Nash began to show symptoms of mental disorder and failed to win the Fields Medal in *Mathematics*.[13] There were many occasions when Nash was hospitalised, with his consent, in hospitals for several months because of the *schizophrenia* from which he was diagnosed.[14]

He eventually, and at a relatively advanced age, managed to return to scientific research.[15] This was in the early 1990s, when new drugs enabled him to regain a satisfactory mental balance.[16]

The highlight of his scientific career was the award of the Nobel Prize in *Economics* in 1994 for his contribution to Game Theory and the definition of the concept of equilibrium, which became known as the 'Nash equilibrium'. Some believe that this was a way of rewarding Nash, not only as a scientist but also for his difficult personal life, much of which was spent in hospitals and away from the university.[17] In addition to Nash, John C. Harsanyi and Reinhard Selten were also awarded the Nobel Prize for their contribution to the theory of non-cooperative games, mainly through their extension of Nash's work.

In 2015, Nash was jointly awarded the Abel Prize in *Mathematics* with Louis Nirenberg for his contributions to the theory of nonlinear partial differential equations and its applications. He received the prize in Oslo, Norway, and on returning to Princeton, he and his wife Alicia, with whom he had separated and remarried, took a taxi home. Unfortunately, the cab overturned on a New Jersey highway, causing the deaths of both of them.[18]

Nash's theories are widely applicable in many fields where there is a strong element of strategic interaction. In particular, Game Theory is now widely used in *Economics*, for example, in the determination of prices between firms in the same industry (e.g. telecommunications) and in *Management*, for example, in the determination of advertising expenses and costs between firms in the same industry (e.g. energy). Also, there is a plethora of applications in *Finance, Political Science, Sociology, Computer Science, Artificial Intelligence* and other fields such as *Medicine, Biology* and even *Sports*. It is noteworthy that a number of academics have won the Nobel Prize in *Economics* for their research on game theory, following Nash's path.[19]

10.2 Game Theory Before John Nash

The application of the 'Nash equilibrium' to an economic model seems to appear for the first time in the work of the French mathematician and economist Antoine-Augustin Cournot.[20] In a pioneering book, Cournot created a theory of oligopolistic competition which includes monopoly and perfect competition as extreme cases. In particular, Cournot showed that the economic outcomes for one firm may depend on the economic outcomes of another firm and, thus, carried out an analysis similar to that of Nash. Although Cournot developed the conceptual distinction between the formulation of a specific game and the general methodology employed for its analysis, he failed to do so in his own research.[21] Also, many economists had created various oligopolistic models, but these were based on questionable assumptions.[22]

The path to Nash's theory begins with an observation in a short article by the mathematician Emile Borel. Given a class of simple two-person games, Borel set out to study whether and to what extent it is possible to develop a method for solving the game that is better than all others.[23] As he presented the structure of his model, Borel observed that a general method was needed that would determine for every possible circumstance, in a game of a finite number of moves, exactly what each player[24] should do. Thus, in this and his subsequent articles, Borel expressed each game in terms of a payoff table that specifies the expected payoff of each player.[25]

Second, John von Neumann (1928)[26] developed a general model of a sequential game in which players have imperfect information of the past moves of the other players.[27] As a follow-up to Borel, von Neumann defined the term 'strategy' as a complete plan that specifies how the player will act depending on the information available to him.[28]

Then, John von Neumann (1928) explicitly formulated a general model of a game in which players play sequentially, over time, with imperfect information about the previous moves of other players. Following Borel, von Neumann defined a strategy for each player to be a complete plan that specifies a move for the player as a function of the information he has.

Furthermore, he believes that a player should be able to choose his strategy before the game starts, that is, before the consequences of other players' decisions are observed. Thus, von Neumann concludes that each player should choose his strategy without being aware of the strategic choices of other players.[29] In this context, he argued that almost any competitive game can be modelled with the following simple structure: There is a set of players, each player has a set of strategies, each player has an expected payoff, and each player chooses his strategy independently of the other players.[30] Von Neumann and Morgenstern called this structure the 'normal form'.[31]

10.3 The Contribution of John Nash

Until Nash's generation, *Economics* was regarded as the social science concerned with the production and distribution of goods and services. Within the prevailing definition of *Economics*, therefore, Nash's work could in principle be seen as a mathematical contribution with limited relevance to *Economics*. But if we broaden this definition and adopt a more 'behavioural' approach, i.e. that *Economics* is that social science which deals with the study of behaviour in the context of a social formation, we see that Nash's theory plays a central role.[32]

Thus, before Nash, economists worked on developing a theory of price determination in free markets, based on models of competitive decision-making by producers and consumers a la Walras. Thus, as economists became familiar with the notion of 'rationality' in a perfectly competitive environment, it remained only to seek the implications and empirical applications of this theoretical construct. Thus, the scope of study and application was extended to issues beyond the determination of resource allocation in perfect competition. However, applications of 'rational' behaviour required a more general analytical framework for it to thrive.

The main reason why Game Theory was developed is precisely to provide the framework in order to study those situations in which individuals determine their decisions not in isolation, but by taking into account the choices of actors in the economy with conflicting interests,[33] but without ultimately depending on the final choice of other players. The importance of this view for *Economics* is shown in its ability to model, first and foremost, situations of conflict between rational decision-makers. Recall that a 'rational' actor in *Economics* is, technically speaking, one who wishes to maximise his subjective expected utility based on his individual preferences.[34]

The basic foundation of Game Theory within *Economics* was laid in 1944 with von Neumann and Morgenstern's work, *Game Theory and Economic Behaviour*, which was the precursor to modern Game Theory. This work introduced a number of new concepts and research areas that are still active today. There is, for example, the concept of cooperative games, where players make agreements with each other, and the formalism of Game Theory applied to a range of economic problems.[35]

▶ Nash defines the equilibrium of a non-cooperative game as a profile of strategies, one for each player in the game, such that each player's strategy maximises his own expected performance, given the strategies of the other players.[36] If we can predict the behaviour of all players in such a game, then our prediction must be a 'Nash equilibrium', or else it would violate the assumption of 'rational' individual behaviour.

Nash's first major contribution was his theory of two-person bargaining in *Econometrica*.[37] Then, on 16 November 1949, the *Proceedings of the National Academy of Science* received a short article by Nash, about one-page long, which was published the following year.[38] In this historic article, Nash gave a general definition of equilibrium for normal form games using the 'fixed point' theorem to prove that equilibrium in random strategies exists for any regular form of game of a finite number of players, each of whom chooses from a finite number of options. In his doctoral dissertation at Princeton, Nash worked further on his idea of non-cooperative equilibrium. Most of his dissertation was published in the *Annals of Mathematics*.[39]

Having formulated the general definition of equilibrium for non-cooperative games, and having proved the general existence of equilibrium for such games in his 1950 article, Nash presented a number of interesting examples, illustrating the problems that still concern game theorists since then, including a particularly important game with Nash equilibrium that is not 'Pareto efficient'— named after Vilfredo Pareto—such as the 'prisoner's dilemma'[40] that we will encounter below.

It should be noted here that Vilfredo Pareto was an Italian engineer from the Polytechnic of Turin who first worked on Italian Railways and then on *Economics* and *General Equilibrium Analysis* and it was he who succeeded Walras in his academic chair in Lausanne. He is considered an important economist who introduced the highly popular concept of Pareto[41] 'efficiency' or 'optimality'. Thus, an equilibrium is called 'Pareto efficient' or 'Pareto optimal' if no player can be in a better position without someone else being in a worse position.

But perhaps, Nash's most important contribution was his realisation that the non-cooperative notion of equilibrium, together with von Neumann's normal form, gives us a complete general methodological framework for the analysis of all games.[42]

10.4 Prisoner's Dilemma

Nash's theory of equilibrium in non-cooperative games is often regarded as one of the most important discoveries of the twentieth century, since the equilibrium of the same name has had a significant impact on *Economics* and other *Social Sciences*. Indeed, the impact is considered by some to be comparable to that of the decoding of DNA in the Biological Sciences.[43] It is, therefore, appropriate to take a practical insight from Nash's work to get a closer look at what is considered one of the most revolutionary discoveries in the history of *Economics*.

Suppose two people, A and B, are arrested and held in separate cells for minor offences. At the same time, however, the authorities do not have sufficient evidence to convict them of a murder in which they suspect these two are involved. So, the police offer each prisoner a bargain: if they both confess to the murder, they will be sentenced to 10 years in prison each. If one denies the charge and the other confesses, then the one who confessed will be released and the other will be sentenced to 25 years in prison. Finally, if both deny the charges, then they will be imprisoned for one year each for minor offences. The game is summarised in the table below and is known as the 'prisoner's dilemma'.

		B	
A		*Confession*	*Denial*
	Confession	(10, 10)	(0, 25)
	Denial	(25, 0)	(1, 1)

For the various possible moves of each player, we see the respective outcomes in brackets. Within the parentheses, the first value represents the years of imprisonment for player A and the second value represents the years of imprisonment for player B. Looking at the above table, many will be tempted to respond that each player would obviously have to deny the charges in order to be sentenced to just one year in prison each. However, the 'Nash equilibrium' does not suggest that. Let's see why.

Based on the Game's Table, player B has two options: either to confess or to deny the charges. So, if player B confesses, then it is in player A's interest to confess as well, in order to get only 10 years in prison, not 25, as would happen if he denies. Now, if player B denies the charges, then it is in player A's interest to confess in

10.4 Prisoner's Dilemma

order to be released and not to deny, because then he will be in prison for one year. Therefore, in either case, that is, in either choice of B, it is in A's best interest to confess. Exactly the same is true for B. Therefore, the best response of each to the other's strategy is to confess. Therefore, they will be in prison for 10 years each.

Now, even if A was hoping for B to deny the charges so that he would deny them himself, in order to sentence them to only one year in prison each, then it is in A's interest to confess in order to get himself released if B denies the charges. In this case, that is, where B has taken a risk by trusting A, B risks 25 years in prison if A confesses. So, everyone has an interest in confessing.

It is striking that even if one player seems willing to cooperate with the other, it is 'rational' for the other player to choose to betray him in order to maximise his self-interest. Or, to put it another way, it is *not* 'rational' for him to cooperate with the other in the mutually beneficial solution (1, 1), but *it is* 'rational' for him to eventually reach the solution (10, 10). Thus, we provide individualists (or 'lone wolves' as a popular phrase puts it) with a very good excuse for their antisocial behaviour.[44]

The above 'solution' to the game (10, 10) is called a 'Nash equilibrium', in the sense that it maximises the level of return a player receives, knowing the possible choices of other players but not depending on them. 'Nash equilibrium' is thus based on the idea that in a state of equilibrium no player wishes to move away from it, given the rational behaviours of the other players.

To begin with, we can see that the basic idea underlying the concept of 'Nash equilibrium' is very attractive, mainly due to its simplicity. More precisely, once the players are in a Nash equilibrium, no one changes their strategic choice at the individual level. They may, of course, be upset because collectively they did not act differently with a much better outcome for each of them, but given the 'rational' behaviour of the other player, no one is upset about their own, individual decisions.[45] Of course, the fact that—once the 'Nash equilibrium' is reached—there is no reason for the players to feel distressed does not in itself imply that the players will necessarily, in the end, seek to move towards that[46] equilibrium.

Looking closely, we see that the 'Nash equilibrium' does not necessarily lead to the best outcome for the group as a whole, nor for the individual, and may even be catastrophic as a choice for everyone involved.[47] If they could, in some way, work together and cooperate, then they could both be in a better position. Indeed, in a well-known critique, Nash's concept of equilibrium has been characterised 'weak' and without offering any further information.[48]

Moreover, the aforementioned Nash equilibrium would also be 'Pareto efficient' if no player could be in a better position without someone else being in a worse position. However, in the end, this particular Nash equilibrium in Prisoner's Dilemma is not 'Pareto efficient', since both can be found in (1, 1), while also improving the position of the other. Indeed, (1, 1) is Pareto efficient, since neither player can be in a better position without the other being in a worse position. However, in other games, some 'Nash equilibria' may indeed be 'Pareto efficient' as well.

Finally, another element that is ignored in individual, 'rational', behaviour is social groupings, collective attitudes and moral concepts. If, for instance, in the above dilemma we had two soldiers arrested and called upon to confess to war crimes (e.g. execution of civilians) against the country that had arrested them, they would in fact be far more likely to refuse to confess to such a heinous act due to patriotism or education, despite their individual 'self-interest', even if Nash's theory suggests confession as the 'equilibrium'. Ignored, therefore, in the 'Nash equilibrium' are elements of collective behaviours, social groupings and moral concepts.

Of course, the above Prisoner's Dilemma is a simplistic presentation of a specific, very simple game, without the use of almost any technical definition or jargon, and was intended to give us a first idea of the concept of 'Nash equilibrium'. Obviously, in Game Theory, much more complex and sophisticated problems, with a huge number of players, preferences and moves, are dealt with, where a large number of concepts, techniques and algorithms, both theoretical and computational, are used.

10.5   The Evolution of Nash's Theory

We have seen that the Prisoner's Dilemma expresses the permanent threat to cooperation when, on the one hand, the collective interest demands cooperation but, on the other hand, individual motives activate forces which tend to destroy it.[49]

▶   Three remarks we believe are relevant here. First, the 'Nash equilibrium' may not always be unique, in which case other criteria would be needed in order to arrive, ultimately, at one of them. Second, we do not know whether players will actually behave 'rationally', because in experiments conducted, only about 50 per cent of the players opted for confession, that is, purely self-interest.[50] Third, the experience that players gain by playing many repetitions (rounds) of the game, according to recent empirical results, keeps cooperation levels high, contrary to what was previously believed.[51]

The impact of Nash's (re)consideration of Game Theory spread very slowly. At first, attention was focused on the analysis of cooperative games. Later, as more and more scholars recognised the importance of Nash's work, it became clear that there were a number of technical issues that needed further analysis. For example, Selten showed that for many normal form games, the analysis can sometimes lead to multiple Nash equilibria. To solve this problem, Selten defined 'perfect equilibrium' and Myerson defined 'proper equilibrium' as an improvement on the concept of 'Nash equilibrium',[52] and Kreps and Wilson defined 'sequential equilibria' as fundamental concepts of non-cooperative solutions for extensive-form games.[53]

A second difficulty with the normal-form game is that it assumes that the game begins at a point in time when all players have the same information.[54] This assumption is highly restrictive, and Harsanyi showed how this difficulty can be avoided by creating Bayesian models,[55] meaning that players formulate the subjective probabilities about whether a specific outcome is likely to occur, based on an individual's personal knowledge and judgement.[56] The interpretation of equilibrium has changed radically since the introduction of these[57] games. Finally, the interpretation of the normal form was modified by Aumann, in his study of the case of cooperation between players.[58]

In general, Nash was an ardent supporter of technology and computers, which he considered superior in some cases to humans, and was fascinated by the idea that algorithms and mathematical models could be created to suggest solutions to various games and problems.[59]

However, even in the field of applications of Game Theory and the computational algorithms that Nash particularly valued, the enthusiasm for the concept of the 'Nash equilibrium' has given way to scepticism as to whether and to what extent such an equilibrium is computationally feasible. Although the Nash equilibrium appears to be a simple concept, this is not the case in practice since Nash did not specify a general method of finding the solution, a process that can be very difficult and time-consuming or even practically impossible.[60] Indeed, as has been shown by Daskalakis, Goldberg and Papadimitriou, there is no efficient algorithm that *computes* Nash[61] equilibria.

▶ Moreover, as shown by Babichenko and Rubinstein,[62] there is no guaranteed method of finding an approximate Nash equilibrium unless they exchange with each other almost all the information they have about their respective preferences. And, as the number of players in a game grows, the time required is prohibitive, making the task impractical, even for approximate Nash equilibria.

Therefore, in some games of increased complexity, finding the Nash equilibrium is, from a computational point of view, practically impossible. And, as Daskalakis et al. have argued[63] 'if your laptop can't find it, neither can the market'.[64]

10.6 The Theoretical Legacy of Nash

In order to understand the significance of non-cooperative Game Theory, we must first understand the concept of 'rationality' in *Economics*. As we know, Game Theory highlights the 'rational player' as the key actor in *Economics,* who operates according to his individual preferences to achieve the best possible outcome with respect to his desires, maximising his utility regardless of whether it is collectively desirable or not, while being aware of the possible strategies of other individuals.

Thus, in the game-theoretic perspective of Nash's analysis, a 'robotic' figure is adopted for the individual, without age, gender, profession, income, social class and emotion, who coldly studies the game in order to calculate, with mathematical precision, the most advantageous strategy for him, which is implicitly reduced to the 'most appropriate' solution, individually. Therefore, it is obvious that the concept of equilibrium suffers, because precisely the model of the 'rational' player cannot actually exist in practice in human society and the economy. It is, therefore, a theoretical assumption based on a highly abstract, theoretical, rationalist construction of an ideal 'player'.

▶ Whenever experimental testing pointed out theoretical inconsistencies in the behaviour and choices of 'rational' individuals, as for example in the work of Nobel Prize-winning economist Daniel Kahneman, who challenged the 'rationality' of the individual with empirical experiments, then various characteristics, such as gender and the role of emotion, began to be taken into account as possible explanatory factors to which these differences could be attributed.[65]

What is the reason, then, for the adoption of the rational behaviour hypothesis, despite these problems, both in Game Theory and in Nash's analysis, as well as in *Economics* more generally? First, there seems to be no other better assumption available to adopt. A second explanation is that 'objectifying' the substance of human existence approximates an ideal individual with known characteristics and behaviours. As a result, we are now able to apply the analytical, mathematical laws and rules of Neoclassical Economics to this ideal atom of society. A third answer involves analysing and evaluating the social and economic system being studied. The result of empirical studies, which test the theory against the available empirical data, may differ from what the mathematical models have predicted, but this does not mean that the models or theories are incorrect. Furthermore, it does not imply that the economic system contains issues that are inconsistent with the abstract, theoretical assumptions and logic of the model. Hence, most people might be driven to believe that these differences between economic 'theory' and 'practice' stem from the 'irrational' behaviour of certain individuals, rather than the theory itself.

It is nevertheless important to note that Nash's work is a valuable contribution to *Economics* due to the fact that he demonstrated another important issue: In the event that each individual acts in accordance with his own self-interest, and believes that the other individuals with whom he interacts will act in a similar manner, it may lead to situations not beneficial to the group and, therefore, to the individual. In other words, blindly pursuing individual interests may eventually result in harm to the collective interest and to the individual himself, as we observed earlier in the Prisoner's Dilemma, a simplistic but typical version of a game, where each prisoner ended up with 10 years in prison versus 1.

As a consequence, in another formulation, it is seen that what is regarded for individuals as 'equilibrium' may not be a desirable state of collective equilibrium, despite attempts to present society as a homogeneous set of rational individuals. Or else, in Margaret Thatcher's words, 'And, you know, there's no such thing as society. There are individual men and women and there are families',[66] overlooking the fact that society consists precisely of the relationships between these individuals.

As a matter of fact, the concept of 'Nash equilibrium' has often been interpreted as an argument in support of the unregulated free market system, which has been associated with the philosopher Thomas Hobbes's view that cooperation would eventually be defeated by 'selfish' acts of self-interest on the part of individuals. As part of a similar theoretical framework, David Hume also expressed his scepticism regarding the role of a third party in social and economic matters, for example, the state.[67]

At precisely this point, Nash is confronted with Smith, whose fundamental claim was that an individual's pursuit of self-interest leads in the long run to the prosperity

10.6 The Theoretical Legacy of Nash

of society ('the invisible hand'). In Game Theory, as we have discussed extensively, when individuals pursue their own self-interest, they are not necessarily advancing the interests of the group.[68] Likewise, similar conclusions can be drawn when considering collective entities, such as firms and trade unions.

Furthermore, Nash's mathematical rigor and his highly restrictive and abstract assumptions are closely related to the essence of the mathematical, Neoclassical approach. Thus, analytic arguments are stripped of their evaluative elements and are wrapped in the attribute of 'objectivity', further reinforced by the eternal validity of abstract mathematical theorems and results.

Despite being mathematically elegant and based upon the relative existence theorem, Nash's theory has not been shown to be computationally feasible in the context of a real and complex economic problem modelled as a game.

There is little hope of calculating the Nash equilibrium in a reasonable amount of time, systematically and generally, when there are too many players, with too many different preferences, with too many available moves, with too many potential outcomes and probability distributions. This finding challenges the strict, Neoclassical equilibrium view of the economic system.

In conclusion, there is an alternative to the blind pursuit of individual interests and autonomous competitive behaviour without any consideration for the collective outcome. The interaction of individuals with one another, the development of mutually beneficial relationships, and the development of cooperative actions.[69] We have seen that this view can lead to a whole new way of approaching social and economic problems, which could result in much better results, both collectively and individually.

Key Takeaways

- Rational players act according to their individual preferences.
- The rational player aims to satisfy his desires as far as possible.
- 'Nash equilibrium' occurs when players behave rationally, and no player wants to leave it.
- 'Nash equilibrium' is not necessarily the 'best' outcome.
- Reaching a 'Nash equilibrium' is not always computationally feasible.
- The development of mutual relationships and cooperative actions may benefit both the rational player and the group.

Revision Questions

- What is the main reason for the development of Game Theory?
- How is the 'prisoner's dilemma' summarised?
- What is the meaning of 'Nash equilibrium'?
- What are the criticisms of 'Nash equilibrium'?
- To what extent is a 'Nash equilibrium' computable?
- What are the characteristics of the 'rational' player in *Economics*?
- Is Nash theoretically close to Smith?
- What is Nash's main contribution to *Economics*?

Notes

1. Nash (1995).
2. Nash (1995).
3. Nash (1996).
4. Nash (1995).
5. Leonard (1994).
6. Fragnelli and Gambarelli (2015).
7. Nash (1995).
8. Nasar (1998).
9. Nash (1995).
10. Nasar (1998).
11. Nash (1995).
12. Nasar (1998).
13. Nasar (1998).
14. Nash (1995).
15. Nash (1995).
16. Fragnelli and Gambarelli (2015).
17. Rubinstein (1995).
18. Fragnelli and Gambarelli (2015).
19. Our discussion follows Myerson (1999).
20. Cournot (1838).
21. Myerson (1999).
22. Leonard (1994).
23. Borel (1921).
24. Myerson (1999).
25. Myerson (1999).
26. von Neumann (1928).
27. Myerson (1999).
28. Myerson (1999).
29. Myerson (1999).
30. Myerson (1999)
31. von Neumann and Morgenstern (1944).
32. Myerson (1999).
33. Screpanti and Zamagni (2005).
34. Screpanti and Zamagni (2005).
35. Screpanti and Zamagni (2005).
36. Nash (1950b).
37. Nash (1950a).

38 Nash (1950b).
39 Nash (1951).
40 Nash (1951).
41 Mornati (2018).
42 Myerson (1999).
43 Myerson (1999).
44 Varoufakis (2007).
45 Varoufakis (2007).
46 Varoufakis (2007).
47 Milnor (1995).
48 Rubinstein (1995).
49 Varoufakis (2007).
50 Economist (2016).
51 Colman et al. (2018).
52 Myerson (1978).
53 Kreps and Wilson (1982).
54 Myerson (1999).
55 Harsanyi (1967–1968).
56 Screpanti and Zamagni (2005).
57 Myerson (1999).
58 Aumann (1974).
59 Nasar (1998).
60 Fellman (2007)
61 Daskalakis et al. (2009).
62 Babichenko and Rubinstein (2020).
63 Daskalakis et al. (2009, p. 196).
64 See also Karlin and Perez (2017, p. 84).
65 Schwartz-Shea (2002)
66 Margaret Thatcher in Brittan (2013).
67 Varoufakis (2007).
68 Nasar (1998).
69 Bix (2007).

References

Aumann, R. J. (1974). Subjectivity and correlation in randomized strategies. *Journal of Mathematical Economics, 1*, 67–96.

Babichenko, Y., & Rubinstein, A. (2020). Communication complexity of approximate Nash equilibria. *Games and Economic Behavior, 134*(July), 376–398.

Bix, B. (2007). *Philosophy of law: Theory and interpretative framework*. Kritiki Publications.
Borel, E. (1921). La théorie du jeu et les equation intégrales à noyau symétrique gauche. *ComptesRendus de l'Académie des Sciences, 173*, 1304–1308.
Brittan, S. (2013, April 18). Thatcher was right—There is no 'society'. *Financial Times*. Retrieved April 1, 2021, from https://www.ft.com/content/d1387b70-a5d5-11e2-9b77-00144feabdc0
Colman, A. M., Pulford, B. D., & Krockow, E. M. (2018). Persistent cooperation and gender differences in repeated Prisoner's Dilemma games: Some things never change. *Acta Psychological, 187*, 1–8.
Cournot, A. (1838). *Recherches sur les Principes Mathématiques de la Théorie des Richesses*. Hachette.
Daskalakis, C., Goldberg, P. W., & Papadimitriou, C. H. (2009). The complexity of computing a Nash equilibrium. *SIAM Journal on Computing, 39*(3), 195–259.
Economist. (2016, August 26). Prison breakthrough. *Game Theory*. Retrieved March 30, 2021, from https://amp.economist.com/schools-brief/2016/08/20/prison-breakthrough
Fellman, P. V. (2007). *The Nash equilibrium revisited: Chaos and complexity hidden in simplicity*. Fellman Southern New Hampshire University.
Fragnelli, V., & Gambarelli, G. (2015). John Forbes Nash (1928–2015). *The European Journal of the History of Economic Thought, 22*(5), 923–926.
Harsanyi, J. C. (1967–1968). Games with incomplete information played by 'Bayesian' players. *Management Science, 14*, 159–182.
Karlin, A., & Perez, Y. (2017). *Game theory, alive*. American Mathematical Society.
Kreps, D., & Wilson, R. (1982). Sequential equilibria. *Econometrica, 50*, 863–894.
Leonard, R. J. (1994). Reading Cournot, Reading Nash: The creation and stabilisation of the Nash equilibrium. *Economic Journal, 104*, 492–511.
Milnor, J. (1995). A Nobel prize for John Nash. *Mathematical Intelligencer, 17*(3), 11–17.
Mornati, F. (2018). *Vilfredo Pareto: An intellectual biography volume I*. Palgrave Studies in the History of Economic Thought.
Myerson, R. B. (1978). Refinements of the Nash equilibrium concept. *International Journal of Game Theory, 7*, 73–80.
Myerson, R. B. (1999). Nash equilibrium and the history of economic theory. *Journal of Economic Literature, 37*(3), 1067–1082.
Nasar, S. (1998). *A beautiful mind*. Simon & Schuster.
Nash, J. (1950a). The bargaining problem. *Econometrica, 18*, 155–162.
Nash, J. (1950b). Equilibrium points in n-person games. *Proceedings of the National Academy of Sciences U.S.A., 36*, 48–49.
Nash, J. (1951). Noncooperative games. *Annals of Mathematics, 54*, 289–295.
Nash, J. (1995). *The Nobel Prizes 1994* (T. Frängsmyr, Ed.) Nobel Foundation.
Nash, J. (1996). *Essays on game theory*. Edward Elgar.
Rubinstein, A. (1995). John Nash: The master of economic modeling. *Scandinavian Journal of Economics, 97*, 9–13.
Schwartz-Shea, P. (2002). Theorizing gender for experimental game theory: Experiments with "Sex Status" and "Merit Status" in an asymmetric game. *Sex Roles, 47*, 301–319.
Screpanti, E., & Zamagni, S. (2005). *An outline of the history of economic thought*. OUP.
Varoufakis, G. (2007). *Game theory*. Gutenberg Publications.
von Neumann, J. (1928). On the theories of parlor games. *MathematischeAnnalen, 100*, 295–320.
von Neumann, J., & Morgenstern, O. (1944). *Theory of games and economic behavior*. Princeton University Press.

Amartya Sen (1933–...) 11

▶ **Learning Objectives**

After having studied this chapter, the reader should be able to:

- Understand the concept of 'capabilities'.
- Explain Sen's ideas on gender inequalities.
- Discuss Sen's work on famine and poverty.
- Analyse Sen's influence on measuring welfare.
- Present briefly Amartya Sen's contribution to *Economics*.

▶ **Summary**

Known for his contributions to the fields of social choice theory, political and moral philosophy, and decision theory, Amartya Sen is an eminent economist, scholar, philosopher and author, as well as the Nobel Prize winner in *Economic Sciences* in 1998. According to Sen's views, *Economics* should be built on the notions of 'functionings' and human 'capabilities'. In general, "capabilities" refer to what it is possible for a person to do or be—in particular, that he or she may be well nourished; avoid unnecessary morbidity or mortality; read, write and communicate; participate in community life. It is important to recognise that while a utilitarian measure of human welfare would suggest that people are worse off when their standard of living is lower, the capability approach may show that with greater freedom and greater choice, individuals may be better off. The work of Sen has contributed to a better understanding of the causes of famines and hunger in the real world. Many international agencies have also changed how they approach famine prevention as a result. Until Sen's research, most development economists believed that famines were caused by insufficient food production. It was pointed out by Sen that issues related to distribution should be considered separately from those related to food supply. A famine may occur due to an insufficient production, but it may also be caused by inefficient or unequal distribution mechanisms. His contention that Gross National Product (GNP) alone was insufficient to assess the standard of living which led him to contribute to the development of the Human Development Index (HDI), the most reliable international metric for assessing welfare levels between countries. He contributed to the global fight against injustice, inequality, diseases and ignorance through his theories of human development and the underlying mechanisms of poverty and famine. His contributions earned him the Nobel Prize in *Economic Sciences* in 1998 and have inspired policies at the United Nations, the World Bank and elsewhere and have also informed the work of other Nobel Laureates.

11.1 Introduction

Amongst his many accomplishments, Amartya Sen is an economist, philosopher, scholar and author of international repute. In addition to his work in social choice theory, political and moral philosophy, and decision theory, he has made numerous important contributions to the field of *Economics* which earned him the Nobel Prize in *Economic Sciences* in 1998.[1]

Generally, Sen's contributions can be divided into the following categories: philosophical criticism of conventional economic ideas and concepts, the development of an *Economic Science* that is grounded in human capabilities, and also practical contributions to economic development, such as understanding poverty and inequality more accurately, understanding famine and hunger, examining gender issues, and explaining the differences between economic growth and economic development.[2]

Amartya was born in 1933 and was the son of a *Chemistry* professor at Dhaka University, the city that is now the capital of Bangladesh. Among his mother's occupations there were several. Although she was quite successful as a dancer once, she worked for more than 30 years as an editor of a magazine.[3] Rabindranath Tagore, a Sanskrit teacher, writer, poet and philosopher, the first non-European to win the Nobel Prize for Literature (1913), founded the school and college that Amartya attended in Santiniketan.[4] And it was Tagore who suggested the name 'Amartya' to Sen's mother.[5]

Financially, the Sens did not have a good situation despite their academic pedigree.[6] In Dacca (now Dhaka), Amartya began his education, but was soon transferred to Santiniketan near Kolkata. In this environment, he was exposed to academic freedom. Thus, Sen was provided with the opportunity to interact with his erudite grandfather, Kisht Mohan, who was a scholar himself and ran the school.[7] During the time that the war was going on with Japan, Amartya spent a considerable amount of time with his grandparents in Santiniketan, where he studied from the age of 7 to the age of 17. His grandparents were with him because the war between Japan and the Allies was in progress at the time.[8]

11.1 Introduction

A number of notable visitors to his school included Mahatma Gandhi and Eleanor Roosevelt. His school was well known for the variety of knowledge it attempted to establish through vigorous discussions and even lively debates and the openness of its campus.[9] As well as India's cultural heritage, analytical and scientific heritage, the school's curriculum was strongly connected to the rest of the world.[10]

In 1943, Sen was nine years old when the Great Bengal Famine took place. Several million people died despite adequate grain being available, and Sen was struck by its deeply class-dependent nature.[11] During the 1970s, he studied famines and developed an interest in economic development.[12]

In 1944, just before British India was split into India and Pakistan, Sen was witness to some of the Hindu–Muslim violence that ravaged British India. While seeking employment in Sen's Dhaka neighbourhood, a Muslim day labourer named Kader Mia was stabbed by Hindus. Therefore, Sen has always considered the murder to be an example of a tragic aspect of human society that happens all too frequently: the killing of members of one group for no other reason than that they are members of that group. In Sen's opinion, Kader Mia's single identity struck a child of 11 as extraordinary. This is discussed by Sen in *Identity and Violence*, in which he brings his razor-sharp intellect and humanist disposition to bear on his earlier sense of astonishment.[13]

During his early years, Sen's intended field of study varied quite a bit, and between 3 and 17years old, he flirted with *Sanskrit*, *Mathematics* and *Physics*. However, he finally chose *Economics*.[14] Between 1951 and 1953, he attended Presidency College. In 1943, he had been a witness to the Bengal famine, in which several million people had died and was struck by its deeply class-dependent nature.[15] Amartya Sen graduated with a BA in *Economics* and a minor in *Mathematics*, from the University of Calcutta. His main concerns in his undergraduate years in Calcutta were *Welfare Economics*, *Economic Inequality* and *Poverty*, and the scope of democratic social choice, as well as the protection of liberty and minority rights.[16]

During his teenage years, Amartya Sen became ill with cancer. He discovered a lump inside his mouth a few months after moving to Calcutta for college. As a student of *Economics* and *Mathematics*, Sen consulted two doctors, who laughed at his suspicions, so he visited a medical library and looked through a few books on cancer. When a squamous cell carcinoma was diagnosed, the question arose as to whether he was really two people with the same name: a patient who had just learned he was dying from cancer, and also the 'agent' who had made the diagnosis. 'I cannot allow the patient to take over completely' Sen decided, 'and I cannot—absolutely cannot—let go of the agent within me'.[17] After undergoing radiation treatment, many of the bones in Sen's mouth were destroyed. This proved to be a difficult experience. He had a 15 per cent chance of surviving for five more years, according to the doctors. After his recovery, his father considered that it might be a good idea for Amartya to travel abroad.[18]

The next step in his education was to attend Cambridge University. As part of his studies at Cambridge, Sen was involved in the work of Maurice Dobb, Joan Robinson and Piero Sraffa in *Economics*.[19] His dissertation was supervised by

Robinson, along with Amiya Dasgupta, who attempted to move his research in the direction of abstract theory.[20] Sen graduated from Trinity College with a BA in 1955 and a PhD in 1959. At the age of 23, Sen became Chairperson of the *Economics* Department at Jadavpur University in Calcutta, while completing his doctoral dissertation (1956–1958).[21] As he was not yet 23 years old, this caused a storm of protest that was entirely foreseeable and understandable. However, he enjoyed the opportunity and took it on with enthusiasm.

After his graduation from Cambridge, he briefly taught at MIT (1960–1961), where he had many stimulating discussions with Paul Samuelson, Robert Solow, Franco Modigliani, Norbert Wiener and others. He gained a greater understanding of the breadth of *Economics* as a result of the summer visit to Stanford.[22] Sen held visiting positions in the United States between 1963 and 1971, while teaching at the University of Delhi. In 1964–1965, he worked for the University of California at Berkeley, and he was at Harvard University[23] between 1968 and 1969.

During this period, he faced several intellectual challenges. In collaboration with K. N. Raj, they attempted to establish an advanced school of *Economics* in Delhi. Together they established the Delhi School as the preeminent centre for economic education in India prior to Sen's departure in 1971 for the London School of Economics.[24]

Upon returning to the United Kingdom in 1971, Sen became a professor at the London School of Economics. Upon moving to Oxford University in 1977, Sen joined Nuffield College. Since 1988, Sen has been teaching *Economics* and *Philosophy* at Harvard University as the Lamont University Professor of Economics and Philosophy. Following his return to England in 1998, Sen joined Trinity College, Cambridge University, as master.[25]

The Nobel Prize in *Economics* was awarded to Sen in 1998 in recognition of his contributions to the understanding of social choice theory, poverty and welfare measurement.[26] A number of academic awards and honours have been bestowed upon Sen throughout his distinguished career. The history of his service to society includes serving as the President of the Human Development and Capability Association and acting as an Honorary Director of the Academic Advisory Committee of the Center for Human and Economic Development Studies in China. His scholarly accomplishments also include being a member of Reporters Without Borders Commission on Information and Democracy. There are also more than 40 honorary doctorates that he has received. He has also produced an impressive body of scholarly work.

Sen has also served on the boards of several leading economic associations. He was president of the Development Studies Association. The Econometric Society appointed him as president in 1984. The International Economic Association elected him as its president in 1986, and the Indian Economic Association elected him as its president in 1989 and 1991, respectively. The American Economic Association elected Sen as its president in 1994.[27] During the year 2021, he was awarded Spain's prestigious Princess of Asturias Award for Social Sciences.[28]

11.2 Capabilities and the Critique to Welfare Economics

According to Sen, the key theme of his work is the development of human potential. Therefore, Sen is generally regarded as the pioneer of the 'capability approach' in the contemporary era, although Sen himself and others have pointed out that Aristotle's definition of a functioning is also crucial in the writings of philosophers and theoreticians who are influenced by Aristotle.[29]

Sen delivered the Tanner lectures in 1980 titled, 'Equality of what?'. The author questioned the effectiveness of measuring equality in terms of marginal or total utility, or primary goods. In addition, he outlined his concept of capabilities for the first time.[30] Capabilities are the alternative combinations of functionings that are feasible to achieve, whereas a functioning describes the activities and states that make up a person's well-being, such as a healthy body, safety, education, a good job and being able to visit loved ones.

The concept of functionings is, in general, closely related to goods and income, but not exclusively. A well-fed population enjoys the benefits of having their basic needs for food (a commodity) met. The fact that functionings are aspects of human fulfilment means that some functionings may be very basic (being fed, clothed, etc.) while others may be quite advanced (being able to play a virtuoso guitar solo, eating expensive caviar). Different dimensions of life can be affected by both basic and complex functioning. Depending on the individual, some may focus on survival, work and material well-being, while others may be concerned with relationships, empowerment and self-expression.[31]

Sen understood that the most important thing in life is to focus on those things that have intrinsic value rather than those that are simply utilitarian. This led him to develop the concept of 'capabilities'. In general, 'capabilities' refer to what is possible for a person to do or be—in particular, that he or she may be well nourished; avoid unnecessary morbidity or mortality; read, write and communicate; participate in community life; and appear in public without embarrassment.[32] It is evident that basic needs are included within this definition, but the term 'capabilities' has to do with a considerably broader concept.

According to this perspective, people are more likely to prosper if they can read, eat and vote. Not only is reading useful, it also contributes to one's development as a person. Food is not precious because people love food, but rather because it is essential. It is not because people wish to maximise their utility that they vote, but because they support certain types of political activities (democracy).[33] Freedom of choice and the availability of a wide range of options also contribute to a person's well-being. Despite having lower incomes and lower security, slaves and people who obtain independence or divorce for the purpose of ending an oppressive marriage will experience greater well-being. The well-being of consumers could also be improved if they were given more choices when purchasing a specific good without any alternatives, even if they did not end up receiving more products. The capability approach to measuring human welfare shows that greater freedom and greater choice can lead to greater individual welfare as a utilitarian measure of human welfare.[34]

▶ Sen argues that *Economics* should involve increasing people's choices in order to improve their capabilities. As such, this stands in stark contrast to traditional economic concerns such as maximising utility by producing more goods more efficiently. Accordingly, he was critical of conventional welfare *Economics*, which assumes that free exchange maximises the well-being of individuals.[35]

According to his first argument, utility maximisation does not accurately describe the behaviour of individuals. It has been argued, for example, that utility maximisation ignores the real reason why people attend polling places and cast their votes. As a result of their commitment, desire to register their preferences, and desire to participate in the elections, people vote. As a practice, *Economics* typically underestimates these human desires because it focuses primarily on the concept of utility that is supposed to be derived from things chosen as opposed to the real decision-making process itself. Traditional economic analysis ignores many human motivations. *Economics* ignores traditional social concerns, fails to take account of the needs of future generations and ignores ethical issues.[36]

A person does not work, according to Sen, because he has conducted some economic calculations and has determined that the value of goods and services that can be purchased with their pay alone is greater than the value of the time they have lost. It is forbidden for employees to work more than 48 hours per week. Aside from providing economic benefits, employment has the potential to facilitate social contact, the development of skills and the achievement of psychological well-being or self-esteem. Consequently, the unemployed are more likely to suffer from health problems, suicide and mortality rates, as well as psychological distress. A higher divorce rate is also associated with unemployment as it weakens family relationships.[37]

Furthermore, traditional welfare analysis has been criticised due to its adherence to rational utility maximisation and its consequences. Based on Sen's reasoning, if people behaved rationally, they would be mocked for their selfish behaviour. The Prisoner's Dilemma constitutes an excellent example of this strange situation. No consideration is given to other individuals, no sense of integrity or any idea of the kind of society one wishes to live in or the type of person one wishes to be. By focusing on rational choices, such as which cereal brand to purchase at the supermarket, economists ignore other, more personal or even interpersonal, factors related to making decisions.[38]

▶ Observations by Sen indicate that in the real-world people do not maximise their own utility for any given set of options. The last piece of dessert on the table, for example, will not be consumed by anyone. This is not to indicate that someone is not interested in the dessert or that eating the dessert would not bring him/her pleasure. However, he/she is more concerned with how others perceive him/her than grabbing the last piece.

11.2 Capabilities and the Critique to Welfare Economics

As this example illustrates, well-being is not solely determined by outcomes. It is important for economists to consider commitments, as well as other social interdependencies in their analyses; however, economists do not take these factors into consideration and consider them to be 'externals', which are major contributors to human welfare. As a result of incorporating these factors back into *Economics*, the subject is broadened, made more realistic and relevant, and its theoretical foundation is strengthened.[39]

In addition to the assumptions about preferences made in traditional welfare *Economics*, there is another issue. There is a possibility that people may not be able to envision the utility of certain actions due to poverty, illness, tyranny or their upbringing or because of their customs. In the absence of early schooling, individuals may become distrustful of schooling and reject all options for education. In spite of their lack of basic reading and writing skills, they may not feel deprived due to their adjustment to their current circumstances.[40]

Additionally, Sen asserts that the welfare *Economics* standard unit of analysis is flawed. In the past, *Psychology* has been viewed as an empirical science that draws general conclusions about human behaviour on the basis of the assumption that individuals are autonomous. It is nevertheless the individual's choice to form a family or household. Thus, household members' well-being is determined not only by household income but also by how household resources are distributed. There may be undesirable results when one member of the family controls most resources or determines how they will be divided within the family. There is no doubt that unequal power prevails in the real world more often than not.[41]

Furthermore, Sen asserts that there are many things that are both useful and un-useful that cannot be exchanged for money. Crime, pollution and social unrest are all inefficient, just as a nice sunset, some good friends and a large family are beneficial. These factors have traditionally been ignored by welfare *Economics*. Best-case scenarios refer to them as externalities; worst-case scenarios dismiss them as insignificant. Although these sources of human welfare are important, *Economics* ignores them. By limiting the scope of *Economics*, welfare *Economics* is unable to address human well-being on a broader scale. For traditional economic theory, the only thing that matters is the goods consumed by a person. It is important to note, however, that this does not take into account the benefits that individuals have from those goods. It is important to keep in mind that some items (such as education) provide the capacity to achieve future goals despite their current utility. In truth, these goods contribute to human welfare and have a welfare component, but traditional welfare *Economics* ignores them. From a logical standpoint, it would be logical to shift the focus from goods themselves to what they do for individuals.[42]

Also, Sen[43] has criticised the use of Pareto efficiency/optimality as a welfare measure. Despite being optimal, outcomes can be disastrous. It is not possible to achieve Pareto efficient/optimal outcomes, such as one where a few people are very wealthy and everyone else is starving, without reducing the income and utility of the wealthy. It is clear, however, that many people are suffering from hunger, which is an undesirable situation. He argues that providing resources to the hungry will enhance their well-being in the long run, even if some of these resources must be derived from multimillionaires and utilities are directly comparable. As a consequence, conventional welfare *Economics* does not reach this conclusion, which represents an important flaw as well as a serious limitation.

Lastly, as noted by Sen,[44] utility maximisation is at odds with the traditional liberal view that individuals are free to pursue their own interests as long as they do not interfere with the interests of others. In spite of this, a concern for freedom would permit each individual to make their own decision. Conventional welfare *Economics* is in jeopardy, as Sen has pointed out. The author has argued that the various policies can contribute to human and societal well-being in contrast with standard welfare *Economics*.

11.3 Gender, Famine and Poverty

Sen has drawn out many of the 'capabilities' approach applications, initially with his attempt to measure poverty at an early stage[45] and continuing through his later research on hunger and famines, work on inequality and works on the role that women play in economic activity.

Economic development can be improved significantly through the use of a capabilities-based approach. This has led to a shift in the paradigm of development from one that promotes economic growth to one that promotes human well-being. Human well-being refers to the expansion of the human capacity to produce and consume goods, regardless of the fate of the people who produce and consume them. Growth refers to the production of more goods regardless of the fate of the individual who produces them and consumes them.[46] Growth in the economy raises per capita incomes and outputs. Consequently, people develop when they are able to accomplish more rather than when they purchase more items. Increasing economic development is associated with an increase in voting, literacy rates and the average number of years of schooling, as well as an increase in life expectancy. Economic development can be defined as the expansion of individual choices and opportunities, as well as the provision of a greater range of positive freedoms.[47]

Throughout his career, Sen has recognised the importance of gender issues in the development process. He has challenged the notion that low levels of development influence men and women equally, as well as the assumption that development policies do not take gender into account.[48] As a result of his research, he has demonstrated that preference for sons leads often to discrimination against women. In order to make the most of their limited income, families are constantly making decisions regarding how to use it. The allocation of income among family members is one of the most important decisions. For more affluent families, these matters are not as important; however, for poor families, these decisions are crucial. Families will die if they are not provided with adequate food and medical care when they are ill.[49]

Furthermore, he has demonstrated that women and men are not equally able to receive health care and nutritional food within their families. As an example, women in India were required to be sicker before being admitted for hospitalisation during

11.3 Gender, Famine and Poverty

famines and had higher chances of dying after being admitted. The availability of adequate food supplies was also less likely to be provided to women.[50]

The consequences[51] of this discrimination have been documented by Sen. The ratio of women to men is approximately 105 in more developed countries. It is estimated that there are 102 women for every man in sub-Saharan Africa. However, the proportion of women to men is only 94 to 96 in countries such as China and India. These countries should also have a sex ratio of about 100 women for every 100 men if men and women were treated equally. Therefore, if women were treated at home according to the same standards as men, there would be an additional 100 million women living today. Moreover, females who have a greater degree of independence are less likely to be missing in countries and areas where they are more independent. Furthermore, in areas with greater control over resources and better employment opportunities, the number of missing women is lower. It is generally believed that women have a greater chance of surviving wherever and whenever they possess greater 'capabilities'.

A number of policy recommendations are derived from this analysis. It is more likely for development projects to be successful when they are designed to assist women. It has been found that direct feeding programmes in India are more effective at improving nutritional status of girls than general food distribution to families at home. Women who are encouraged to work outside the home are able to negotiate and receive a greater share of the family's resources due to programmes encouraging them to work outside the home.[52] According to numerous empirical studies, empowering women with their own income contributes to both their own and their children's well-being.

As a result of Sen's research, the community of economists has been able to gain a better understanding of real-world issues. It has also influenced the approach taken by various organisations in the prevention of famines. Famines had previously been believed to be caused by insufficient food production by most development economists before Sen's work. In his view, the distribution of food is a separate issue from the supply of food. There are several causes of famine, including insufficient or unequal production, as well as insufficient or unequal distribution mechanisms.

The primary cause of famines, according to Sen, is distributional problems, and his empirical studies have demonstrated that distributional problems are more often involved than supply problems in causing famines.[53] This work is the result of the author's experience regarding the 1943 Bengal famine. There, millions of people were killed in front of well-stocked food stores that were protected by the government during the Great Bengal Famine. Wage earners with low incomes were not affected by food; rather, they were deprived of an income source as a result of food shortages. If they did not have income, they were unable to purchase food. Workers lost their entitlements as a result of losing the ability to feed themselves and their families. The lack of adequate wages resulted in a number of deaths among poor rural workers. Furthermore, during the Bangladesh famine, there were record levels of food supply; however, workers lost their jobs as a result of flooding and, as a result, lost their entitlement to food.

By demonstrating the impact of traditional concerns about economic incentives, Sen illustrates that famine can be greatly exacerbated.[54] A lack of income and low demand contributed to the movement of food from famine areas during the Irish famine (1840s) and the Wollo famine of Ethiopia (1973). Sen[55] and Dreze and Sen[56] noted that famines do not often occur in democracies or in countries with a free press. They[57] demonstrated that although China has generally done a better job eliminating hunger than India, India has never experienced a famine since gaining independence, while China suffered from a catastrophic famine from 1958 to 1961.

They noticed[58] that military regimes in sub-Saharan Africa were not so sensitive to victims of famine and have experienced more famines than other forms of government. A democratic government produces a greater amount of output, which reduces the risk of famine, and more importantly, democratic governments must respond to pressure from their electorates. It has also been reported that countries with a free press do not suffer from famines so often.

A result of the 'capabilities approach' is the way in which poverty is measured. In the past, researchers have attempted to analyse poverty by determining the minimum level of income required to support a family of varying size and composition.[59] Families with fewer adults, small families and those living in rural areas are likely to require more income and are likely to experience higher poverty rates than families with larger numbers of adults, urban families and families with more adults. An individual or family qualifies as poor if they fall below the poverty line, irrespective of their size or type of family. As a percentage of families living below the poverty line, poverty rates are calculated.

According to Sen, this approach to calculating poverty has numerous flaws. In the first instance, more income is linked to better health. There are many factors besides income that contribute to utility or well-being, as Sen has repeatedly emphasised. It is not considered poor under traditional standards if a person is in poor health and has a significant income that can be spent on health care. By applying the 'capability approach', deprivation is defined as the absence of capabilities, therefore, the 'wealthy but unhealthy' may be considered to be poor.

In addition to the conventional measure of poverty, the use of alternative scales presents another challenge. It has been noted by Sen many times that the distribution of family resources is highly influenced by a household with only one primary income earner. It may be possible for members of a household to receive unequal or equivalent shares or may not be able to participate in the household's average welfare. Assuming the household head has purely benevolent intentions (which contradicts other economic assumptions), equivalence scales should be used to measure household welfare, and it should be assumed that everyone in the household will have a similar level of welfare. Despite the fact that households are not always cooperative, sometimes they work together, while at other times they disagree on allocations.[60] The family is experiencing a cooperative conflict, according to Sen. A household may have different needs due to a variety of factors, including its environment, its social situation and its consumption patterns.[61]

Regardless of the demographic composition of a family, the same poverty line cannot be applied to them all. Last but not least, due to the way poverty rates are

11.3 Gender, Famine and Poverty

calculated today, if funds were taken from one family that is extremely poor and given to another family that is below poverty line, the poverty rate would decrease. According to Sen, this will worsen the lives of the very poor and should not be considered as 'poverty-reducing' or even 'welfare-enhancing'. Sen recommended the use of another method to measure poverty.

In the 1970s, Sen[62] formulated a relevant measure. In the study, it was examined not only the proportion of poor families but also the extent to which those families fell below the poverty line. There has been considerable attention paid to people who live below the poverty line. It is the most serious aspects of poverty that are given the greatest weight in this method of measuring poverty. Aside from its importance from a policy perspective, it has other implications as well. According to Sen's poverty index, government efforts will not be able to reduce poverty if they are focused on those who are just below poverty line. In order to reduce poverty, it is necessary to dedicate more resources to the ones who require the most assistance. Sen,[63] in addition to his poverty measure, has developed a measure of inequality. The Sen inequality measure also emphasises those at the bottom of the income distribution, as opposed to the Gini coefficients and coefficients of variation, that treat all components of the income distribution equally. Sen's index indicates that redistributions benefiting the poorest will probably result in greater income equality.[64]

In recent years, Sen has shifted his focus from income to capabilities as a measure of human well-being. The purpose of Sen's income is not to provide for his needs in and of itself but rather to facilitate his goals. In order to achieve this goal, individuals must be able to function and perform better. It is essential to measure welfare in this manner. To measure the degree to which people in a country were able to access basic opportunities, Sen constructed a simple summary index over the course of many years. His argument is that a measure of human well-being of this type would be more meaningful. The development of various countries and over time can also be analysed more comprehensively in a comparative manner. A measure of human development is the Human Development Index (HDI), which adjusts income for factors such as distribution, purchasing power, life expectancy, literacy and education. Therefore, HDI is an index with 1 being the highest value possible and 0 being the lowest value possible. A gender development index (GDI) and a gender empowerment metric (GEM) are also available. Human Development Reports have included these two indicators. In terms of key capabilities, the HDI is the most influential attempt to quantify success and failure in development in a variety of countries.

Through the use of the HDI, we are able to change many of our previous conclusions regarding development projects. Human development, rather than income, is a better indicator of performance for Canada. The HDI indices of Canada are one of the highest in the world, despite the fact that the country has a lower per capita income than many other developed countries. The reason for this can be attributed to Canada's income equality, literacy and longevity.

Real-world implications are also associated with HDI rankings. The majority of people tend to adopt policies that promote economic growth only whenever a country focuses primarily on income and income growth. It is likely that distributional issues will be discounted; education will be neglected; the environment will be neglected; and long-term growth will be compromised. The HDI has shifted the policy efforts on different ends as a result of its emphasis on other factors promoting well-being, including the provision of health care and education for all citizens, as well as the promotion of a sustainable environment and standard of living.[65]

11.4 The Theoretical Legacy of Sen

The theories of Sen regarding human development and the causes of poverty and famine contributed to the global fight against injustice, inequality, disease and ignorance.[66] Awarded the Nobel Prize in *Economics* in 1998 is widely recognised as a leading economist globally. Probably, the most notable contribution Sen made to welfare *Economics* was his investigation into the causes of food shortages, leading to solutions for preventing or limiting food shortages, real or perceived.

Sen has had a significant influence on the work of other Nobel laureates, as well as the United Nations (UN) and the World Bank (WB).[67] In his case, he is one of the few intellectuals who have made significant contributions to *Politics*. As a result of his work on famines, he changed public perceptions by demonstrating why people can starve despite a country's food production not declining, and his analysis of poverty significantly influenced society. Having argued that measures of Gross National Product (GNP) are insufficient to express the standard of living, he was instrumental in the development of the United Nations Human Development Index (HDI). This index is today one of the most prominent sources of comparative data on the standard of living in different countries.[68]

His work has contributed to many areas during the course of his career. As a result of his book *Collective Choice and Social Welfare*, he is widely recognised as one of the founders of contemporary social choice theory. A measure of social well-being based on different individuals' well-being was proposed in the book, which sparked interest and expanded on the ideas of the famous economist Kenneth Arrow.

His work has also had a profound impact on the fields of *Philosophy* and *Economics*. Freedom of expression is inherently at odds with the principle that people should always have a better quality of life. In particular, he has had a profound impact on *Development Economics* and *Welfare Economics* as a result of his research on famines and his novel perspective that economists must consider factors beyond income to accurately determine people's well-being. The 'capabilities approach', an area of *Economics* that has gained popularity over the past few years, focuses on how policy affects an individual's future opportunities, based on ideas Amartya developed many years ago.[69]

The work of Sen has been more than just a critique of conventional *Economics*. In order to develop a realistic and plausible theory, he developed a respective set of realistic and plausible assumptions. As part of Sen's philosophy, relationships, human potential and things other than those that can be bought and sold on the market are of utmost importance. In traditional welfare *Economics*, the importance of all of this is overlooked because it begins with the rationality assumption and ends with justifying the results of free exchange since it is unable to compare individual utility. Over Sen's career, he has focused on enhancing human potential and showing how this leads to a greater sense of well-being in society and at home. According to him, the objective of economic development is the cultivation of human capabilities. In order to understand such a perspective, it is necessary to have a broader understanding of *Economics*.[70]

The work of Sen has resulted in an entirely new perspective on human economic behaviour. The results of his research have demonstrated that individuals are shaped by the environment in which they live and possess internal value. They are more than utility maximisers. A well-functioning economic system should offer a greater variety of goods and services, as well as make life better for both men and women. This rich perspective has resulted in a more humane and broader approach to *Economics*.[71]

Key Takeaways

- Sen focuses on poverty, famine and welfare *Economics*.
- Individuals are shaped by the environment in which they live.
- What a person can do and be is called a 'capability'.
- Individuals are more than 'utility maximisers'.
- Improper distribution and production can lead to famines.
- Freedom and options are expanded through economic development.
- Men and women should both benefit from a good economic system.

Revision Questions

- Which areas do Sen's contributions fall under?
- What effect does Sen's work have on famines and hunger?
- How did Sen contribute to the creation of the HDI?
- What is Sen's main criticism of Neoclassical *Economics*?
- What is Sen's main contribution to *Economics*?

Notes

1 Nti (2022).
2 Pressman and Summerfield (2000).
3 Pazzanese (2021).
4 Steele (2001).
5 Pressman and Summerfield (2000).
6 Gaertner and Pattanaik (1988).
7 Sivaraman (2022).
8 Pazzanese (2021).

9 Sivaraman (2022).
10 Sen (1998).
11 Sen (1998).
12 Pressman and Summerfield (2000).
13 Chakrabarty (2009).
14 Sen (1998).
15 Sen (1998).
16 Sen (1998).
17 Chakraborty (2021).
18 Pazzanese (2021).
19 Sen (1960).
20 Klamer (1989).
21 Pressman and Summerfield (2000).
22 Sen (1998).
23 Pressman and Summerfield (2000)
24 Sen (1998).
25 Pressman and Summerfield (2000).
26 Pazzanese (2021).
27 Pressman and Summerfield (2000).
28 Sen (2021).
29 Basu et al. (2019).
30 Alkire and Deneulin (2009).
31 Sen (1999).
32 Sen (1990a).
33 McPherson (1992).
34 Sen (1990a).
35 Pressman and Summerfield (2000).
36 Sen (1987).
37 Sen (1987).
38 Pressman and Summerfield (2000).
39 Sen (1997).
40 Pressman and Summerfield (2000).
41 Sen (1990a).
42 Pressman and Summerfield (2000).
43 Sen (1985).
44 Sen (1970, 1976b).
45 Sen (1976a, 1983).
46 Sen (1984).
47 Sen (1984, 1985).

48 Sen (1990b).
49 Sen (1993).
50 Sen (1984).
51 Sen (1990b, 1992b, Sen (1993).
52 Dreze and Sen (1990–1991).
53 Sen (1981b), Dreze and Sen (1989) and Dreze and Sen (1990–1991).
54 Sen (1981a) and Dreze and Sen (1989).
55 Sen (1981b).
56 Dreze and Sen (1989).
57 Dreze and Sen (1996).
58 Sen (1981b), Sen (1994), Dreze and Sen (1989) and Dreze and Sen (1990–1991).
59 Ruggles (1990).
60 Sen (1990a).
61 Foster and Sen (1997), Sen (1983) and Sen (1992a).
62 Sen (1976a).
63 Sen (1973a).
64 Sen (1973b).
65 Pressman and Summerfield (2000).
66 Sen (2021).
67 Sen (2021).
68 Steele (2001).
69 Pazzanese (2021).
70 Pressman and Summerfield (2000).
71 Pressman and Summerfield (2000).

References

Alkire, S., & Deneulin, S. (2009). *Introducing the human development and capability approach. An introduction to the human development and capability approach*. Earthscan.

Basu, K., Ravi, R., & Robeyns, I. (2019). Introduction to the special issue in celebration of Amartya Sen's 85th birthday. *Journal of Human Development and Capabilities, 20*, 2.

Chakrabarty, D. (2009). Identity and violence: The illusion of destiny, by Amartya Sen. *South Asian History and Culture, 1*(1), 149–154.

Chakraborty, A. (2021). Home in the World by Amartya Sen review—The making of a Nobel laureate.

Dreze, J., & Sen, A. K. (1989). *Hunger and public action*. Clarendon Press.

Dreze, J. & Sen, A. K. (Eds). (1990–1991). The political economy of hunger (3 Vols.). Clarendon Press.

Dreze, J., & Sen, A. K. (Eds.). (1996). *Indian development: Selected regional perspectives*. Oxford University Press.

Foster, J., & Sen, A. K. (1997). On economic inequality after a quarter century. In A. K. Sen (Ed.), *On economic inequality* (2nd ed., pp. 107–219). Clarendon Press.

Gaertner, W., & Pattanaik, P. K. (1988). An interview with Amartya Sen. *Social Choice and Welfare, 5*(1), 69–79.

Klamer, A. (1989). A conversation with Amartya Sen. *Journal of Economic Perspectives, 3*(1), 135–150.
McPherson, M. (1992). Amartya Sen. In W. Samuels (Ed.), *New horizons in economic thought: Appraisals of leading economists* (pp. 294–309). Edward Elgar.
Nti.org. (2022). Amartya Sen. Retrieved June 7, 2022, from https://www.nti.org/about/people/amartya-sen/
Pazzanese, C. (2021). Amartya Sen's nine-decade journey from colonial India to Nobel Prize and beyond.
Pressman, S., & Summerfield, G. (2000). The economic contributions of Amartya Sen. *Review of Political Economy, 12*(1), 89–113.
Ruggles, P. (1990). *Drawing the line.* Urban Institute.
Sen, A. (1998). Biographical Nobel Prize.
Sen, A. (2021). A conversation with Amartya Sen. Retrieved June 9, 2022, from https://www.youtube.com/watch?v=27lcM8bYOFg&t=5s
Sen, A. K. (1960). *Choice of techniques.* Basil Blackwell.
Sen, A. K. (1970). The impossibility of a Paretian liberal. *Journal of Political Economy, 78*(1), 152–157.
Sen, A. K. (1973a). *On economic inequality.* Clarendon Press.
Sen, A. K. (1973b). On ignorance and equal distribution. *American Economic Review, 63*(5), 1022–1024.
Sen, A. K. (1976a). Poverty: An ordinal approach to measurement. *Econometrica, 44*(2), 219–231.
Sen, A. K. (1976b). Liberty, unanimity and rights. *Economica, 43*(171), 217–245.
Sen, A. K. (1981a). Ingredients of famine analysis: Availability and entitlements. *Quarterly Journal of Economics, 95*, 433–464.
Sen, A. K. (1981b). *Poverty and famines: An essay on entitlement and depression.* Oxford University Press.
Sen, A. K. (1983). Poor, relatively speaking. *Oxford Economic Papers, 35*(2), 153–169.
Sen, A. K. (1984). *Resources, values and development.* Blackwell & Harvard University Press.
Sen, A. K. (1985). The moral standing of the market. In E. F. Paul, F. D. Miller Jr., & J. Paul (Eds.), *Ethics and economics* (pp. 1–19). Basil Blackwell.
Sen, A. K. (1987). Justice. In J. Eatwell, M. Milgate, & P. Newman (Eds.), *The new Palgrave: A dictionary of economics* (Vol. 2, pp. 1039–1043). Macmillan.
Sen, A. K. (1990a). Gender and cooperative conflict. In I. Tinker (Ed.), *Persistent inequalities* (pp. 123–149). Oxford University Press.
Sen, A. K. (1990b). More than 100 million women are missing. *New York Review of Books, 37*(20), 61–66.
Sen, A. K. (1992a). *Inequality re-examined.* Clarendon Press & Harvard University Press.
Sen, A. K. (1992b). Missing women. *British Medical Journal, 304*(6827), 587–588.
Sen, A. K. (1993). The economics of life and death. *Scientific American, 268*(5), 40–47.
Sen, A. K. (1994). Population and reasoned agency. In K. Lindahl-Kiessling & H. Landberg (Eds.), *Population, economics development, and the environment* (pp. 51–78). Oxford University Press.
Sen, A. K. (1997). Maximization and the act of choice. *Econometrica, 65*(4), 745–779.
Sen, A. K. (1999). *Development as freedom.* Oxford University Press.
Sivaraman, M. (2022). *Home in the world: A memoir*: by Amartya Sen, London, Allen Lane, 2021, xv–464 pp.
Steele, J. (2001, March 31). Food for thought. London, England. *The Guardian.* Retrieved December 24, 2022, from https://www.theguardian.com/books/2001/mar/31/society.politics

Joseph Stiglitz (1943–…) 12

▶ **Learning Objectives**

After having studied this chapter, the reader should be able to:

- Understand the role of 'asymmetric information' in the economy.
- Analyse Stiglitz's view on 'sticky prices'.
- Describe the main point that the Shapiro and Stiglitz model makes.
- Discuss Stiglitz's views on globalisation.
- Present briefly Stiglitz's contribution to *Economics*.

▶ **Summary**

A very influential economist of our times and Nobel Prize laureate who is well known for his often critical views of fully unregulated free-market policies and insightful vision on globalisation is Joseph Stiglitz. It became a central focus of his research to understand the limitations of the market, known as 'market failures'. Stiglitz and his colleagues showed that even small imperfections of information could have profound effects on how the economy behaved. As a result of the failure of the socialist economies, Stiglitz concluded that the competitive equilibrium model was insufficient. Just as the socialists failed to recognise the complexity of the information problem facing the economy, the standard competitive market equilibrium model did not account for the complexity of the information problem. In a similar manner, their view of decentralisation was oversimplified. Asymmetries of information refers to the imperfection of information caused by the fact that different people in a market have different levels of knowledge. Stiglitz makes the connection between asymmetries of information and asymmetries of economic power. Besides correcting market failures, government has a role to play in redressing power imbalances. Despite the fact that government is subject to the same information imperfections as the private sector, Stiglitz demonstrated that government intervention into the market can make everyone better off in an economy. Joseph Stiglitz amongst others tried to show that the invisible hand 'is not there'. Stiglitz explained why some prices were naturally 'sticky', thereby creating market inefficiencies and preventing the effective functioning of the 'invisible hand'. The main point that the Shapiro and Stiglitz model makes is that involuntary unemployment is a potential outcome even in a competitive labour market. The purpose of Stiglitz's work was to explain why developing countries were so dissatisfied with globalisation. Simply put, many individuals believed that the system was 'rigged' against them, with global trade agreements being singled out as being especially unfair. The goal of globalisation, according to Stiglitz, was to weaken the bargaining power of workers. Regardless of how it could be obtained, corporations were looking for cheaper labour.

12.1 Introduction

Joseph Stiglitz is a highly influential economist and a Nobel Prize laureate known for his critical views on fully unregulated free-market policies as well as his insight into globalisation. It was his theory of asymmetric information in markets[1] that led to the Nobel Prize for *Economics* in 2001, and he was named by *Time* magazine in 2011 as one of the 100 most influential people in the world.[2] Among his many publications are a number of bestsellers and scholarly articles.[3]

A native of Gary, Indiana, Stiglitz was born into a Jewish family in 1943[4] and attended a public school with many immigrants. He was raised by a mother who was a teacher and a father who was an insurance agent. He grew up in an environment that deeply influenced him, one where unemployment, poverty and discrimination were all present. He also discussed political issues openly with his family and debated them. In addition to the teachers who greatly motivated him, he was left to take responsibility for his learning, and debate was his favourite extracurricular activity. As a National Merit Scholar attending Amherst College, he learned that 'asking the right question' is vitally important through the Socratic method of teaching where teachers ask questions and respond with new questions.[5]

It was during these three years from 1960 to 1963 that he attended Amherst College, where he majored in *Physics* until late in his third year, that he experienced the most intellectually formative experiences. He enrolled at MIT for graduate studies and left Amherst for MIT without receiving a degree. At MIT, he was a student for two years, completing his generals in a year and a half before beginning to write his thesis. Among his colleagues were at least four Nobel laureates, namely Samuelson, Solow, Modigliani and Arrow. With its simple and concrete models designed to answer important questions, the famous MIT style suited him well, with the models presented as more benchmarks than full descriptions. While studying, he also became aware that economists usually belong to 'circles', which are based on the 'school' and/or the 'subject'.[6]

12.2 Asymmetry of Information

The MIT graduate, after two years of study, moved to Cambridge, United Kingdom, at a time when the city was on the left. The colleges of Cambridge were populated among others by Joan Robinson, Nicky Kaldor and Piero Sraffa; Joan Robinson was initially assigned to be his tutor. Eventually, Frank Hahn became his tutor. Throughout his career, he has remained concerned with inequality, which he pursued as he began to dissect the asymmetry of information in *Economics*, as we shall see later.[7]

At Cambridge, Stiglitz also worked on an important project related to the interaction of income distribution and macroeconomic behaviour. Macroeconomic models at the time were based on the assumption that wages and prices are fixed. However, the problem was the dynamics of adjustment, as wages and prices fell significantly during the Great Depression. Together with George Akerlof, he demonstrated that such dynamics can lead to cyclical fluctuations.[8] After Cambridge, he became an Assistant Professor at MIT. He then went to Yale, where his work earned him an indefinite exemption from the draft. There, he continued to work on the dynamics of the economy and delved into the *Economics of Uncertainty*, which led to his theory on the Asymmetry of Information.[9]

Professor Stiglitz has held a number of academic positions, both permanent and visiting, at Yale, Stanford and Oxford, Princeton and Columbia, Sciences Po, the Ecole Polytechnique de Paris, and in addition he served as the chair of the Brooks World Poverty Institute at the University of Manchester. His other positions include being senior vice president of the President's Council of Economic Advisers (Clinton administration), advising Barack Obama, serving as chief economist for the World Bank, president of the International Economic Association and member of its economic advisory committee, as well as advising the Greek government during the Euro crisis. As of 2009, he served as the chair of at least two United Nations' Commissions. Stiglitz's work has been recognised widely, and he has received a large number of honorary degrees and awards.[10]

12.2 Asymmetry of Information

Stiglitz was greatly assisted by his education at Amherst and MIT in approaching the problems now known as the *Economics of Information*. His childhood was marked by the cold war. The communist system promised fast growth, but with limited liberty. Also, large segments of the population were living in poverty as a result of repeated periods of unemployment. The question that mattered most was how, and how effectively, various systems addressed the problem of making decisions based on incomplete information. One of the focuses of his research was to understand market limitations, the so-called market failures.[11]

▶ In the past, economists have employed models assuming that information is 'perfect', that is, that all actors are aware of the relevant factors in an equal and transparent manner. Even though they knew that information was imperfect, they argued that a world with a certain degree of imperfections of information could be comparable to one with perfect information. Stiglitz and his colleagues demonstrated that even a small error in information could have a profound effect on the behaviour of the economy.[12]

In the opinion of Stiglitz,[13] a number of early economists were aware of the importance of information and, in Smith's observation, as interest rates rise, borrowers leave the market. Because it is difficult to observe precisely what workers do, Marshall argued that workers are not necessarily paid according to the effort they undertake, and he thought that information imperfections 'greatly complicate' economic analysis.[14]

Friedrich Hayek, who previously won a Nobel Prize, is also included on the Stiglitz list. Hayek, according to Stiglitz, did not appreciate the problem of information, preferring instead to think of prices as effective signals of relative scarcity. However, it was during his involvement in socialist planning that he became interested in dispersed and tacit information. It was debated whether socialist planners fulfil the role of an auctioneer in the Walrasian sense by gathering centralised information to develop an efficient general equilibrium. In Hayek's view, socialist planners are incapable of planning efficiently. His argument ultimately rested on the concept of 'asymmetric information'. In his view, the central planner cannot learn the hidden information in the economy, and therefore will not be able to assume the role of an auctioneer.[15]

When Stiglitz discussed transition problems in *Whither Socialism?*, he specifically focused on such information issues.[16] As a consequence, he concluded that the failure of the so-called socialist economies was related to beliefs concerning the competitive equilibrium model. Similar to the socialists, the competitive market model was not able to adequately describe the complexity of the information problem. They also oversimplified the concept of decentralisation.[17]

Stiglitz's work on the Asymmetry of Information refers to imperfection of knowledge because of the fact that different people have different perspectives. For instance, the seller of a motorbike may have more information about the motorbike than the buyer; the purchaser of insurance might be able to estimate his chances of having an accident based on his driving style than the insurer; the worker may be able to estimate his capabilities better than a prospective employer; the borrower may be able to assess his chances of repaying the loan better than the lender. However, information asymmetries are only one aspect of information imperfections, and all of them may have substantial consequences.[18]

Furthermore, bankruptcy would not exist in a world with perfect information. What is the point of lending to someone who is known to be unable to repay their loan? Generally, privatisation failures can be traced in part to a lack of corporate governance, as well as information asymmetries between managers and owners. Consequently, concerns about bankruptcy are based on a theory of corporate finance, which is a theory of asymmetric information. Nonetheless, Stiglitz argues that asymmetries in information are linked to asymmetries in economic market power.

Additionally, government plays a crucial role in redressing power imbalances as well as correcting market failures.[19]

In this vein, another important result of his work was the finding that Adam Smith's 'invisible hand' was not visible, it actually did not exist. Despite the government facing the same information imperfections as the private sector, Stiglitz demonstrated that government interventions can be beneficial to all parties involved. Furthermore, economists have recognised for many years that market solutions are often inefficient when faced with externalities to economic activity. Often, some commodities are produced in excess, such as pollution-generating steel, while others are produced insufficiently, such as research that advances knowledge. In his analysis, he demonstrated that as soon as one acknowledges that information is not perfect, externalities become evident, as well as market failures becoming apparent.[20]

As a student, Stiglitz was taught that demand equalled supply, which led to strange results. For example, if the supply of labour equalled the demand, unemployment would not be possible. In addition, Stiglitz grew up in Gary, Indiana, a manufacturing town on Lake Michigan's southern shore that experienced poverty, unemployment and discrimination. In fact, he studied *Economics* in order to gain a deeper understanding and to take action regarding these phenomena. He was taught mathematical models which assumed that unemployment did not exist, and this is likely what led Stiglitz to work on these topics and develop his theory of 'sticky prices'.[21]

12.3 Sticky Prices

For decades and even centuries, conventional *Economics* assumed that Adam Smith's 'invisible hand' operated seamlessly. Due to the demand outpacing supply, prices moved smoothly upward and then fell, maintaining equilibrium. Joseph Stiglitz is one of the individuals who tried to prove that the 'invisible hand' does not exist.[22]

Indeed, the truth was somewhat different—that prices, wages and interest rates, among others, were frequently 'sticky', a fact which prevented the market from 'clearing'. These factors contributed to prolonged unemployment among unemployed workers. However, some experts responded that 'unemployment' did not actually exist, but was the result of stubborn workers who refused to accept the going wage.[23]

John Maynard Keynes recognised the reality of involuntary unemployment early on, believing that wages do not respond to labour supply gluts and remain above what workers earn. Price stickiness was a concept that Keynes used in his work. However, it was only an assumption since he did not explain analytically why wages and interest rates were resistant to supply and demand.[24] The puzzle, however, was solved by Joseph Stiglitz. In a series of ground-breaking papers, Stiglitz drew together some facts about the economy, combined them, and demonstrated why some prices are naturally 'sticky', leading to market inefficiencies and impeding the effective functioning of the invisible hand.[25]

In his famous argument, Stiglitz laid out his case over a 10-year period. This research on price rigidities was based on the work of other economists, such as George Akerlof. A series of articles by Stiglitz authored in the 1970s and 1980s, however, radically altered the conventional, mainstream approach to microeconomic theory. More specifically, Stiglitz wrote an article[26] explaining the causes of wage rigidity. Other important works followed, including an article on credit rationing and interest rate rigidity with Andrew Weiss, one on the efficiency wage[27] and, he also co-authored a seminal article on 'endogenous unemployment' with Carl Shapiro.[28]

According to Stiglitz, rigid prices can be explained by an intuitive logic. As we can see, people often 'shirk', that is, put in little or no effort, if there are no consequences, and that the most common consequence for 'shirking' in the workplace is losing employment. However, if one assumes that the market operates without friction and reaches the equilibrium of full employment, this penalty is ineffective. When workers can immediately find a new position, threatening them with the loss of their job will have no impact.[29]

If we want to provide incentives to workers in order not to shirk, we must pay them above market wages, in order to make job losses more costly. There is no doubt that if this works for one company, it will work for others, leading to a rise in wages and eventually an increase in supply over demand. This will result in joblessness. In the case where all firms pay the same wage, a potential threat to fire a worker would still be effective, since the worker who loses a job faces the prospect of being unemployed. Consequently, the market is about to reach a new equilibrium position where unemployment does exist, but where wages do not decrease. The Shapiro–Stiglitz equilibrium can, in brief, be described in this way.[30] Shapiro and Stiglitz's model makes the significant point that involuntary unemployment is indeed a labour market outcome regardless of the level of competition. As a consequence, we are led to Stiglitz's work on globalisation, which has been widely discussed.

12.4 On Globalisation

Stiglitz explained how the globalisation process had been managed, particularly by international financial institutions such as the IMF. His book *Globalization and Its Discontents* was translated into 35 languages.[31] With regard to this work, Stiglitz was not very supportive of the IMF, which he considered to be most ineffective when it came to dealing with developing economies or former communist nations. In his book, Stiglitz posed the following question: People in developing countries were led to believe that globalisation would increase their well-being. However, why had so many individuals become so hostile towards it? By way of example, according to data that Stiglitz cites, income stagnation for the bottom 90 per cent of the population in the United States has lasted for more than three decades, while the median income regarding full-time male workers is lower when adjusted for inflation, when compared to that four decades ago. Additionally, this has affected the life expectancy of Americans. Stiglitz's book attempted to explain why developing countries were so dissatisfied with globalisation. A number of people have expressed concerns about the unfairness of the global trade agreements, and they have claimed that the system is rigged against them.[32]

Assuming that markets function perfectly, as is the standard assumption in most conventional approaches, free trade would equalise wages worldwide. The reason for this is that the movement of goods replaces the movement of people. If, for example, goods are imported from China that require many labourers to produce, then the need for labourers in other parts of the world, such as Europe and the United States, will be reduced. As a result, it is as if workers from China continue to migrate to Europe and the United States until wage disparities are eliminated. As a consequence, the inability of globalisation to satisfy the promises of conventional analyses undermines trust and confidence in the concept and the process.[33]

All of this openness was supposed to lead to greater prosperity for people, and the economies were to implement policies to make sure that the benefits would be shared widely. Stiglitz's analysis focuses on the case of the U.S. trade negotiations, which he has been following closely for more than three decades. There is no doubt that U.S. trade negotiators achieved most of their goals. However, they faced difficulties in obtaining what they desired. Stiglitz contends that corporations set the agenda behind closed doors. It was a plan authored by and for large, usually multinational, corporations, and not for ordinary citizens around the globe.[34] According to Stiglitz,[35] one of the objectives of globalisation was to weaken the bargaining power of workers. It was in the interests of the corporate agenda to find cheaper labour at any cost.

Additionally, the generous government bailouts for the banks following the financial meltdown of 2007 gave the impression that this failure was not simply due to economic mistakes made by the banks. Rather than promoting policies to increase equality, it proposed reorganising markets in a way that slowed economic growth; as a result, banks, big corporations and the wealthy benefited from the changes. There was a reduction in workers' bargaining power. Meanwhile, financialisation was accelerating. Stiglitz's message was that globalisation itself is not the problem, but rather how it was being managed.[36]

12.5 The Theoretical Legacy of Stiglitz

Based on asymmetric information models, Stiglitz views the economic system through the macroeconomic lens of (New) Keynesian macroeconomics.[37] The evidence indicates that Keynes was right in his assertion that there exists persistent involuntary unemployment and that fluctuations in aggregate demand can cause fluctuations in unemployment. Meanwhile, he was probably right that savings do not drive investment, and fiscal policy can be used to address these issues, following Greenwald and Stiglitz.[38]

Stiglitz's work rebuked the part of macroeconomic theory, which puts a heavy burden on 'rational expectations'. When there is asymmetry in information, the policy approaches will differ significantly even though 'rational expectations' prevail. As a consequence, Keynes' reputation in *Economics* has been restored to a significant extent.[39]

Lastly, there is a growing field of dynamic economic analysis. As a result, a variety of Keynesian macroeconomists, as well as a number of the so-called New Classical economists are becoming interested in this area of analysis.[40] According to Stiglitz and his colleagues, asymmetric information models are backed by a high level of certainty, and there is a high probability of observing the outcome. With an ever-increasing degree of uncertainty, the question of how those who are involved learn these probabilities, and whether they are capable of doing so, has become pressing, especially in an increasingly complex world plagued by nonlinearity.[41]

Stiglitz believed that the government had a significant role to play in the economic recovery. In light of this, he focused on how it could fulfil that role efficiently.[42] First, the *Economics of information* offers a theoretical context within which to consider the issue in an appropriate manner.[43]

The concept of 'rational expectations' was once very popular among economists. These models made the assumption that all participants would have the same (if not perfect) information and act 'rationally'. Also, among other things, they assumed that markets would be efficient and unemployment would not occur. These models still persist.[44]

There is, therefore, a paradox of contemporary *Economics* that despite the commonplace nature of lessons regarding the limits of the markets in macroeconomic environments, most international institutions continue to emphatically ignore them. Consequently, there can be friction between these international agencies and local communities and societies.[45]

To sum up, with Stiglitz's work, we gained a better understanding of numerous economic models and what their limitations may be, especially when asymmetric information prevails. Aside from his pioneering work on asymmetric information, Joseph Stiglitz has made substantial contributions to our understanding of unemployment in market economies, as well as had constructive criticisms of globalisation and a variety of other topics of great interest such as inequality and fully unregulated markets. Therefore, Stiglitz's impact has been immense, as he has profoundly influenced the fields of microeconomics, macroeconomics and the global political economy.

Key Takeaways

- Information asymmetries are related to power asymmetries.
- Information imperfections can have profound consequences.
- As a rule, the 'invisible hand' doesn't exist.
- In competitive markets, involuntary unemployment is highly likely.
- Globalisation aims to weaken workers' power.

> **Revision Questions**
> - What was Joseph Stiglitz awarded the Nobel Prize for?
> - What is Stiglitz's view of the asymmetry of information?
> - What is the concept of 'sticky prices'?
> - What is his opinion of the role of the state in the market?
> - How does Stiglitz view 'the invisible hand'?
> - What is his opinion of globalisation?
> - What is Stiglitz's main contribution to *Economics*?

Notes

1 Britannica (2022a).
2 Brown (2011).
3 Columbia (2022).
4 Kern (2003).
5 Stiglitz (2002a).
6 Stiglitz (2002a).
7 Stiglitz (2002a).
8 Stiglitz (2002a).
9 Stiglitz (2002a).
10 Columbia (2022).
11 Stiglitz (2002a).
12 Stiglitz (2001).
13 Stiglitz (1987, 2000, 2002c).
14 Rosser (2003).
15 Rosser (2003).
16 Stiglitz (1994).
17 Stiglitz (2002a).
18 Stiglitz (2001).
19 Stiglitz (2001).
20 Stiglitz (2001).
21 Stiglitz (2001).
22 Basu (2015).
23 Basu (2015).
24 Basu (2015).
25 Basu (2015).
26 Stiglitz (1974).
27 Stiglitz (1976).

28 Basu (2015).
29 Basu (2015).
30 Basu (2015).
31 Columbia (2022).
32 Stiglitz (2017).
33 Stiglitz (2016).
34 Stiglitz (2017).
35 Stiglitz (2017).
36 Stiglitz (2016).
37 Rosser (2003).
38 Greenwald and Stiglitz (1987).
39 Rosser (2003).
40 Brock and Hommes (1998), Sargent (1993).
41 Rosser (2003).
42 Stiglitz (1991, 1997).
43 Stiglitz (2002a).
44 Stiglitz (2002b).
45 Stiglitz (2001).

References

Basu, K. (2015, December 15). Stiglitz's sticky prices. *Project Syndicate*.
Brock, W. A., & Hommes, C. H. (1998). Heterogeneous beliefs and routes to chaos in a simple asset pricing model. *Journal of Economic Dynamics and Control, 22*, 1235–1274.
Brown, G. (2011, April 21). The 2011 TIME 100. *time.com*. Retrieved May 9, 2022, from http://www.time.com/time/specials/packages/article/0%2C28804%2C2066367_2066369_2066440%2C00.html
Columbia University. (2022). Faculty homepages: Joseph Stiglitz. Retrieved May 9, 2022, from https://www8.gsb.columbia.edu/faculty/jstiglitz/bio
Encyclopedia Britannica. (2022a). Joseph E. Stiglitz. https://www.britannica.com/biography/Joseph-Stiglitz
Greenwald, B., & Stiglitz, J. E. (1987). Keynesian, new Keynesian, and new classical economics. *Oxford Economic Papers, 39*, 119–133.
Kern, J. (2003, September 18). Interview with Professor Joseph Stiglitz. *Social Enterprise News*. Retrieved May 9, 2022, from https://www8.gsb.columbia.edu/socialenterprise/newsn/423/interview-with-professor-joseph-stiglitz
Rosser, B. J., Jr. (2003). A Nobel Prize for Asymmetric Information: The economic contributions of George Akerlof, Michael Spence and Joseph Stiglitz. *Review of Political Economy, 15*(1), 3–21.
Sargent, T. J. (1993). *Bounded rationality in macroeconomics*. Clarendon Press.
Stiglitz, J. (1974). Alternative theories of wage determination and unemployment in LDC's: The labor turnover model. *The Quarterly Journal of Economics, 88*(2), 194–227.

Stiglitz, J. E. (1976). The efficiency wage hypothesis, surplus labour, and the distribution of income in L.D.C.s. *Oxford Economic Papers, 28*(2), 185–207.
Stiglitz, J. E. (1987). The causes and consequences of the dependence of quality on price. *Journal of Economic Literature, 25*, 1–48.
Stiglitz, J. E. (1991). The economic role of the state: Efficiency and effectiveness. In T. P. Hardiman & M. Mulreany (Eds.), *Efficiency and effectiveness in the public domain, the economic role of the state* (pp. 37–59). Institute of Public Administration.
Stiglitz, J. E. (1994). *Whither socialism?* MIT Press.
Stiglitz, J. E. (1997, May). Looking out for the National Interest: The Principles of the Council of Economic Advisers. *American Economic Review, 87*(2), 109–113.
Stiglitz, J. E. (2000). The contributions of the economics of information to twentieth century economics. *Quarterly Journal of Economics, 115*, 1441–1478.
Stiglitz, J. E. (2001, December 4). Asymmetries of information and economic policy. *Project Syndicate*.
Stiglitz, J. E. (2002a). *The Nobel Prizes 2001* (T. Frängsmyr, Ed.). Nobel Foundation.
Stiglitz, J. E. (2002b, December 11). Celebrating the irrational. *Project Syndicate*.
Stiglitz, J. E. (2002c). Information and the change in the paradigm in economics. *American Economic Review, 92*, 460–501.
Stiglitz, J. (2016, August 5), Globalization and its new discontents. *Project Syndicate*.
Stiglitz, J. E. (2017, December 5). Globalization: Time to look at historic mistakes to plot the future, *The Guardian*.

Paul Krugman (1953–…) 13

▶ **Learning Objectives**

After having studied this chapter, the reader should be able to:

- Understand the term 'New Economic Geography'.
- Analyse Krugman's ideas on free trade.
- Describe Krugman's point of view on the role of the state.
- Discuss the Keynesian resurgence of 2008–2009.
- Present briefly Krugman's contribution to *Economics*.

▶ **Summary**

Krugman is perhaps most famous for his contributions on international trade and economic geography. He is well known for having incorporated economies of scale into the so-called General Equilibrium models so that we may better understand both the determinants of international trade as well as where production takes place. The results of his research assisted in the formation of New Economic Geography (NEG) and attempt to explain the unequal spatial development of economic regions on a global scale through a new area of economic research. Krugman's model shows that when trade barriers are lowered, firms have access to larger markets, which is important for expanding production and seeking profitability internationally and achieving economies of scale. Consequently, trade benefits are not derived from specialisation, but rather from economies of scale, more intensive competition and the possibility of obtaining a large variety of products and services. Despite the positive effects of globalisation, Krugman points out that since the 1980s, there has been a rise in inequality as a result of 'hyper-globalisation'. There are many benefits to trade even between similar countries, including the possibility of firms cutting costs by producing at a larger, more efficient scale, as well as an increase in the number of brands available and a sharpening of competition among them. Based on his approach, Krugman distinguished between a 'core' and a 'periphery'. It is a result of the interaction between economies of scale and transportation costs that geographical concentration occurs. As Krugman explains, he was interested in explaining why manufacturing tends to concentrate in one or a few regions of a country (core) while the remaining regions are used as agricultural suppliers (periphery).

13.1 Introduction

In recent years, Paul Krugman has been recognised as one of the most influential economists and opinion makers in the field of *Economics*, both globally and in the United States. Krugman is perhaps most famous for his contribution in international trade and economic geography. In a globalised economy following World War II, he is well-known for having incorporated 'economies of scale' into General Equilibrium models so that we may better understand both the determinants of international trade as well as where production takes place.[1] The results of his research assisted in the formation of New Economic Geography (NEG), an area of economic research that attempts to analyse the uneven development of economic regions on a global scale.[2]

Paul Robin Krugman was born in 1953 to a Jewish family[3] in Albany, New York. In 1974, he received a Bachelor of Arts degree with a major in *Economics* from Yale University and a PhD with a major in *Economics* from MIT in 1977. During the writing of his thesis, Krugman worked under the supervision of Rüdiger Dornbusch (1942–2002), who Krugman described as 'one of the great economics teachers of all time' who 'attracted the best and the brightest students at MIT at a time when MIT had the best and brightest anywhere' and 'almost everyone in macro or international [economics] who has since risen to some reputation was a Rudi Dornbusch student'.[4] The idea of a monopolistically competitive trade model was one of the ideas Krugman presented to Dornbusch in 1978. Krugman wrote on this: 'I went home to work on it the next day—and knew within a few hours that I had the key to my whole career in hand. I distinctly remember staying up all night in excitement'.[5] Of course, it was by no means an easy task. 'It took a while to convince anyone else of the truth of that vision. In fact the next year and a half was deeply frustrating: rejections by journals, lack of interest by most of my senior colleagues […], and a decision by the Yale department not to give me a research fellowship'.[6] But he never gave up.

In 1978, Krugman wrote 'The Theory of Interstellar Trade'. In that work, he explored how interest rates could be computed on goods in transit that are travelling at near the speed of light! He said that this essay cheered himself up as 'an oppressed assistant professor, caught up in the academic rat race'.[7] After all, Krugman's suggestion has always been to 'start with an informal verbal story, often one drawn from casual empiricism or from non-mainstream economic literature'.[8] And maybe,

13.1 Introduction

this is because: 'conventional wisdom [...] very heavily tends to reflect the preferences and interests of the elite'.[9]

His career as an assistant professor at Yale began in 1975, and he worked there until 1980. In addition, between 1979 and 1980, he served as a visiting assistant professor at MIT. In the following years, he served as an associate professor at the same institute until 1984. In 1982 and 1983, he served as an international policy economist at the Council of Economic Advisers. During the period 1984–2000, he served as a professor at MIT and Stanford University, as well as at the famous London School of Economics. Princeton University hosted him as a professor since 2000.[10] When he retired from Princeton in 2015, he wrote that while he still cherished and respected Princeton, he wished to relocate to New York City to give voice to public policy concerns.[11]

What Krugman most characteristically remembers from the early stages of his academic career time is 'going to conferences. These were not lavish affairs: we are talking about flying economy class, taking the bus in from the airport, and staying on the sixth floor of a hotel with no elevator or in a conference center with bathrooms down the hall'.[12] He described himself as 'very shy and lonely, and [...] hoped that getting out into the real world would help me break out of my personal shell'.[13]

Of course, Krugman has also served in other important roles, including research associate at the National Bureau of Economic Research and member of the Group of Thirty. A number of organisations and countries have retained him as a consultant, including the Federal Reserve Bank of New York, the World Bank, the International Monetary Fund and the United Nations, as a member of the Board of Advisors, Institute of International Economics, and as a fellow of the American Academy of Arts and Sciences, and the Econometric Society.[14]

Krugman wrote several books in addition to his seminal academic articles. He also contributed hundreds of articles to professional journals and news magazines. Columns in *Fortune* and *The New York Times* were among his most popular pieces. As part of his prolific career, he wrote the textbook *International Economics* (with Maurice Obstfeld), as well as a number of non-academic bestsellers including *The Return of Depression Economics*, which draws a comparison between the current financial crisis and the Great Depression and the return of depression economies in the wake of the Asian crisis and Japan's so-called lost decade. An updated version of *The Return of Depression Economics and the Crisis of 2008* includes the crisis and the related measures, comparing it to the Great Depression. A study of the last decades of American history and the inequalities created was presented in Krugman's book *The Conscience of a Liberal*, which became the title of his blog in *The New York Times*.[15]

He has received many accolades for his career, including the title 'Most Important Political Columnist in America' by *The Washington Monthly*. Aside from this, Krugman has an international reputation that extends far beyond the United States. According to the *Asia Times*, Krugman is the 'Mick Jagger of political/economic punditry'. *The Economist* argued that he is the 'most celebrated economist of his generation'. He also received a prize commonly known as the European Pulitzer Prize, the Asturias Award, awarded by the King of Spain.[16]

As a result of his accomplishments, in 1991 the American Economic Association awarded him with the John Bates Clark Prize for economists under the age of 40. He was awarded the George Eccles Prize that same year. His work was recognised with the Adam Smith Award in 1995. A Nikkei Prize was awarded to Krugman, Fujita and Venables in 2001. The North American Regional Science Council recognised Krugman with the William Alonso Memorial Prize a year later. Finally, it was his contribution to international trade and economic geography that earned him the Nobel Prize in *Economics* in 2008, an honour that recognised his lifetime of work.[17]

13.2 International Trade

Theorists have long struggled with the problem of increasing returns and economies of scale. It follows that, in principle, in the event that larger firms have lower costs, one firm could supply the entire market. Consumers' love for variety, however, negates the advantages of standard models. There is a higher level of satisfaction associated with having a variety of goods as opposed to having many products of one type. Consequently, firms are motivated to produce a wide range of products as a result of this situation. The Krugman paper assumed that the CES utility function fits a model of a 'preference for diversity' that had been developed by Avinash Dixit and Joseph Stiglitz in 1977.[18] Production of a new variety, however, involves various types of costs, such as setup costs, which result in a decline in the average costs, since a greater quantity is produced, which limits the varieties that the market can supply with profit. Therefore, the market is fragmented between competing companies, each offering distinctive products.[19]

In the context of the aforementioned setup, Krugman was presented with a tool that allowed him to open the long-closed 'black box'. As a result of his use of this tool, Krugman was able to save *Economics* from counterfactual doctrines. As per one of the founding doctrines of the discipline, countries are best served by specialising as well as exchanging. They should focus on what they are good at and import the rest. Traditionally, trade theory was highly influenced by the 'comparative advantage' approach, expressed by the relative costs of labour in David Ricardo's model and the relative endowments of the factors in Heckscher–Ohlin's model. As a result of the difference in the countries, trade is triggered in both cases. A country exports a product in which comparative labour costs (or labour productivity) differ from one country to another, whereas one country exports products that are intensive in a factor that it is abundantly stocked with.[20]

Is there a reason, for instance, that Italy would import French cars while France would import Italian cars? He showed that when barriers are lowered, firms gain access to larger markets, which is important for expanding production and seeking profitability internationally and achieving economies of scale. They are, however, exposed to competition from competing foreign firms, which reduces their operating margins. Although several firms may be forced to exit the market due to losses,

13.2 International Trade

consumers will still have a greater selection of products because of the domestic survivors as well as the foreign competitors. Consequently, trade benefits are not derived from specialisation, but rather from the so-called scale economies, intensive competition and the possibility of obtaining various products.[21]

Of course, Krugman pointed out that the 'hyper-globalisation' has led to rising inequality.[22] It is nevertheless clear that trade is beneficial in general, because it increases the available volume of goods and services.[23] Krugman's support of globalisation and free trade is largely based on this framework.[24]

In the meantime, consumers' love for variety explains the existence of different types of cars such as French and Italian ones. Nevertheless, due to economies of scale, it is practically not quite profitable to expand the production of French or Italian cars all over the world; instead, each car's production is 'concentrated' in a few specific factories and, consequently, in a few specific countries. He demonstrated in his 1979 paper that when consumer preferences are structured in a way that encourages a love of variety (i.e. Dixit–Stiglitz preferences), and production costs are set in a manner that leads to an average cost decline across a production scale, trade patterns can be derived that go hand in hand with statistical data. He also discussed the impediments to trade when labour is interregionally mobile. Core–periphery (CP) models would be based on such considerations.[25]

As part of the new trade theory, the so-called comparative advantage approach is acknowledged as one of the reasons for international trade. In addition to this, it emphasises the role played by increased returns as a source of trade. Comparative advantage is the basis for trade among rich and poor countries. In spite of this, the trade between advanced economies depends on economies of scale or increasing returns in which manufactured goods exchange for manufactured goods. It is common for countries to specialise in a narrow range of products so as to exploit economies of scale. As a result of international trade, consumers are able to choose from a greater variety of goods, leading to greater choice for them. There are increasing returns on investment as a result of specialisation in this type of trade.[26]

The previous analysis has paved the way for models studying the impact of returns to scale and (monopolistic) competition in more sophisticated set ups. Transportation costs have decreased substantially in recent years, which has contributed to the growth of trade. However, most trade models do not address this issue. An important contribution was made here by Krugman:[27] it is convenient for goods to be shipped abroad, but a portion of those goods 'melt away' while in transit. Krugman was able to identify the so-called 'home market effect', stating that firms 'concentrate' more heavily in large markets than in small ones. Scale economies are realised as a result of increasing returns and reducing transportation costs by concentrating production in the largest markets. A number of relevant contributions include Krugman (1981) as well as Helpman and Krugman (1985), providing models of inter-industry and/or intra-industry trade. A combination of the new and old trade theories has been crucial in order to make empirical analyses about cross-country differences.[28]

Hence, New Trade Theory (NTT) was developed as a way of modelling trade. NTT has deeply affected trade policy. It enables accurate modelling concerning the effect of 'liberalisation' on trade, the location of production and the remuneration of factors. In addition, it can be used to analyse the welfare of an individual. There has been a tremendous amount of literature on calibrated numerical models in recent years as realistic models have become too complex to be assessed with econometric models and several institutions have used the model developed by Baldwin and Krugman (1988).[29]

13.3 New Economic Geography

Paul Krugman's contributions in the field of New Trade Theory (NTT) eventually led to what is commonly known as the 'New Economic Geography' (NEG), developed in his article 'Increasing Returns and Economic Geography' (1991), in *The Journal of Political Economy*. As Krugman himself describes it, the transition from NTT to NEG was 'obvious in retrospect; [...] the only good news is that nobody else picked up that $100 bill lying on the sidewalk during this period'.[30] And regarding his idea on NEG he wrote: 'Coming up with a good idea, with an insight into the way the world works that is really new and that you really believe in, is a deeply satisfying experience. [...] When that happens, never mind if you are a shy and mild-mannered professor: you feel like some archetypal hero on a mythic quest'.[31]

As Krugman demonstrated in his seminal article in 1991, regional imbalances are the result of a variety of factors. Developing an explanation was hampered by the existing dominant paradigms based on constant returns to scale.[32] Starret (1978) presented several limitations associated with constant returns.[33] A competitive equilibrium with inter-locational trade (i.e. transportation) cannot exist in an Arrow–Debreu (1954) framework characterised by: (i) constant returns to scale, (ii) finite agents and locations, (iii) homogeneous space and (iv) costly transportation. It is understood that homogeneous space refers to the absence of location-based preferences or production technologies. In the case of fully divisible economic activities, there exists a competitive equilibrium where each location is autonomous and no trade takes place among locations.[34]

It is therefore necessary to violate at least one assumption to analyse regional specialisation and spatial inequalities. Therefore, *Economics* has seen the appearance of models based on Ricardian advantages, agglomeration externalities and imperfect competition. Agglomeration and very high spatial imbalances cannot be explained by the first type of model. For the second type, the principle of constant returns and perfect competition is applied. The result is that models incorporating agglomeration externalities are unable to explain the microeconomic interactions that are the source of the spatial externalities. In such models, imperfect competition is considered, and monopolistic models of competition in the spirit of Dixit–Stiglitz can be especially useful in this regard.[35]

Firms make pricing decisions based on the spatial distribution of consumers and competitors. There is an appeal to monopolistic competition models. Given that no strategic interaction exists among the firms, the issue of equilibrium in oligopolistic competition cannot arise. Furthermore, monopolistic competition is more tractable

13.3 New Economic Geography

than competitive markets. In view of the framework's assumptions that increasing returns to scale are derived at the plant level, along with the fact that transportation is a costly operation, location decisions are not straightforward. Therefore, any model attempting to explain spatial imbalances must include both of these ingredients.[36]

Price competition is regarded as one of the strongest dispersive forces. However, by differentiating products, firms are able to access a wider market, meet greater demand and reduce transport costs, thereby reducing price competition. It has already been mentioned that the 'home market' effect is also at work. Firms are generally more attracted to large markets. Nevertheless, this view assumes that consumers cannot migrate between markets, so the size of the market is exogenous.

The Krugman model describes an industrial 'core' surrounded by an agricultural 'periphery'. Economies of scale, as well as transportation costs are responsible for geographical concentration. He is concerned with determining why manufacturing tends to be concentrated in a country (core) while the rest serve as agricultural suppliers (periphery). Another assumption is that the external economies that cause the core–periphery pattern are external economies that are the result of a shock to demand or supply.[37]

CP (Core–Periphery) is probably the most important contribution Krugman (1991) made to this issue, which established the foundation of the New Economic Geography (NEG). There are the same fundamental elements of the CP model as those in NTT: monopolistic competition, growing returns and a love of variety. In addition to these elements, Krugman emphasised the importance of free movement of workers across sectors and space, as well as transportation costs. A key issue that must be addressed is how to allocate economic activity and population among the two regions. Do you anticipate that manufacturing will be concentrated in one region? Is there going to be a core and a periphery in terms of the population? Economic experts were provided with a relevant framework through which we can understand the world in which we live. It is the central tendency of firms and workers to gather in the same location in order to lower the costs of transporting goods. As a result, a tendency for individuals to seek out natural inputs such as farmland is pulling them apart.[38]

The impact of some workers' migration on global welfare, as a result of this model, impacts the relative attractiveness of origin and destination regions. The CP model generally consists of two regions, two sectors—the first with monopolistic competition according to Dixit–Stiglitz and the second with perfect competition—and two factors of production. In the agricultural sector, there is one input that is not regionally mobile. In addition, there is another form of input that is mobile regionally and used in the industrial sector. A combination of market size and cost of living leads to the agglomeration of industries. In conjunction with the growth of this region, as well as the market, more industries are attracted to this area. This circular causation generates a 'centripetal' force.[39]

However, the crowding effect in a more concentrated market leads to an increase in price competition, which acts as a dispersant force. As a result of all factors taken into consideration, transportation costs are the most important factor to consider when analysing the spatial distribution of industry. CP models account for both convergence and divergence, in contrast with most conventional models which predicted only convergence.[40] If trade relies heavily on economies of scale, Krugman supports the conclusion that regions with the highest production will have a higher profitability and, hence, attract more production. It is expected that instead of distribution of production evenly throughout the globe, it will be concentrated in several geographic areas that will become densely populated as well as have an increased level of income as a result of this trend.[41]

According to Krugman and Venables (1995) and Venables (1996), vertical linkages are a factor that contributes to agglomeration and dispersion. There is a basic concept here that the sectoral agglomeration in a region exists because there is already an agglomeration of an adjacent vertically connected sector in that region. In comparison to the CP approach, this framework involves a different set of forces. In this instance, higher income leads to higher consumer demand, which in turn results in a market expansion effect. It is also possible, however, that there will be a dispersion force if wages are too high. As a result of this framework, an agglomeration process may, in fact, turn out to be a non-perpetual process. A bell-shaped curve of spatial development results from economic integration. As a result, this model anticipates the possibility of gradual desertification being followed by re-industrialisation of the periphery.[42]

In the years following the publication of NEG, it has made such an impression in the economic geographer's field that Krugman's contributions have often been viewed with harshness.[43] Krugman, for example, has engaged in a lively discussion with economists who specialise in geography.[44] Even so, he has always maintained an awareness of the limitations associated with NEG.[45]

▶ While the field has crossed over the boundaries of conventional Economics, the fact that it did so only signifies the enormous impact Paul Krugman has had on scientific scholarship as a whole.[46]

13.4 Depressions, Inequality and Growth

His 1979 article in the *Journal of Money, Credit, and Banking* represents a seminal contribution on currency crises. As Krugman discussed in this article, misaligned fixed exchange rate regimes have a high probability of ending in a sudden speculative attack rather than a smooth exit.[47] As part of the original generation of models for currency crises, his work is probably one of the most significant articles in the field.[48] The latter part of the 1990s was probably Krugman's first time writing for a wide audience, he increasingly focused on policy issues that he deemed important. *The Age of Diminished Expectations*, for example, discusses the income inequality during the 'New Economy' of the 1990s in the United States and attributes it primarily to changes in the political environment during that time.

13.4 Depressions, Inequality and Growth

In 1994, in an article in *Foreign Affairs*, Krugman wrote that it was an urban legend that the East Asian economies had accomplished a 'miracle'. The rise of these countries was fuelled by the mobilisation of production factors, and their growth trajectories would slow as a consequence.[49] The article he published contributed to the popularisation of a famous argument that the growth path of East Asian countries was not attributable to innovative or completely new economic models, but rather to increasing capital investment and labour. However, the total factor productivity had not improved. Based on Paul Krugman's argument, the sole way to sustain economic growth in the long run is to increase total factor productivity (TFP). It is important to note that many of his conclusions have been challenged by subsequent research. In addition, the government provided incentives to encourage technological advancement, which stimulated a great deal of research.[50]

Krugman argued that Japan was doomed in *The Return of Depression Economics* because the central bank was unable to lower interest rates any more in order to escape stagnation. For the purpose of addressing Japan's liquidity trap, his policy proposal is 'to provide adequate demand'. In subsequent remarks, he drew comparisons between the 'lost decade' in Japan and the late 2000s crisis, emphasising the need for fiscal expansion.[51] According to Krugman, Japan's recovery was based on an export-driven boom.[52]

During the twentieth century, Krugman wrote *The Conscience of a Liberal*, a work that discusses inequality in the United States. A significant decline was observed over the middle of the century in the gap between rich and poor, but this gap widened again over the last decades to levels higher than those of the 1920s. It is Krugman's contention in this book that government policies played an important role in both reducing and increasing inequality during the 1930s through 1970s. It is included in Krugman's book that he proposes a 'new New Deal', a programme that focuses on social and medical programmes.[53] Accordingly, it is noteworthy that Krugman calls for state intervention in places that have uninsured workers to create trade unions while advocating for a public and universal healthcare system in his book.[54]

According to the Pulitzer Prize-winning and well-known historian David Kennedy, 'Krugman's chapter on the imperative need for health care reform is the best in this book, a rueful reminder of the kind of skilled and accessible economic analysis of which he is capable', and Kennedy also noted that Krugman puts emphasis on 'the manipulation by the richest Americans to rig the game in their favor'.[55]

The book *Return of Depression Economics and the Crisis of 2008* was Krugman's publication that substantially extended an earlier work. According to the author, the U.S. regulatory system has been unable to keep pace with an out-of-control financial system, and he discusses the causes and solutions of the financial crisis. A book titled *End This Depression Now!* was published by Krugman in 2012. By analysing historical economic data, the book claims that austerity measures and fiscal cuts simply deprive the economy of funds which could otherwise be circulated and further contribute to the contraction of the economy. People are unable to spend, markets cannot operate, and if there is no adequate consumption, it is impossible for the economy to flourish. The author makes the argument that although it is necessary to reduce debt, doing so at a time when a country has just suffered a severe financial shock is the worst choice. Reduced government spending is more appropriate when the economy is close to full employment and the private sector is capable of absorbing the reduction in government spending. If neither the public nor private sectors are able to stimulate the economy, the current economic depression will only be unnecessarily prolonged and exacerbated.

Krugman was a leading advocate of the Keynesian resurgence that emerged during the recession of 2008–2009, a phenomenon that was referred to by the economic commentator Noah Smith as the 'Krugman insurgency'.[56] During the 2006–2009 global financial crisis, Krugman wrote that he is 'gravitating towards a Keynes–Fischer–Minsky view of macroeconomics',[57] and in this context, Krugman and his co-author Eggertsson developed a Keynesian-type model of debt-overhang, in the spirit of Fischer, Minsky and Koo, where they proudly argued that their approach 'sheds considerable light both on current economic difficulties and on historical episodes, including Japan's lost decade [...] and the Great Depression itself'.[58] Meanwhile, several thousand people signed his *Manifesto for Economic Sense*, launched in 2012 with Richard Layard, calling for fiscal stimulus in order to reduce unemployment and promote growth.[59]

Anti-globalisation groups have expressed their anger over his support for free trade.[60] In 1987, Krugman famously argued, 'If there were an Economist's Creed, it would surely contain the affirmations "I understand the Principle of Comparative Advantage" and "I advocate Free Trade"'.[61] A number of reasons support Krugman's view that free trade is a good thing, including the enormous political costs of pursuing effective trade policy and the fact that there is no readily available process for governments to identify which sectors will eventually produce results. The underlying fact of comparative advantage cannot be disproved by increasing returns or strategic trade theory, according to him.

A tariff on Chinese imports, however, was advocated by Krugman during the Great Recession as a retaliation for Chinese decision of keeping a low renminbi value, artificially increasing export competitiveness, just as a 'drag on global economic recovery'.[62] As Krugman noted in his 2015 commentary, he is ambivalent regarding the Trans-Pacific Partnership, since the agreement does not primarily concern trade issues and 'whatever you may say about the benefits of free trade, most of those benefits have already been realized' [by existing agreements]. And 'you want reassurance that the people negotiating the deal are listening to valid concerns, that they are serving the national interest rather than the interests of well-connected corporations'.[63]

According to Krugman, economists did not accurately measure the impact of globalisation on jobs in countries such as the United States in the 1990s, thanks to the models used by scholars to measure the impact.[64] The author stated that despite the fact that free trade has had ill effects on several industries and labourers, it remains a so-called 'win-win' situation in the long run, resulting in prosperity for both parties. A trade war, on the other hand, is equally detrimental to the nations involved, even if it results in benefits to some individuals or sectors within each economy in the short term.[65]

13.5 The Theoretical Legacy of Krugman

The question Krugman (1987) posed is: *Is Free Trade Passé*? According to him, the doctrine based on comparative advantage has been sacred to economists since Ricardo's *Principles of Political Economy*. Nevertheless, there is some doubt being cast on free trade in the current context. Rather than being influenced by political factors, this has been a result of significant changes in global trade that focuses on increasing returns as well as imperfect competition. In addition to doubting the extent to which trade could be analysed and explained by comparative advantage, these new models argue that import restrictions and subsidies may contribute to greater national welfare under certain conditions.[66]

It is evident that international trade is a well-established topic in the field of *Economics*, and for most of its past trajectory, trade has been explained by factors endowment and comparative advantage. Trade patterns in the early twentieth century can be explained by these theories. Comparative advantages, however, are becoming less relevant in the modern world. Today, a large portion of trade takes place between countries that possess similar technologies and resources; exports and imports of similar products can take place between countries of the same type. Krugman wrote important articles which provided a clear explanation for the fact that most economies export cars and TVs, but import them as well. The extent of trade between countries with comparable endowments of capital and labour was greater than the extent of trade between countries with different initial endowments, a fact that was not adequately explained by the standard theory.[67]

According to Krugman, monopolistic competition is a framework in which consumers pursue variety, where a Japanese consumer may occasionally prefer a car made in Germany, even if he or she resides in Japan. Furthermore, the combination of these ingredients has provided a framework that is likely to fit global trade patterns better than David Ricardo's theory of the nineteenth century.

Krugman's models became valuable references in *Economics* because they were more realistic as well as great pieces of mathematical modelling. 'His models are among the most elegant: lean and thin and transparent. They have all the required parts but no unnecessary fat' as Columbia Professor of *Economics* Arvind Panagariya (2008) wrote in *Forbes*.[68] Or, in Paul Krugman's own words: 'small models applied to real problems, blending real-world observation and a little mathematics to cut through to the core of an issue'.[69]

In addition to being realistic, elegant and tractable, his models served as foundations for innumerous articles that followed on trade, economic development, and most significantly economic geography. A small proportion of standard *Economics* is devoted to economic geography, according to Krugman.[70] He was probably the first researcher to publish a paper which presents a mathematically rigorous framework for the simultaneous consideration of trade and the spatial distribution of people and businesses in space[71] in *Journal of Political Economy*, titled 'Increasing Returns and Economic Geography'.

Economies of scale have long been recognised as crucial for the location of economic activity in economic geography, which primarily studies migration flows across the geographical landscape. It should be noted, however, that models of General Equilibrium did not support these insights. This would require waiting until 1991, when Krugman published his seminal article that signified the beginning of the New Economic Geography (NEG).[72]

Meanwhile, besides academic papers and textbooks, Paul Krugman contributes extensively to the general public with his books and articles concerning issues he considers important, such as crises, inequality and growth, and has made significant contributions to explaining and popularising economic principles and ideas. He has certainly criticised a variety of positions on economic issues from various political viewpoints, a characteristic which has often been used as proof of his 'controversial' views. Even so, he has maintained an appealing writing style, and when needed, has demonstrated an excellent ability to develop compact, elegant and informative mathematical models. After all, in his own words:[74] 'Economics is a social science about what people do and how it turns out. And that means that you're telling a story, a narrative about people, even if you're doing it in a very stylized way', since 'any economic argument that has *not* been expressed in that form [i.e. mathematical model] tends to remain invisible'.[75]

Key Takeaways

- Trade increases the variety of products available and sharpens competition.
- When trade barriers are lowered, firms may achieve economies of scale.
- 'Hyper-globalisation' has contributed to rising inequality.
- Increasing total factor productivity is essential to sustaining economic growth.

Revision Questions

- What is Krugman's position on free trade?
- What is the 'home market effect' in the economy?
- What is Krugman's opinion on 'globalisation' and 'hyper-globalisation'?
- What is 'New Economic Geography' (NEG) about?
- Why does manufacturing get concentrated in one or a few regions (core) and the remaining regions play the role of agricultural suppliers (periphery)?
- Why firms achieve economies of scale when trade barriers are lowered?
- What is the more appropriate time to reduce debt?
- What is Krugman's main contribution to *Economics*?

Notes

1 Britannica (2022b).
2 Gaspar (2018).

Notes

 3 Solomon (2015).
 4 Krugman (2002).
 5 Krugman (2022).
 6 Krugman (2022).
 7 Krugman (2008a).
 8 Krugman (2022).
 9 Krugman (2008b).
10 Gaspar (2018).
11 Krugman (2014).
12 Krugman (2022).
13 Krugman (2022).
14 Krugman (2008c).
15 Gaspar (2018)
16 Krugman (2008c).
17 Gaspar (2018).
18 Dixit and Stiglitz (1977).
19 Our discussion draws from Gaspar (2018).
20 Chandra (2022).
21 Gaspar (2018).
22 Krugman (1981).
23 Krugman (2008b).
24 Krugman (1997).
25 Krugman (1991).
26 Chandra (2022).
27 Gaspar (2018).
28 Gaspar (2018).
29 Gaspar (2018).
30 Krugman (1999).
31 Krugman (2022).
32 Gaspar (2018).
33 Gaspar (2018).
34 Gaspar (2018).
35 Gaspar (2018).
36 Gaspar (2018).
37 Chandra (2022).
38 Gaspar (2018).
39 Krugman (1991).
40 Gaspar (2018).

41 Panagariya (2008).
42 Gaspar (2018).
43 Gaspar (2018).
44 Krugman (2010a).
45 Fujita and Krugman (2004).
46 Gaspar (2018).
47 Krugman (1979).
48 Sarno and Taylor (2002).
49 Krugman (1994).
50 van den Berg and Lewer (2006).
51 Krugman (2000).
52 Krugman (2009a).
53 Krugman (2007).
54 Milios and Sotiropoulos (2009).
55 Kennedy (2007).
56 Smith (2012).
57 Krugman (2009b).
58 Eggertson and Krugman (2012, abstract).
59 Blanchflower (2012), van den Heuvel (2012).
60 Leigh and Gilbert (2007).
61 Krugman (1987); see also Gupta (1997).
62 Krugman (2010b).
63 Krugman (2015).
64 Krugman (2019).
65 Krugman (2017).
66 Chandra (2022).
67 Gaspar (2018).
68 Panagariya (2008).
69 Krugman (2022).
70 Chandra (2022).
71 Gaspar (2018).
72 Gaspar (2018).
73 Krugman (2008b).
74 Krugman (1990, p. 3, emphasis added).

References

Baldwin, R., & Krugman, P. (1988). Market access and international competition: A simulation study of 16K random access memories. In R. C. Feenstra (Ed.), *Empirical models for international trade*. MIT Press.

Blanchflower, D. (2012, July 2). David Blanchflower: Yet more nails in Osborne's economic coffin. *The Independent*. Retrieved June 13, 2022, from https://www.independent.co.uk/news/business/comment/david-blanchflower/david-blanchflower-yet-more-nails-in-osborne-s-economic-coffin-7902990.html

Chandra, R. (2022). Paul Krugman, new trade theory and new economic geography. In *Endogenous growth in historical perspective* (pp. 221–249). Palgrave Macmillan.

Dixit, A., & Stiglitz, J. E. (1977, June). Monopolistic competition and optimum product diversity. *The American Economic Review, 67*(3), 297–308.

Eggertsson, G., & Krugman, P. (2012, August). Debt, deleveraging, and the liquidity trap: A Fisher-Minsky-Koo approach. *The Quarterly Journal of Economics, 127*(3), 1469–1513.

Encyclopedia Britannica. (2022b). Paul Krugman. https://www.britannica.com/biography/Paul-Krugman

Fujita, M., & Krugman, P. (2004). The new economic geography: Past, present and the future. *Papers in Regional Science, 83*, 139–164.

Gaspar, J. (2018, January). A biography of Paul Krugman: Contributions to geography and trade. FEP Working Papers, No. 600. ISSN: 0870-8541.

Gupta, S. D. (1997). *The political economy of globalization*. Springer.

Helpman, E., & Krugman, P. (1985). *Market structure and foreign trade: Increasing returns, imperfect competition, and international economy*. MIT Press.

Kennedy, D. M. (2007, October 21). Malefactors of Mega wealth. *Sunday Book Review*. Retrieved June 13, 2022, from https://www.nytimes.com/2007/10/21/books/review/Kennedy-t.html

Krugman, P. (1979b). A model of balance of payments crises. *Journal of Money, Credit, and Banking, 11*, 311–325.

Krugman, P. (1981, April). Trade, accumulation and uneven development. *Journal of Development Economics, 8*(2), 149–161.

Krugman, P. (1990). *Rethinking international trade*. MIT Press.

Krugman, P. (1991). Increasing returns and economic geography. *Journal of Political Economy, 99*, 483–499.

Krugman, P. (1994, December). The myth of Asia's miracle. *Foreign Affairs, 73*(6), 62–78.

Krugman, P. (1997, March 21). In praise of cheap labor: Bad jobs at bad wages are better than no jobs at all. *Slate*. Retrieved June 13, 2022, from https://slate.com/business/1997/03/in-praise-of-cheap-labor.html

Krugman, P. (1999, October). Was it all in Ohlin? Retrieved June 13, 2022, from http://web.mit.edu/krugman/www/ohlin.html

Krugman, P. (2000). Thinking about the liquidity trap. *Journal of the Japanese and International Economies, 14*(4), 221–237.

Krugman, P. (2002, July 26). Rudi Dornbusch, Originally published on the Official Paul Krugman Site. Retrieved June 13, 2022, from http://www.pkarchive.org/theory/Rudi.html

Krugman, P. (2007). *The conscience of a liberal*. W.W. Norton & Co.

Krugman, P. (2008a, March 11). Economics: The final frontier, The conscience of a liberal. *The New York Times*. Retrieved June 13, 2022, from https://krugman.blogs.nytimes.com/2008/03/11/economics-the-final-frontier/

Krugman, P. (2008b). In UBS Nobel perspective interview. Retrieved June 13, 2022, from https://www.ubs.com/microsites/nobel-perspectives/en/laureates/paul-krugman.html

Krugman, P. (2008c). *The Nobel Prizes 2008* (K. Grandin, Ed.). Nobel Foundation.

Krugman, P. (2009a, April 2). Japan's Recovery. *The New York Times* from https://archive.nytimes.com/krugman.blogs.nytimes.com/2009/04/02/japans-recovery/

Krugman, P. (2009b, May 19). Actually existing Minsky, The conscience of a liberal. *The New York Times*. from https://archive.nytimes.com/krugman.blogs.nytimes.com/2009/05/19/actually-existing-minsky/

Krugman, P. (2010a). The new economic geography, now middle aged. Mimeo, Paper presented at the Association of American Geographers.

Krugman, P. (2010b, March 14). Taking on China, opinion. *The New York Times* from https://www.nytimes.com/2010/03/15/opinion/15krugman.html?src=me

Krugman, P. (2014, February 28). Changes (Personal/Professional), the conscience of a liberal. *The New York Times*. Retrieved June 13, 2022, from https://krugman.blogs.nytimes.com/2014/02/28/changes-personalprofessional/

Krugman, P. (2015, May 22). Trade and trust, opinion. *The New York Times*. Retrieved June 13, 2022, from https://www.nytimes.com/2015/05/22/opinion/paul-krugman-trade-and-trust.html?_r=0

Krugman, P. (2017, July 3). Oh! What a lovely trade war. *Opinion, The New York Times*. Retrieved June 13, 2022, from https://www.nytimes.com/2017/07/03/opinion/trump-trade-war.html

Krugman, P. (2019, October 10). What economists (including me) got wrong about globalization. *Bloomberg*, www.bloomberg.com. Retrieved June 13, 2022, from https://www.bloomberg.com/opinion/articles/2019-10-10/inequality-globalization-and-the-missteps-of-1990s-economics#xj4y7vzkg

Krugman, P. (2022). Incidents from my career. Retrieved June 13, 2022, from https://www.princeton.edu/~pkrugman/incidents.html

Krugman, P., & Venables, A. (1995). Globalization and the inequality of nations.

Krugman, P. R. (1987). Is free trade passé? *Journal of Economic Perspectives, 1*(2), 131–144.

Leigh, D., & Gilbert, H. (2007). *Economies of representation, 1790–2000: colonialism and commerce* (pp. 200–201). Ashgate Publishing, Ltd.

Milios, J., & Sotiropoulos, D. P. (2009). *Rethinking imperialism: A study of capitalist rule*. Palgrave Macmillan.

Panagariya, A. (2008). Paul Krugman, Nobel. *Forbes*. Retrieved June 13, 2022, from https://www.forbes.com/2008/10/13/krugman-nobel-economics-oped-cx_ap_1013panagariya.html?sh=79e4ad23172e

Sarno, L., & Taylor, M. P. (2002). *The economics of exchange rates* (pp. 245–264). Cambridge University Press.

Smith, N. (2012, March 21). Did the Krugman insurgency fail? *Noahpinion*. Retrieved June 13, 2022, from http://noahpinionblog.blogspot.com/2012/03/did-krugman-insurgency-fail.html

Solomon, R. (2015, September). American Jews in economics. In S. H. Norwood & E. G. Pollack (Eds.), *Encyclopedia of American Jewish History* (Vol. 1, p. 721).

Van Den Berg, H., & Lewer, J. (2006). *International trade and economic growth* (pp. 98–105). M.E. Sharpe.

Van den Heuvel, K. (2012, July 9). Krugman's Manifesto for economic common sense. *The Nation*. Retrieved June 13, 2022, from https://www.thenation.com/article/archive/krugmans-manifesto-economic-common-sense/

Venables, A. J. (1996). Equilibrium locations of vertically linked industries. *International Economic Review, 37*, 341–335.

References

Abramovitz, M. (1956). Resource and Output Trends in the United States since 1980. *American Economic Review, 46*(2), 5–23.
Aghion, P., & Howitt, P. (1998). *Endogenous growth theory*. Cambridge, MA: MIT Press.
Alkire, S., & Deneulin, S. (2009). Introducing the human development and capability approach. *An introduction to the human development and capability approach*. Earthscan.
Andersen, E. (1991). *Schumpeter's Vienna and the Schools of Thought*. Smaskrift No. 70, August, Aalborg University.
Arrow, K. J., & Debreu, G. (1954). Existence of an equilibrium for a competitive economy. *Econometrica, 22*, 265–290.
Aumann, R. J. (1974). Subjectivity and correlation in randomized strategies. *Journal of Mathematical Economics, 1*, 67–96.
Babichenko, Y., & Rubinstein, A. (2020). Communication complexity of approximate Nash equilibria. *Games and Economic Behavior, 134*(July), 376–398.
Backhouse, R. E. (2009). *The evolution of economic thought*. Kritiki.
Baldwin, R., & Krugman, P. (1988). Market access and international competition: A simulation study of 16K random access memories. In R. C. Feenstra (Ed.), *Empirical models for international trade*. MIT Press.
Ballandonne, M., & Rubin, G. (2020). Robert Solow's Non-Walrasian conception of economics. *History of Political Economy, 52*, 827–861.
Barro, R. J., & Sala-i-Martin, X. (1995). *Economic growth*. McGraw-Hill.
Barry, N. P. (1979). *Hayek's social and economic philosophy*. Macmillan.
Basu, K. (2015, December 15). Stiglitz's sticky prices. *Project Syndicate*.
Basu, K., Ravi, R., & Robeyns, I. (2019). Introduction to the special issue in celebration of Amartya Sen's 85th birthday. *Journal of Human Development and Capabilities, 20*, 2.
Bentham, J. (1948). *The principles of morals and legislation*. Hafner Press.
Beranek, W., & Kamerschen, D. (2016). Examining two of Keynes's most popular statements-wasteful public spending can be acceptable, and, in the long run we are all dead-yields some surprising implications. *The American Economist, 612*, 263–267.
Bix, B. (2007). *Philosophy of law: Theory and interpretative framework*. Kritiki Publications.
Blanchflower, D. (2012, July 2). David Blanchflower: Yet more nails in Osborne's economic coffin. *The Independent*. Retrieved June 13, 2022, from https://www.independent.co.uk/news/business/comment/david-blanchflower/david-blanchflower-yet-more-nails-in-osborne-s-economic-coffin-7902990.html
Blaug, M. (1995), Why is the quantity theory of money the oldest surviving theory in economics. In: *The quantity theory of money, from Locke to Keynes and Friedman*. Edward Elgar Publication Company.
Bodin, J. (1578). *Discours sur le rehaussement et diminution des monnoyes*. Dupuys.

Boianovsky, M., & Hoover, K. (2014). In the kingdom of Solovia: The rise of growth economics at MIT: 1956–70. *History of Political Economy, 46*, 198–228.

Borel, E. (1921). La théorie du jeu et les equation intégrales à noyau symétrique gauche. *ComptesRendus de l'Académie des Sciences, 173*, 1304–1308.

Bowles, S., & Edwards, R. (2005). *Understanding capitalism: Competition, command, and change* (3rd ed.). Oxford University Press.

Encyclopedia Britannica. (2021). Leon Walras from https://www.britannica.com/biography/Leon-Walras

Encyclopedia Britannica. (2022a). Joseph E. Stiglitz from https://www.britannica.com/biography/Joseph-Stiglitz

Encyclopedia Britannica. (2022b). Paul Krugman, from https://www.britannica.com/biography/Paul-Krugman

Brittan, S. (2013, April 18). Thatcher was right—There is no 'society'. *Financial Times*. Retrieved April 1, 2021, from https://www.ft.com/content/d1387b70-a5d5-11e2-9b77-00144feabdc0

Brock, W. A., & Hommes, C. H. (1998). Heterogeneous beliefs and routes to chaos in a simple asset pricing model. *Journal of Economic Dynamics and Control, 22*, 1235–1274.

Brown, G. (2011, April 21). The 2011 TIME 100. *time.com*. Retrieved May 9, 2022, from http://www.time.com/time/specials/packages/article/0%2C28804%2C2066367_2066369_2066440%2C00.html

Caldwell, B. (2004). *Hayek's challenge: An intellectual biography of F.A. Hayek*. University of Chicago Press.

Chakrabarty, D. (2009). Identity and violence: The illusion of destiny, by Amartya Sen. *South Asian History and Culture, 1*(1), 149–154.

Chakraborty, A. (2021). Home in the World by Amartya Sen review—The making of a Nobel laureate.

Chamberlin, E. (1933). *The Theory of Monopolistic Competition*. Harvard University Press.

Chandra, R. (2022). Paul Krugman, new trade theory and new economic geography. In *Endogenous growth in historical perspective* (pp. 221–249). Palgrave Macmillan.

Colman, A. M., Pulford, B. D., & Krockow, E. M. (2018). Persistent cooperation and gender differences in repeated Prisoner's Dilemma games: Some things never change. *Acta Psychological, 187*, 1–8.

Columbia University. (2022). Faculty homepages: Joseph Stiglitz. Retrieved May 9, 2022, from https://www8.gsb.columbia.edu/faculty/jstiglitz/bio

Committee on Science and Technology, Subcommittee on Science and Technology. (1983). *Hearings*, U.S. House of Representatives, Ninety-Eighth Congress, First Session on H.R., National Science Foundation Authorization 1984, February 23, 25, March 1, 8, 10, No. 21.

Cournot, A. (1838). *Recherches sur les Principes Mathématiques de la Théorie des Richesses*. Hachette.

Daskalakis, C., Goldberg, P. W., & Papadimitriou, C. H. (2009). The complexity of computing a Nash equilibrium. *SIAM Journal on Computing, 39*(3), 195–259.

Denison, E. (1967). *Why growth rates differ*. The Brookings Institution.

Dixit, A., & Stiglitz, J. E. (1977, June). Monopolistic competition and optimum product diversity. *The American Economic Review, 67*(3), 297–308.

Dizikes, P. (2011, October 25). The office next door. *MIT Technology Review*. Retrieved April 8, 2021, from https://www.technologyreview.com/2011/10/25/21338/the-office-next-door/

Dizikes, P. (2019, December 27). The productive career of Robert Solow. *MIT Technology Review*. Retrieved April 8, 2021, from https://www.technologyreview.com/2019/12/27/131259/the-productive-career-of-robert-solow/

Dornbusch, R., & Fischer, S. (1990). *Macroeconomics*. McGraw-Hill.

Drakopoulos, S., & Karagiannis, A. (2003). *History of economic thought: An overview*. Kritiki Publications.

Dreze, J., & Sen, A. K. (1989). *Hunger and public action*. Clarendon Press.

Dreze, J. & Sen, A. K. (Eds). (1990–1991). The political economy of hunger (3 Vols.). Clarendon Press.

Dreze, J., & Sen, A. K. (Eds.). (1996). *Indian development: Selected regional perspectives*. Oxford University Press.
Economist. (2016, August 26). Prison breakthrough. *Game Theory*. Retrieved March 30, 2021, from https://amp.economist.com/schools-brief/2016/08/20/prison-breakthrough
Eggertsson, G., & Krugman, P. (2012, August). Debt, deleveraging, and the liquidity trap: A Fisher-Minsky-Koo approach. *The Quarterly Journal of Economics, 127*(3), 1469–1513.
Fellman, P. V. (2007). *The Nash equilibrium revisited: Chaos and complexity hidden in simplicity*. Fellman Southern New Hampshire University.
Foster, J., & Sen, A. K. (1997). On economic inequality after a quarter century. In A. K. Sen (Ed.), *On economic inequality* (2nd ed., pp. 107–219). Clarendon Press.
Fragnelli, V., & Gambarelli, G. (2015). John Forbes Nash (1928–2015). *The European Journal of the History of Economic Thought, 22*(5), 923–926.
Freud, S. (n.d.). *Introduction to psychoanalysis*. Govostis Publications.
Friedman, M. (1969). *The optimum quantity of money*. In: The optimum quantity of money and other Essays. Aldine Press: Chicago, IL.
Friedman, M. (1992). In A. Lindbeck (Ed.), *Nobel lectures, economics 1969–1980*. World Scientific Publishing Co..
Fujita, M., & Krugman, P. (1995). When is the economy monocentric? von Thünen and Chamberlin unified. *Regional Science and Urban Economics, 25*, 505–528.
Fujita, M., & Krugman, P. (2004). The new economic geography: Past, present and the future. *Papers in Regional Science, 83*, 139–164.
Fujita, M., Krugman, P., & Mori, T. (1999). On the evolution of hierarchical urban systems. *European Economic Review, 43*, 209–251.
Fujita, M., Krugman, P., & Venables, A. J. (1999). *The spatial economy. Cities, regions and international trade*. The MIT Press.
Fujita, M., & Thisse, J.-F. (2009). New economic geography: An appraisal on the occasion of Paul Krugman's 2008 Nobel Prize in economic sciences. *Regional Sciences and Urban Economics, 39*(2), 109–119.
Gaertner, W., & Pattanaik, P. K. (1988). An interview with Amartya Sen. *Social Choice and Welfare, 5*(1), 69–79.
Gaspar, J. (2018, January). A biography of Paul Krugman: Contributions to geography and trade. FEP Working Papers, No. 600. ISSN: 0870-8541.
Glaeser, E. (2008, October 13). Honoring Paul Krugman. *Economix* blog of *The New York Times*.
Goodhart, C. (1988). *The evolution of central banks*. The MIT Press.
Greenwald, B., & Stiglitz, J. E. (1987). Keynesian, new Keynesian, and new classical economics. *Oxford Economic Papers, 39*, 119–133.
Gupta, S. D. (1997). *The political economy of globalization*. Springer.
Haberler, G. (1950). Joseph Alois Schumpeter: 1883–1950. *Quarterly Journal of Economics, 64*, 333–372.
Hanusch, H., & Pyka, A. (2007). Principles of Neo-Schumpeterian Economics. *Cambridge Journal of Economics, 31*, 275–289.
Harsanyi, J. C. (1967–1968). Games with incomplete information played by 'Bayesian' players. *Management Science*, 14, 159–182.
Harsanyi, J. C. (1973). Games with randomly disturbed payoffs: A new rationale for mixed-strategy equilibria. *International Journal of Game Theory, 2*, 1–23.
Hayek, F. A. (1935). The present state of the debate. In F. A. Hayek (Ed.), *Collectivist economic planning: Critical studies on the possibilities of socialism*. Routledge & Kegan Paul Ltd.
Hayek, F. A. (1937). Economics and knowledge. *Economica, 4*, 33–54.
Hayek, F. A. (1940). Socialist calculation III: The competitive solution. In F. A. Hayek (Ed.), *Individualism and economic order*. The University of Chicago Press.
Hayek, F. A. (1942). The facts of the social sciences. In F. A. Hayek (Ed.), (1949), *Individualism and economic order*. Routledge & Kegan Paul Ltd.
Hayek, F. A. (1953). *The counter-revolution of science*. Collier-Macmillan.
Hayek, F. A. (1960). *The constitution of liberty*. University of Chicago Press.

Hayek, F. A. (1968). Competition as a discovery procedure. In F. A. Hayek (Ed.), *New studies in philosophy, politics, economics and the history of ideas*. Routledge [1978].

Heilbroner, R. L. (2011). *The worldly philosophers: The lives, times and ideas of the great economic thinkers*. Simon and Schuster.

Helpman, E., & Krugman, P. (1985). *Market structure and foreign trade: Increasing returns, imperfect competition, and international economy*. MIT Press.

Henderson, D. (2008). Robert Merton Solow. In D. Henderson (Ed.), *The concise encyclopedia of economics*. Library of Economics and Liberty. Retrieved March 3, 2021, from https://www.econlib.org/library/Enc/bios/Solow.html

INFORMS. (2021). Robert Solow. Retrieved March 3, 2021, from https://www.informs.org/Explore/History-of-O.R.-Excellence/Biographical-Profiles/Solow-Robert

Itoh, M., & Lapavitsas, C. (1999). *Political economy of money and finance*. Macmillan.

Jaffe, W. (Ed.). (1965). *Correspondence of Leon Walras and related papers* (3 vols.). North-Holland Publishing Company.

Johnson, H. G. (1971). The Keynesian Revolution and the monetarist counter-revolution. *American Economic Review, 61*(2), 1–14.

Jones, H. (1993). *Introduction to modern theories of economic growth*. Kritiki Publications.

Karagiannis, A. (2001). *Economic methodology*. Kritiki Publications.

Karlin, A., & Perez, Y. (2017). *Game theory, alive*. American Mathematical Society.

Kennedy, D. M. (2007, October 21). Malefactors of Mega wealth. *Sunday Book Review*. Retrieved June 13, 2022, from https://www.nytimes.com/2007/10/21/books/review/Kennedy-t.html

Kern, J. (2003, September 18). Interview with Professor Joseph Stiglitz. *Social Enterprise News*. Retrieved May 9, 2022, from https://www8.gsb.columbia.edu/socialenterprise/newsn/423/interview-with-professor-joseph-stiglitz

Keynes, J. M. (2001). *The general theory of employment, interest and money*. Papazisis Publications.

Keynes J. M. (2009). *The general theory of employment, interest and money, management laboratory press*. Unabridged Edition.

Kirzner, I. M. (1992). *The meaning of market process: Essays in the development of modern Austrian economics*. Routledge.

Klamer, A. (1989). A conversation with Amartya Sen. *Journal of Economic Perspectives, 3*(1), 135–150.

Klein, P. (2007). *Biography of F. A. Hayek (1899–1992)*. Articles of Interest, Mises Institute. Retrieved March 17, 2021, from https://mises.org/library/biography-f-hayek-1899-1992

Kreps, D., & Wilson, R. (1982). Sequential equilibria. *Econometrica, 50*, 863–894.

Krugman, P. (1979a). Increasing returns, monopolistic competition and international trade. *Journal of International Economics, 9*, 469–479.

Krugman, P. (1979b). A model of balance of payments crises. *Journal of Money, Credit, and Banking, 11*, 311–325.

Krugman, P. (1980). Scale economies, product differentiation and the pattern of trade. *American Economic Review, 70*, 950–959.

Krugman, P. (1981, April). Trade, accumulation and uneven development. *Journal of Development Economics, 8*(2), 149–161.

Krugman, P. (1990). *Rethinking international trade*. MIT Press.

Krugman, P. (1991a). Increasing returns and economic geography. *Journal of Political Economy, 99*, 483–499.

Krugman, P. (1991b). *Geography and trade*. MIT Press.

Krugman, P. (1993). First nature, second nature, and metropolitan location. *Journal of Regional Science, 33*, 129–144.

Krugman, P. (1994, December). The myth of Asia's miracle. *Foreign Affairs, 73*(6), 62–78.

Krugman, P. (1995). *Development, geography and economic theory*. MIT Press.

Krugman, P. (1997, March 21). In praise of cheap labor: Bad jobs at bad wages are better than no jobs at all. *Slate*. Retrieved June 13, 2022, from https://slate.com/business/1997/03/in-praise-of-cheap-labor.html

Krugman, P. (1998). Space: The final frontier. *Journal of Economic Perspectives, 12*, 161–174.

Krugman, P. (1999, October). Was it all in Ohlin? Retrieved June 13, 2022, from http://web.mit.edu/krugman/www/ohlin.html

Krugman, P. (2000). Thinking about the liquidity trap. *Journal of the Japanese and International Economies, 14*(4), 221–237.

Krugman, P. (2002, July 26). Rudi Dornbusch, Originally published on the Official Paul Krugman Site. Retrieved June 13, 2022, from http://www.pkarchive.org/theory/Rudi.html

Krugman, P. (2007). *The conscience of a liberal*. W.W. Norton & Co.

Krugman, P. (2008, December 10). *Incidents from my career*. Princeton University Press.

Krugman, P. (2008a, March 11). Economics: The final frontier, The conscience of a liberal. *The New York Times*. Retrieved June 13, 2022, from https://krugman.blogs.nytimes.com/2008/03/11/economics-the-final-frontier/

Krugman, P. (2008b). In UBS Nobel perspective interview. Retrieved June 13, 2022, from https://www.ubs.com/microsites/nobel-perspectives/en/laureates/paul-krugman.html

Krugman, P. (2008c). *The Nobel Prizes 2008* (K. Grandin, Ed.). Nobel Foundation.

Krugman, P. (2009a, April 2). Japan's Recovery. *The New York Times* from https://archive.nytimes.com/krugman.blogs.nytimes.com/2009/04/02/japans-recovery/

Krugman, P. (2009b, May 19). Actually existing Minsky, The conscience of a liberal. *The New York Times* from https://archive.nytimes.com/krugman.blogs.nytimes.com/2009/05/19/actually-existing-minsky/

Krugman, P. (2010a). The new economic geography, now middle aged. Mimeo, Paper presented at the Association of American Geographers.

Krugman, P. (2010b, March 14). Taking on China, opinion. *The New York Times* from https://www.nytimes.com/2010/03/15/opinion/15krugman.html?src=me

Krugman, P. (2015, May 22). Trade and trust, opinion. *The New York Times*. Retrieved June 13, 2022, from https://www.nytimes.com/2015/05/22/opinion/paul-krugman-trade-and-trust.html?_r=0

Krugman, P. (2014, February 28). Changes (Personal/Professional), the conscience of a liberal. *The New York Times*. Retrieved June 13, 2022, from https://krugman.blogs.nytimes.com/2014/02/28/changes-personalprofessional/

Krugman, P. (2017, July 3). Oh! What a lovely trade war. *Opinion, The New York Times*. Retrieved June 13, 2022, from https://www.nytimes.com/2017/07/03/opinion/trump-trade-war.html

Krugman, P. (2019, October 10). What economists (including me) got wrong about globalization. *Bloomberg*, www.bloomberg.com. Retrieved June 13, 2022, from https://www.bloomberg.com/opinion/articles/2019-10-10/inequality-globalization-and-the-missteps-of-1990s-economics#xj4y7vzkg

Krugman, P. (2022). Incidents from my career. Retrieved June 13, 2022, from https://www.princeton.edu/~pkrugman/incidents.html

Krugman, P., & Venables, A. (1995). Globalization and the inequality of nations.

Krugman, P. R. (1987). Is free trade passé? *Journal of Economic Perspectives, 1*(2), 131–144.

Kurz, H., & Salvadori, N. (2000). The dynamic Leontief Model and the theory of endogenous growth. *Economic Systems Research, 12*(2), 255–265.

Lacan, J. (1973–1974). *Seminaire XXI, Les non dupes errent*. Retrieved April 10, 2021, from http://staferla.free.fr/S21/S21%20NON-DUPES.pdf

Lacan, J. (1974). *La troisième*. VIIèmeCongrès De l'Écolefreudienne de Paris Rome, 31 octobre–3 novembre. Retrieved April 10, 2021, from http://staferla.free.fr/Lacan/La_Troisieme.pdf

Lange, O. (1936). On the economic theory of socialism: Part one. *The Review of Economic Studies, 4*(1), 53–71.

Lavoie, M. (1984). The endogenous flow of credit and the post Keynesian theory of money. *Journal of Economic Issues, 18*, 771–797.

Leigh, D., & Gilbert, H. (2007). *Economies of representation, 1790–2000: colonialism and commerce* (pp. 200–201). Ashgate Publishing, Ltd.

Leonard, R. J. (1994). Reading Cournot, Reading Nash: The creation and stabilisation of the Nash equilibrium. *Economic Journal, 104*, 492–511.

Lucas, R., Jr. (1988). On the mechanisms of economic development. *Journal of Monetary Economics, 22*(1), 3–42.
Mariolis, T. (2010). *Essays in the logical history of political economy*. Matura.
Marx, K. (1990). *Capital* (Vol. 1). Penguin Classics.
Marx, K. (1991). *Capital* (Vol. 3). Penguin Classics.
Marx, K. (1993). *Grundrisse. Foundations of the critique of political economy*. .
Marx, K., & Engels, F. (1985). *The communist manifesto*. Penguin Cvlassics.
McPherson, M. (1992). Amartya Sen. In W. Samuels (Ed.), *New horizons in economic thought: Appraisals of leading economists* (pp. 294–309). Edward Elgar.
Milios, J., Dimoulis, D., & Economakis, G. (2018 [2002]). *Karl Marx and the classics, an essay on value, crises and the capitalist mode of production*. Routledge.
Milios, J., & Sotiropoulos, D. P. (2009). *Rethinking imperialism: A study of capitalist rule*. Palgrave Macmillan.
Milnor, J. (1995). A Nobel prize for John Nash. *Mathematical Intelligencer, 17*(3), 11–17.
Mollo, M. L. R. (1999). The endogeneity of money: Post-Keynesian and Marxian concepts compared. In P. Zarembka (Ed.), *Economic theory of capitalism and its crises, research in political economy* (Vol. 17, pp. 3–26). Jai Press.
Moore, B. J. (1988a). *Horizontalists and verticalists: The macroeconomics of credit money*. Cambridge University Press.
Moore, B. J. (1988b). Keynes and the endogeneity of money stock. In J. C. Wood (Ed.), *John Maynard Keynes, critical assessment* (Vol. 6, pp. 1–38). Second Series.
Moore, B. J. (1994, September). The demise of the Keynesian multiplier: A reply to cottrell. *Journal of Post Keynesian Economics, 17*(1), 121–133.
Morgenstern, O. (1976). The collaboration between Oskar Morgenstern and John von Neumann on the theory of games. *Journal of Economic Literature, 14*(3), 803–816.
Mornati, F. (2018). *Vilfredo Pareto: An intellectual biography volume I*. Palgrave Studies in the History of Economic Thought.
Myerson, R. B. (1978). Refinements of the Nash equilibrium concept. *International Journal of Game Theory, 7*, 73–80.
Myerson, R. B. (1999). Nash equilibrium and the history of economic theory. *Journal of Economic Literature, 37*(3), 1067–1082.
Nasar, S. (1998). *A beautiful mind*. Simon & Schuster.
Nash, J. (1950a). The bargaining problem. *Econometrica, 18*, 155–162.
Nash, J. (1950b). Equilibrium points in n-person games. *Proceedings of the National Academy of Sciences U.S.A., 36*, 48–49.
Nash, J. (1951). Noncooperative games. *Annals of Mathematics, 54*, 289–295.
Nash, J. (1995). *The Nobel Prizes 1994* (T. Frängsmyr, Ed.) Nobel Foundation.
Nash, J. (1996). *Essays on game theory*. Edward Elgar.
New World Encyclopedia. (n.d.). *Vilfredo Pareto*. Retrieved April 1, 2021, from https://www.newworldencyclopedia.org/entry/Vilfredo_Pareto
Nti.org. (2022). Amartya Sen. Retrieved June 7, 2022, from https://www.nti.org/about/people/amartya-sen/
O.E.C.D. (1996). *Research and development expenditures in industry*.
Ohlin, B. (1933). *Interregional and international trade*. Harvard University Press. Revised version published in 1968.
Oser, J., & Blanchfield, W. 1975. *The evolution of economic thought*. New York: Harcourt Brace Jovanovich.
Panagariya, A. (2008). Paul Krugman, Nobel. *Forbes*. Retrieved June 13, 2022, from https://www.forbes.com/2008/10/13/krugman-nobel-economics-oped-cx_ap_1013panagariya.html?sh=79e4ad23172e
Papadogonas, Th. (1996). *Research and development expenditure in Greek industry*. Department of International and European Economic Studies, Athens, Athens University of Economics and Business.

Pazzanese, C. (2021). Amartya Sen's nine-decade journey from colonial India to Nobel Prize and beyond.
Pressman, S., & Summerfield, G. (2000). The economic contributions of Amartya Sen. *Review of Political Economy, 12*(1), 89–113.
Reppas, P. (2002). *Economic development: Theories and strategies (vol. A)*. Papazisis Publications.
Romer, P. (1986). Increasing Returns and Long-Run Growth. *Journal of Political Economy, 94*, 1002–1037.
Romer, P. (1990). Endogenous technological change. *Journal of Political Economy, 98*, 71–102.
Rosser, B. J., Jr. (2003). A Nobel Prize for Asymmetric Information: The economic contributions of George Akerlof, Michael Spence and Joseph Stiglitz. *Review of Political Economy, 15*(1), 3–21.
Rousseas, S. (1986). *Post Keynesian monetary economics*. M. E. Sharpe.
Rubin, I. I. (1979). *A history of economic thought*. Ink links.
Rubinstein, A. (1995). John Nash: The master of economic modeling. *Scandinavian Journal of Economics, 97*, 9–13.
Ruggles, P. (1990). *Drawing the line*. Urban Institute.
Samuelson, P. (1947). *Foundations of economic analysis*. Harvard University Press.
Sargent, T. J. (1993). *Bounded rationality in macroeconomics*. Clarendon Press.
Sarno, L., & Taylor, M. P. (2002). *The economics of exchange rates* (pp. 245–264). Cambridge University Press.
Schumpeter, J. A. (1934). *1912*. Harvard University Press.
Schumpeter, J. A. (1937). Preface to Japanese Edition of *Theorie der wortschaftlichen Entwicklung, in essays on economic topics* (R. V. Clemence, Ed.) Kennikat Press, 158–163 [1951].
Schumpeter, J. A. (1939). *Business cycles*. McGraw-Hill.
Schumpeter, J. A. (1949). Economic history and entrepreneurial history. In R. Clemence (Ed.), *Essays: Joseph Schumpeter*. Transaction Publishers.
Schumpeter, J. A. (1954). *History of economic analysis*. Routledge.
Schumpeter, J. A. (2010). *Capitalism, socialism and democracy*. Routledge.
Schwartz-Shea, P. (2002). Theorizing gender for experimental game theory: Experiments with "Sex Status" and "Merit Status" in an asymmetric game. *Sex Roles, 47*, 301–319.
Scott, M. F. (1989 [1998]). *A new view of economic growth*. New York and Oxford: Oxford University Press.
Screpanti, E., & Zamagni, S. (2005). *An outline of the history of economic thought*. OUP.
Selten, R. (1965). Game-theoretic treatment of an oligopoly model with demand-sustainability. *Journal of Sampled Political Science, 301–329*.
Selten, R. (1975). Reexamination of the perfectness concept for equilibrium points in extensive games. *International Journal of Game Theory, 4*, 25–55.
Sen, A. (1998). Biographical Nobel Prize.
Sen, A. (2021). A conversation with Amartya Sen. Retrieved June 9, 2022, from https://www.youtube.com/watch?v=27lcM8bYOFg&t=5s
Sen, A. K. (1960). *Choice of techniques*. Basil Blackwell.
Sen, A. K. (1970a). *Collective choice and social welfare*. Holden Day.
Sen, A. K. (1970b). The impossibility of a Paretian liberal. *Journal of Political Economy, 78*(1), 152–157.
Sen, A. K. (1973a). *On economic inequality*. Clarendon Press.
Sen, A. K. (1973b). On ignorance and equal distribution. *American Economic Review, 63*(5), 1022–1024.
Sen, A. K. (1976a). Poverty: An ordinal approach to measurement. *Econometrica, 44*(2), 219–231.
Sen, A. K. (1976b). Liberty, unanimity and rights. *Economica, 43*(171), 217–245.
Sen, A. K. (1977a). Rational fools: A critique of the behavioral foundations of economic theory. *Philosophy and Public Affairs, 6*(4), 317–344.
Sen, A. K. (1977b). Social choice theory: A re-examination. *Econometrica, 45*(1), 53.
Sen, A. K. (1981a). Ingredients of famine analysis: Availability and entitlements. *Quarterly Journal of Economics, 95*, 433–464.

Sen, A. K. (1981b). *Poverty and famines: An essay on entitlement and depression*. Oxford University Press.
Sen, A. K. (1983). Poor, relatively speaking. *Oxford Economic Papers, 35*(2), 153–169.
Sen, A. K. (1984). *Resources, values and development*. Blackwell & Harvard University Press.
Sen, A. K. (1985). The moral standing of the market. In E. F. Paul, F. D. Miller Jr., & J. Paul (Eds.), *Ethics and economics* (pp. 1–19). Basil Blackwell.
Sen, A. K. (1987). Justice. In J. Eatwell, M. Milgate, & P. Newman (Eds.), *The new Palgrave: A dictionary of economics* (Vol. 2, pp. 1039–1043). Macmillan.
Sen, A. K. (1990a). Gender and cooperative conflict. In I. Tinker (Ed.), *Persistent inequalities* (pp. 123–149). Oxford University Press.
Sen, A. K. (1990b). More than 100 million women are missing. *New York Review of Books, 37*(20), 61–66.
Sen, A. K. (1992a). *Inequality re-examined*. Clarendon Press & Harvard University Press.
Sen, A. K. (1992b). Missing women. *British Medical Journal, 304*(6827), 587–588.
Sen, A. K. (1993). The economics of life and death. *Scientific American, 268*(5), 40–47.
Sen, A. K. (1994). Population and reasoned agency. In K. Lindahl-Kiessling & H. Landberg (Eds.), *Population, economics development, and the environment* (pp. 51–78). Oxford University Press.
Sen, A. K. (1997). Maximization and the act of choice. *Econometrica, 65*(4), 745–779.
Sen, A. K. (1999). *Development as freedom*. Oxford University Press.
Shapiro, C., & Stiglitz, J. E. (1984). Equilibrium unemployment as a worker discipline device. *The American Economic Review, 74*(3), 433–444.
Sivaraman, M. (2022). *Home in the world: A memoir*: by Amartya Sen, London, Allen Lane, 2021, xv–464 pp.
Skidelsky, R. (1995). J. M. Keynes and the quantity theory of money. In *The quantity theory of money, from Locke to Keynes and Friedman*. Edward Elgar Publication Company.
Smith, A. (1981). *An inquiry into the nature and causes of the Wealth of Nations*. Liberty Classics.
Smith, N. (2012, March 21). Did the Krugman insurgency fail? *Noahpinion*. Retrieved June 13, 2022, from http://noahpinionblog.blogspot.com/2012/03/did-krugman-insurgency-fail.html
Solomon, R. (2015, September). American Jews in economics. In S. H. Norwood & E. G. Pollack (Eds.), *Encyclopedia of American Jewish History* (Vol. 1, p. 721).
Solow, R. (1956). A contribution to the theory of economic growth. *Quarterly Journal of Economics, LXX*, 65–94.
Solow, R. (1957, August). Technical change and the aggregate production function. *Review of Economics and Statistics, 39*(3), 312–320.
Solow, R. (1988). *The Nobel Prizes 1987* (W. Odelberg, Ed.). Nobel Foundation.
Sotiropoulos, D. P., Milios, J., & Lapatsioras, S. (2013). *A political economy of contemporary capitalism and its crisis: Demystifying finance*. Routledge.
Stamatis, G. (1977). *Die 'spezifisch kapitalistischen' Produktionsmethoden und der tendenzielle Fall der Profitrate bei Karl Marx*, Berlin.
Starrett, D. (1978). Market allocations of location choice in a model with free mobility. *Journal of Economic Theory, 17*, 21–37.
Steele, J. (2001, March 31). Food for thought. London, England. *The Guardian*. Retrieved December 24, 2022, from https://www.theguardian.com/books/2001/mar/31/society.politics
Stiglitz, J. (1974). Alternative theories of wage determination and unemployment in LDC's: The labor turnover model. *The Quarterly Journal of Economics, 88*(2), 194–227.
Stiglitz, J. E. (1976). The efficiency wage hypothesis, surplus labour, and the distribution of income in L.D.C.s. *Oxford Economic Papers, 28*(2), 185–207.
Stiglitz, J. E. (1987). The causes and consequences of the dependence of quality on price. *Journal of Economic Literature, 25*, 1–48.
Stiglitz, J. E. (1991). The economic role of the state: Efficiency and effectiveness. In T. P. Hardiman & M. Mulreany (Eds.), *Efficiency and effectiveness in the public domain, the economic role of the state* (pp. 37–59). Institute of Public Administration.
Stiglitz, J. E. (1994). *Whither socialism?* MIT Press.

Stiglitz, J. E. (1997, May). Looking out for the National Interest: The Principles of the Council of Economic Advisers. *American Economic Review, 87*(2), 109–113.

Stiglitz, J. E. (2000). The contributions of the economics of information to twentieth century economics. *Quarterly Journal of Economics, 115*, 1441–1478.

Stiglitz, J. E. (2001, December 4). Asymmetries of information and economic policy. *Project Syndicate*.

Stiglitz, J. E. (2002a). *The Nobel Prizes 2001* (T. Frängsmyr, Ed.). Nobel Foundation.

Stiglitz, J. E. (2002b, December 11). Celebrating the irrational. *Project Syndicate*.

Stiglitz, J. E. (2002c). Information and the change in the paradigm in economics. *American Economic Review, 92*, 460–501.

Stiglitz, J. E. (2002d). *Globalization and its discontents*. W.W. Norton & Company.

Stiglitz, J. E. (2016, August 5). Globalization and its new discontents. *Project Syndicate*.

Stiglitz, J. E. (2017, December 5). Globalization: Time to look at historic mistakes to plot the future, *The Guardian*.

Stiglitz, J. E., & Weiss, A. (1981). Credit rationing in markets with imperfect information. *The American Economic Review, 71*(3), 393–410.

The New York Times. (1987, October 22). Man in the news: Robert Meton Solow; Tackling Everyday Economic Problems. Retrieved March 3, 2021, from https://www.nytimes.com/1987/10/22/business/man-in-the-news-robert-merton-solow-tackling-everyday-economic-problems.html

Thirlwall, A. (2001). *Growth and development*. Papazisis Publications.

Thornton, P. (2014). *The great economists: Ten economists whose thinking changed the way we live*. Pearson UK.

Tobin, J. (1972, September/October). Friedman's theoretical framework. *Journal of Political Economy, 80*, 852–863.

Tsoulfidis, L. (2007). Classical economists and public debt. *International Review of Economics, 54*(1), 1–12.

Tsoulfidis, L. (2008). *History of economic theory and policy*. University of Macedonia Publications.

Tsoulfidis, L. (2010). *Competing schools of economic thought*. Springer Science & Business Media.

Tsoulfidis, L., & Paitaridis, D. (2012). Revisiting Adam Smith's theory of the falling rate of profit. *International Journal of Social Economics, 39*(5), 304–313.

Van Den Berg, H., & Lewer, J. (2006). *International trade and economic growth* (pp. 98–105). M.E. Sharpe.

Van den Heuvel, K. (2012, July 9). Krugman's Manifesto for economic common sense. *The Nation*. Retrieved June 13, 2022, from https://www.thenation.com/article/archive/krugmans-manifesto-economic-common-sense/

van Staveren, I. (2021). *Alternative ideas from 10 (almost) forgotten economists*. Springer Nature Press.

Varoufakis, G. (2007a). *Political economy: The economy in the light of criticism*. Gutenberg Publications.

Varoufakis, G. (2007b). *Game theory*. Gutenberg Publications.

Varoufakis, G., & Theocharakis, N. (2005). *Microeconomic models of partial and general equilibrium*. Typotheo—GiorgosDardanos.

Venables, A. J. (1996). Equilibrium locations of vertically linked industries. *International Economic Review, 37*, 341–335.

von Neumann, J. (1928). On the theories of parlor games. *MathematischeAnnalen, 100*, 295–320.

von Neumann, J., & Morgenstern, O. (1944). *Theory of games and economic behavior*. Princeton University Press.

Walker, D. A. (1987). Walras, Leon. In J. Eatwell, M. Milgate, & P. Newman (Eds.), *The new Palgrave: A dictionary of economics* (Vol. 4 (Q to Z)). Macmillan Press.

Walras, L. (1954). *Elements of pure economics* (W. Jaffe, Trans.). Allen and Unwin.

Walsh, V. (2000). Smith after Sen. *Review of Political Economy, 12*(1), 5–25.

White, L. H. (1999). Hayek's Monetary theory and policy: A critical reconstruction. *Journal of Money, Credit, and Banking, 31*(1), 109–120.

Yueh, L. (2018). *What would the great economists do?* Picador.

Index

A
Absolute advantage, 22
Accumulation, 33, 36, 40
Asymmetric information, 148, 150, 153, 154
Asymptotically stable, 111
Auctioneer, 45, 49, 50

B
Business cycle, 79–82, 87, 89

C
Capabilities, 131, 132, 134–141, 143
Capital, 29, 31, 33–38, 40
Capitalism, 67, 68, 70, 72–74, 76
Capitalist, 2, 6–10, 17–24, 29, 30, 32–40
Capitalist mode of production, 29, 33, 36–38
Class struggle, 29, 32–33, 39
Comparative advantage, 17, 22, 24
Conservative, 2, 9, 11
Convergence, 111
Cooperation, 124–126
Core-periphery (CP), 163, 165, 166
Creative destruction, 67, 68, 73, 76
Credit, 31, 34–36, 79, 82, 83, 87
Crisis, 29, 38–40

D
Demand, 55, 57–62
Distribution, 131, 132, 139–141, 143
Division of labour, 1, 3, 5–8, 11, 12

E
Economic development, 67, 68, 70

Economies of scale, 159, 160, 162, 163, 165, 166, 170
Entrepreneur, 71, 72, 74
Expanded reproduction, 29, 36

F
Famine, 131–133, 138–143
Fluctuations, 62
Freedom, 131, 132, 135, 138, 142, 143
Free market, 1, 9, 12, 79, 81, 83–89
Free trade, 159, 163, 168, 169

G
Game Theory, 117–121, 124–127
Gender, 132, 138–142
General equilibrium, 45, 47–51
Globalisation, 147, 148, 152–154
Great Depression, 55–57, 60
Great Recession, 96, 102

H
Helicopter money, 97, 100
Human Development Index (HDI), 132, 141, 142
Hunger, 131, 132, 137, 138, 140
Hyper-globalisation, 159, 163, 170

I
Income distribution, 60
Individualism, 4
Inflation, 93, 96–98, 102
Information, 83–85
Innovation, 67, 68, 70–76
Instability, 89

Interest rates, 79, 81–83
Invisible hand, 1, 3, 5, 148, 151, 154

K
Keynesian resurgence, 159, 168
Knowledge, 79, 80, 83–85, 87, 89

L
Labour theory, 1, 5–8, 17, 19–20
Landlord, 17–22, 24

M
Macroeconomics, 55, 57–58, 61, 62
Market, 45–52
Market socialism, 79, 83, 84, 87
Monetarism, 93, 95–97, 101
Monetary policy, 79, 82, 89
Money, 29, 31, 33–35, 39, 93–97, 99–102
Money demand, 55, 61
Monopolies, 68, 74–76

N
Nash equilibrium, 117, 119, 121–127
Neoclassical Economics, 47, 48
New Deal, 59
New Economic Geography (NEG), 159, 160, 164–166, 170
New Growth Theory (NGT), 111, 114
New Trade Theory (NTT), 163–165
Non-accelerating inflation rate of unemployment (NAIRU), 93, 97, 102

O
Oligopolies, 68, 74, 76
Over-accumulation, 29, 38

P
Permanent income, 96, 102
Physics, 80–82, 86, 89
Poverty, 132, 134, 137–143
Prisoner's dilemma, 121–124, 126
Production, 58–62
Production function, 107, 110–114
Profit, 17, 20–24

Profitability, 59, 60
Profit rate, 29, 37, 40

Q
Quantity Theory of Money, 93, 96, 97, 101

R
Rational player, 125, 127

S
Say's law, 57, 58
Schumpeterian hypothesis, 67, 74–75
Scientism, 86
Shapiro and Stiglitz, 147, 148, 152
Simple reproduction, 29, 36
Socialism, 73, 74
Society, 1–9, 11, 12
Solow growth model, 109–112
Solow residual, 107, 112
Solution, 50, 51
State intervention, 58–60, 62, 88, 167
State interventionism, 98, 101
Sticky prices, 151–152
Strategy, 117, 120, 121, 123, 125
Surplus value, 29, 31, 35–37, 40

T
Technological progress, 107, 111–114
Technology, 22–24, 37, 40
Total Factor Productivity (TFP), 107, 112–113
Trade, 17, 22–24

U
Uncertainty, 58, 59, 61–63
Unemployment, 148, 149, 151–154
Utility maximisers, 143

V
Value, 1, 3, 5–7, 12, 33–35, 37, 40
Variety, 159, 162–165, 169, 170

W
Welfare, 131, 132, 134, 138, 140–142

The manufacturer's authorised representative in the EU is Springer Nature Customer Service Centre GmbH, Europaplatz 3, 69115 Heidelberg, Germany. If you have any concerns regarding our products, please contact ProductSafety@springernature.com

Printed and bound by CPI Group (UK) Ltd, Croydon, CR0 4YY

23/03/2026

02076457-0012